THE TIME BENEATH
THE CONCRETE

THE TIME BENEATH THE CONCRETE

PALESTINE BETWEEN CAMP AND COLONY

NASSER ABOURAHME

Duke University Press   Durham and London   2025

© 2025 DUKE UNIVERSITY PRESS
All rights reserved
Printed and bound by CPI Group (UK) Ltd, Croydon, CR0 4YY
acid-free paper ∞
Project Editor: Liz Smith
Designed by Matthew Tauch
Typeset in Merlo Tx and Retail
by Copperline Book Services

Library of Congress Cataloging-in-Publication Data
Names: Abourahme, Nasser, [date] author.
Title: The time beneath the concrete : Palestine between
camp and colony / Nasser Abourahme.
Description: Durham : Duke University Press, 2025. |
Includes bibliographical references and index.
Identifiers: LCCN 2024031940 (print)
LCCN 2024031941 (ebook)
ISBN 9781478031444 (paperback)
ISBN 9781478028239 (hardcover)
ISBN 9781478060512 (ebook)
Subjects: LCSH: Refugee camps—Palestine. | Refugees,
Palestinian Arab—Government policy—Israel. | Palestinian
Arabs—Colonization. | Settler colonialism—Israel. | Arab-Israeli
conflict—Social aspects. | Palestine—Colonization. | Gaza Strip—
Social conditions.
Classification: LCC HV640.5.P36 A25 2025 (print) |
LCC HV640.5.P36 (ebook) | DDC 362.87095694—dc23/eng/20241118
LC record available at https://lccn.loc.gov/2024031940
LC ebook record available at https://lccn.loc.gov/2024031941

Cover art: *(Front)* Basel Abbas and Ruanne Abou-Rahme,
Until we became fire and fire us, 2023. *(Back)* Basel Abbas
and Ruanne Abou-Rahme, *Gilboa, we haunt them*, 2023.
Courtesy of the artists.

Publication of this book is supported by Duke University
Press's Scholars of Color First Book Fund.

To the Salmas

CONTENTS

ix		PREFACE
xi		ACKNOWLEDGMENTS
1		**INTRODUCTION. CAMP/COLONY** In the Open Time of Dispossession
33	1	**THE CAMP, INEVITABLE** Technomorality and Racialization in the Prehistory of the Camp Regime
63	2	**THE CAMP, FORMALIZED** Authority and the Built in the Management of the Interim
93	3	**THE CAMP, OVERCOME** Revolution and Movement in the Impossible Present
126	4	**THE CAMP, UNDONE** Negation and Return in the Vanishing Horizon of Settler Permanence
164		**CODA. THE POLITICS OF INHABITATION**
183		NOTES
207		REFERENCES
223		INDEX

PREFACE

I sat down to finalize this manuscript in the fall of 2023, amid the images and sounds of genocide in Palestine. That is, when all there was were the images and sounds of thousands of lifeless children being pulled out of the rubble day in, day out for months on end; the images and sounds of breathless people digging for bodies with their bare hands and nails; of the cries of endless bereaved parents in morgues and hospitals; of countless massacres in neighborhoods, schools, and refugee camps; of the siege of one hospital after the next; of story after story of summary executions; of millions displaced and starved; of our enveloping, almost suffocating grief. All of it not only aided and abetted by the world's biggest state powers but also accompanied by an enthusiastic dehumanization of Palestinians by nearly the entirety of the mainstream media and political establishments in the West. There was a brutality and a connivance here that even in the long history of the colonization of Palestine was arresting.

This kind of violence and radical indifference has its own way of foreclosing thought. What does it mean to write, and write in English, in the face of all this? What can this writing do? What can it offer a people—a people I happen to owe my entire existence to—who are subject to active annihilation and who need food and weapons before words and thoughts? Even for those of us committed to critical thought, to history and theory, as the scaffolding of our action and activism, writing amid genocide can seem a futility at best. Given the complicity of not just universities and epistemic structures in the West but the very conventions of liberal academic writing, always working to sanitize our language, it might feel compromised at worst. And yet we still write. We write to figure out what we think; to take stock of our own strength when it seems most distant; and to insist on our existence when it is most denied. We write to make sense of the world and ourselves in it, even, or especially, when that world seems to have no place for us in it at all. We write against writing. We write not as a turn from action, but as an incitement to movement.

In truth, for all the shock of the moment, for how deeply we all felt scarred and changed by it, genocidal violence has long been both a formative history and a constant potential horizon in Palestinian life. We've always lived under its sign. And this book was always written as a way of grappling with the political structures that were formative of this violence and made its reproduction all but inevitable. The only way to really understand how we came to be faced with a frenzied genocidal campaign in Gaza at the end of 2023 is to think about the historical and temporal contradictions of Zionism as a settler colonial project faced with renewed forms of struggle and refusal. That is, the conjuncture could only be understood if located in the *foundational impasse* of the Zionist project, as that impasse had been shaped by a long century of anticolonial struggle. If political Zionism is, as this book argues, a project stuck at its foundational moment of conquest, unable to move past the past, it is not simply because its own immanent contradictions have risen to the surface, but because the Palestinian insistence on remaining and not disappearing amounts to a refusal to abide by the closure of time, a refusal of the rendering of the past into settler futurity, a refusal to allow the impasse to be overcome.

This book is largely about that impasse and the refusals that have formed it. But it is also written as a commitment to the ordinary dispossessed people whose forms of life demonstrate a world beyond settler colonialism and its degradations every single day. A commitment to those who even from the midst of genocide continue to insist—and insist with force—on life.

ACKNOWLEDGMENTS

The statement that all writing is autobiography is by now a truism but is no less relevant for being so. Even at its most archivally aloof or conceptually abstract, this book is a personal inventory of the relations and conversations that have over years shaped the questions I ask, the political commitments I make, and the struggles I join. People haven't so much left their marks on this text, as much as they have left their marks on me.

I was blessed at Columbia to work with not just brilliant but generous minds. Joseph Massad marshaled an incisive conceptual rigor and offered a model of political courage and clarity. Tim Mitchell upended so many assumptions and always had a knack of putting his finger on exactly what was missing. Reinhold Martin broadened the book's ambitions and taught an attentiveness to the work of theory. Gil Hochberg and Saskia Sassen pushed me to account for terms and absences I'd taken for granted. Sudipta Kaviraj taught me how to read (again).

In a year of on and off residency in Princeton, Julia Elyachar offered refuge and warmth, alongside an always sharp critical eye. Samera Esmeir hosted me and then gifted the type of reading that renders the work in an entirely new light, opening up dimensions I didn't even know the text had; I'm deeply grateful for her engagements and friendship. Helga Tawil-Souri read and gave the kind of creative insight only she can. Liron Mor was my effective writing group and read pretty much the entire thing; the meetings we had and her feedback improved the final text immeasurably. Sharif Elmusa read at least one part of the book and offered comments replete with his own poetic sensibilities. I'm grateful also to Beshara Doumani and the special space he's cultivated for Palestinian scholarship and community at Brown in the New Directions of Palestinian Studies forum; he and Alex Winder have been both supportive hosts and insightful and supple readers. Anooradha Iyer Siddiqi, Anupama Rao, and Casey Primel invited me to present some preliminary thoughts on inhabitation in a workshop that was immensely productive, and their engagements have stayed with me a long time. Teresa Caldeira and AbdouMaliq Simone both gave me platforms to explore some of the ideas in this book, and they always help remind me of the connections of my work to the broader questions posed by the lifeworlds of the global urban poor. Heba Alnajada kindly invited me to present a version of one chapter at the Race and Architecture series at Berkeley, which was generative, not least because it allowed me to reconnect with Sharad Chari, whose insights I treasure.

A two-year fellowship at the Mellon Interdisciplinary Fellows Program at Columbia was a huge boon; I'm grateful to all the other fellows, especially Emily Yao, who's one of the most perceptive readers I've ever come across, and the director Bill McAllister, who was always supportive and whose style and writing lessons were invaluable (today I teach them myself, using his same handouts). A one-year fellowship at the Princeton-Mellon Initiative in Architecture, Urbanism, and the Humanities also afforded me some space and time to work on the book; I'm grateful to Aaron Shkuda, Alisson Isenberg, and Mario Gandelsonas for the opportunity. I'm also grateful to Elizabeth Ault at Duke University Press, who read closely but capaciously and always knew what had to be done. My thanks also to Benjamin Kossack at Duke for his deft and patient editorial guidance.

The bulk of the research for this book was done in archives. It demanded a fair bit of persistence and a whole load of help and luck. I'm grateful to Helga Baumgarten, whose political history of the Palestinian national movement has been hugely informative and who also generously shared her collection of the Arab National Movement's early newspaper *al-Thaʿr*. I promise to pay it forward. Matan Cohen was the key that unlocked access to documents in the Israel State Archives; without him I'd still be waiting to get in. Muna Budeiri helped me navigate the formidable bureaucracies that guard the central records of the United Nations Relief and Works Agency.

Along the way, friends, accomplices, and fellow travelers have enriched my world, and their engagements with the ideas in this book have been formative. To note them here in a list is close to a betrayal of their importance, but I hope they each know their mark on this work is singular: Ahmad Dia, Ali Ugurlu, Brenna Bhandar, Deen Sharp, Eduardo Rega

Calvo, Emilio Dabed, Enas Alsafadi, Foad Torshizi, Henny Ziai, Kareem Rabie, Katia Hall, Khalid al-Hilli, Max Weiss, Nicola Perugini, Nikolas Kosmatopolous, Nora Akawi, Omar Jabary-Salamanca, Omar Sirri, Omar Tesdell, Pascal Menoret, Peter Lagerqvist, Rana Baker, Raof Haj Yahya, Ricardo Cardoso, Samar Maqusi, Saphe Shamoun, Sarah Hawas, Sarah El-Kazaz, and Taimoor Shahid. I finished this book while at Bowdoin, and I'm grateful for the support and friendship of some wonderful people there: Oyman Basaran, Meryem Belkaid, Ángel Saavedra Cisneros, Barbara Elias, Zahir Janmohamed, Paige Milligan, Salar Mohandesi, Robert Morrison, Brian Purnell, Shreyas Sreenath, Dharni Vasudevan, Bianca Williams, and Túlio Zille.

I owe an infinite debt to family. To my parents, May Jayyusi and Tawfiq Abourahme, who began my political education from the very start and have never stopped adding to it. That their radicalism has not dimmed or ebbed with time, not even for a minute, is a political consistency I can only aspire to. My mother, and her sharpest of intellects, charted this course long before I even knew it existed. To my aunt Lena Jayyusi, who pored over key chapters and mobilized her full formidable intellectual powers to enrich them. To my grandmothers: Salma Khadra Jayyusi, who passed in the spring of 2023, leaving us bereft but rich beyond measure with an inheritance of a lifetime of love, poetry, and feminist defiance; and Maryam Abourahme, who in 1948, after being ethnically cleansed, somehow "smuggled" herself and her six children back across the lethal border between what had just become Israel and Lebanon to make sure that we might hold on to but a piece of our land. All of them instances of a Palestinian will to live, of lives miraculously reassembled from the shards of fragmentation and displacement. All of them models of life lived in the anticolonial key. To my sister Ruanne Abou-Rahme and Basel Abbas, from whom I continue to learn, and who take the familiar and make us see and hear it otherwise every time they create. To Laura Ribeiro Rodrigues Pereira and that bundle of curiosity and beauty we brought into this world, Salma Pereira-Abourahme, who remind me every day that, ultimately, the power of life is all we have with which to fight and that the road to freedom always traverses the personal and the political. May we forever travel that road together.

INTRODUCTION. CAMP/COLONY
IN THE OPEN TIME OF DISPOSSESSION

"The Camp Is the Issue"

The primary claim of this book is a simple one—to read the question of Palestine, we have to read the camp. "The camp *is* the issue" (*al-mukhayyam huwa al-qadiyya*). In one sense, this rhetorical statement, often repeated in the refugee camps, operates as a straightforward metaphor. The term *al-qadiyya* (issue, cause, or question) is shorthand for the question of Palestine, and the refugee camp, this statement says, is just another name for this question—Palestine as camp. As such, one can read it as saying not only that displacement is still *the* constitutive Palestinian experience (such that "we Palestinians" is always at some level "we refugees") but also that *all* Palestinians are encamped one way or another: those who live in Israel proper as formal citizens but not nationals of the Jewish State in constricted towns and villages, many of which are legally "unrecognized" and denied basic infrastructure; those under long-term military occupation in the enclosed cities and villages of the West Bank or the entirely besieged Gaza Strip; or those living stateless or as second-class citizens in permanent exile in the surrounding states. The camp is the issue because all are effectively encamped. All live in the permanent temporariness of camptime, with varying degrees of extraterritorial dislocation and extralegal vulnerability. Camps within camps, abutting or within a larger voluntary encampment—the settler colony itself.

But there is something else in this statement, beyond the figurative (and not always helpful) movement of the camp image as metaphor or synecdoche. There is an insistence in it, I would argue, that the question of Palestine *remains*, at heart, a story of colonial dispossession. In the early pages of *The Question of Palestine* ([1979] 1992), Edward Said wrote that among the different ways we use the English word *question*, one important sense implies the persistent duration of a problem—a question is often something long-standing, intractable, and insistent. The statement "the camp is the issue/question" urges us to locate that sense of temporal persistence at a particular point; it urges us to read this duration of intractability from and in the camp itself. If the camp is the effect of an ongoing and contested dispossession, and if dispossession is the modus operandi of the colonial, then what this statement in effect does is call out the issue for what it *still* is. For encamped refugees, once the backbone of the national liberation movement but now the principal losers in the geopolitical restructuring of the occupation regime still somehow called "the peace process," the statement insists on a reckoning with the open history of the foundational violence of the settler polity that cannot be sutured through the (indefinitely deferred) promise of Palestinian statehood. It is a rhetorical move that insists on the openness of the time of dispossession.

The camp is the issue not because it represents or marks anything outside of itself (as a paradigm or exemplum) or because it can stand in for a larger whole, but because it is materially and politically installed at the center of the *ongoing* history of colonial struggle in Palestine. At the center of this book, then, is the claim that we can tell the story of the Palestinian question by telling the story of the camp as a political object. From and through the camps, we can approach the heart of this story—and this is my main argument—as not only a struggle over land and its (dis)possession *but also a struggle over historical time itself*. Settler colonialism everywhere is a particularly, even peculiarly, fraught struggle over time: perhaps nowhere more so than here. From the camps, we come to see Israel as a settler colonial project defined by its inability to move past the past, a project *stuck* at its foundational moment of conquest. And we come to see the Palestinian insistence on return as a refusal to abide by the closure of the past into settler futurity; we see that Palestinian struggle does not just happen *in* the open time of dispossession: it happens *over* this time. Palestinian refusal impinges on settler time, denies it closure and consolidation, surrounds it and smuggles its fugitive temporalities beneath and above it, all the while and with every passing day chipping away at this order's certainties and keeping the question, a question.

"At Best an Arab Encampment"

In Palestine's encounter with Zionism, the camp, at least as image, has been there almost from the beginning. Writing at the end of the second decade of the twentieth century, an English playwright, novelist, and eventual president of the Jewish Territorial Organization, Israel Zangwill, would, while celebrating Zionism's gains, reflect on the challenges it faced. Zangwill—who is credited, somewhat erroneously, with generalizing what came to be one of the emblematic mottos of Zionism, "a land without a people, for a people without a land"—would later come to a break with and oppose the Zionist movement, embracing first what came to be known as "the Uganda option" and then any territorial settlement that allowed for Jewish self-government, even delivering a speech in 1923 at the American Jewish Congress that declared political Zionism to be dead. But in his 1921 Zionist treatise *The Voice of Jerusalem*, Zangwill remained focused on the conquest of Palestine, albeit with an important twist—he refuted his own earlier descriptions of Palestine as "wilderness" or "ruin" and insisted that the movement square up to the fact that the territory was not literally empty. On this, it's fair to say he was blunt, citing a 1904 speech he gave in New York in which he reminded his audience that "there is, however, a difficulty from which the Zionist dares not avert his eyes, though he rarely likes to face it. Palestine proper has already its inhabitants" (1921, 92).

For Zangwill, whose palimpsestic treatise reads like an uneasy mixture of tightly coiled English mannerisms and romantic, biblical literary flourishes, that Palestine was quite clearly inhabited only clarified the necessary course of action. "There is no example in history of an inhabited country being acquired except by force" (94). Even if this conquest was the stuff of righteousness, without force it was a nonstarter: "A race, therefore, that desires a land of its own must—if it sets its eye on a land already inhabited—be prepared to face war" (95). Zangwill would square open conquest with the pretension to universality the same way every early liberal did, by racially limiting the terms of inclusion: "The only solution for this difficulty lies in the consideration that Palestine is not so much *occupied* by the Arabs as *over-run* by them. They are *nomads*, who have created in Palestine neither material nor spiritual values. To treat them therefore on the same basis as, say, the Belgians, would be to follow an analogy which does not exist" (97, emphasis added).

Though he was insistent on the need for force, Zangwill hoped persuasion would do the trick, and here he appeals to what he insists is the existing transience of "the Arabs": "We cannot allow the Arabs to block so valuable a piece of historic reconstruction, so romantic a reparation to the sorely-tried race of the Apostles. And therefore we must gently persuade them to 'trek.'... 'To fold their tents' and 'silently steal away' is their proverbial habit: let them exemplify it now" (97–98).

Zangwill's imagery of Palestinian Arabs as tent-dwelling nomads, proverbial or otherwise, is no outlier. Seraje Assi (2018), for one, shows that the Zionist national enterprise in Palestine eventually came to be defined in its very opposition to what it identified as nomadism. Patrick Wolfe came to a similar conclusion: "The new Jew's formative Other was the nomadic Bedouin rather than the *fellaheen* farmer" (2006, 396). But the reproach of nomadism was not merely figurative—it worked to render Palestinians removable. For Labor Zionists, so invested in the sedentary cultivation and settlement of land, nomadism became the paradigmatic lens that shaped Zionist discourse and attitudes about native Palestinians as foreign, marauding desert tribes. This image acted, writes Assi, as double repression, negating both sedentary Arab culture and nomadic Jewish traditions.

And yet, given Zionism's "lateness" as a colonial enterprise, the construction of nomadism had to contend with a land not just populated but also built-up. If settler colonialism is everywhere a struggle to capture and commodify land by replacing forms of inhabitation, then Zionism's lateness was not inconsequential. Here, settler colonialism had to face—and somehow negate—existing forms of inhabitation that spanned towns, villages, and, given Palestine's integration into global markets and its already articulated class formations (with proletarianized peasants, merchant classes, and an emergent bourgeoisie), urbanized cities.

If *nomadism* was a primary form of figuration through which colonial discourse everywhere rendered native presence, the camp or *encampment* would, here, be its spatial accessory. We need only note the sheer frequency of the image of the tented encampment that was such a staple—maybe even one of the defining motifs—of Orientalist and Zionist textual and visual accounts of Palestine. And at one level, this imagery of tents functioned *only* to highlight the absence of any imagery of buildings, towns, or cities. A little later in Zangwill's work, he gets at the heart of the intersection between dispossession and this image of nomadic life: "If Lord Shaftesbury was literally inexact in describing Palestine as a country without a people, he was essentially correct, for there is no Arab people living in intimate fusion with the country, *utilizing its resources* and stamping it with a characteristic impress: *there is at best an Arab encampment*" (1921, 109, emphasis added). Encampment here is meant to underline the passing temporariness or transience of physical and built native life. In a discursive move with almost immaculate settler colonial (and Lockean) overtones, it constructs not only the excessive and irrational movement of native bodies ("over-running") but also the essential transience of their relation to land; their built spaces are not cities, towns, and villages but something like bedouin caravans and mobile camps. Native peoples do not—indeed, cannot—inhabit the land "in intimate fusion": they merely "over-run" it in mobile and passing encampments.[1] Zangwill may have conceded the land was not actually empty, but neither was it inhabited or owned in any meaningful sense; it was vacant.

The camp here is not yet a mark of confinement but is something like a *placeless form*. We might say it stands as the inverse or opposite of a Hebrew word that in Zionist discourse would become steeped in an almost mystical aura: *yishuv* (settlement or territory). If the term *yishuv*, which came to refer to the entirety of Jewish settlement or territory in Palestine, and tellingly comes from the causative verb *le-yashev*, meaning "to settle" (from the root *y-sh-v*, which also gives us the verb *la-shavet*, meaning "to sit"), marked the settled, rooted, and possessed, then the images of camps were its photographic negatives, marking the unsettled, unrooted, and unpossessed. The camp is the *nonsettlement*. It is an image of negation, one that was put to direct use in the racialization of Palestinians (always strictly generic "Arabs") as alien interlopers in Palestine, naturally and incorrigibly nomadic, unrooted, and—above all—eminently removable.

Already we can see how an image of the camp sits at the center of the definitive biopolitical sites of settler colonial struggle: bodily movement and land (dis)possession. Yet the *projected* placelessness and unrootedness that Zangwill, through the racial image of the encampment, superimposed on the Palestinian landscape would *only* eventually be engendered in the ethnic cleansing and subsequent *actual* encampment of Palestinians after 1948. Zangwill's discourse was, ultimately, performative. It was an image—like all those of nomadism and vacancy in colonial history—that was to have real material effects, the effects of removing people from and severing their connections with the land.

And yet, in the long colonization of Palestine, the camp form would play a very different role. From the beginning, the camp was not just a projected negative image of Zionist colonialism but also one of its formative spatial instruments. That is, beneath the discourse, the camp form wasn't just the opposite of Zionism's settled colony or city but was its overlapping *accomplice*. It's somewhat ironic that in the years after Zangwill's observations, camps would come to play a critically formative role for both Zionism and British imperialism. Put simply, both British and Zionist colonization relied on a variety of camp forms: forms that brought together a flexible mixture of penal-carceral, extractive, labor exploitative, demographic, and territorial logics. There was here a very basic, primary, and elective affinity between camp and colony forms, especially in the early stages of settlement, and in ways that drew on the existing repertoires and networks of imperial history.

The list is extensive. We can think, for example, of the racially pure cooperative settlements, the *kibbutzim*, so critical to the entire "conquest of land" doctrine, which in many instances began precisely as tented encampments; these were themselves heavily influenced by early twentieth-century German agricultural colonies in the mainly Polish province of Posen, knowledge of which was brought to Palestine by figures like Arthur Ruppin (a eugenicist and race theorist known as "the father of Zionist settlement") who was deeply involved in both contexts.[2] Or take the "wall and stockade" (*homa u-migdal*) formations of the *yishuv*, which themselves often began as tented camps, constructed in a single day between sunrise and sundown; this practice was informed in turn by British colonial counterinsurgent architecture of the Mandate period like the Tegart Forts and their military watchtowers (which still make up the insignia of the Israeli Border Police).[3] These formations, fifty-seven of which were spread out across Palestine during the Great Revolt between 1936 and 1939, were essential to the establishment of the state and became the very *conceptual* model not only of Israeli architecture but arguably of the state project itself, with their two essential functions, fortification and observation, replicated on every scale (Rothbard 2003).

Earlier still we can think of the British Mandate's prison labor camps. Built between 1920 and 1947 and often run as jail labor companies, these labor camps straddled and brought together British and Zionist imperatives in Palestine (al-Saleh 2022). Sited near quarries, railroads, or major road works, they were the sites of a forced labor regime in which criminalized landless peasants worked to build the infrastructure that would both facilitate the extraction of resources and mineral wealth *and* lay the infrastructural foundations for the emergent settler state. In many instances, these same camps would be taken over when the emergent Zionist state operated its own labor and concentration camps in Palestine; at least one, Nur al-Shams, adjacent to the city of Tulkaram's major stone quarries, would itself become a refugee camp for ethnically cleansed Palestinians.[4]

These British prison labor camps foreshadowed Zionist labor camps and also were their incubators (except the Zionist state had the decency to drop the pretense of criminality entirely). Over the course of 1948, Zionist forces established at least five major labor camps (and some sixteen smaller ones) across Palestine that detained and put to work about twenty-five thousand Palestinians who had just been expelled from their towns and villages, in conditions that the International Committee of the Red Cross called "slavery" (Abu Sitta and Rempel 2014); these camps remained active until 1955, when these Palestinians too would be expelled. Around the same time, in depopulated Palestinian cities, the small numbers of Palestinians that remained after 1948 were confined for months behind barbed wire in urban encampments that Israeli officials themselves described as "fenced concentration camps" (Raz 2020). In Haifa, for example, the roughly three thousand Palestinians that remained from a population of more than seventy thousand were rounded up on David Ben-Gurion's orders and confined in a camp in the neighborhood of Wadi Nisnas; in Jaffa, the 'Ajami quarter (today the site of aggressive gentrification by Israeli real estate capital) was fenced off and designated as a zone of concentration for remaining Palestinians.

After the establishment of the state, absorption camps (*ma'abarot*) held hundreds of thousands of Arab and Middle Eastern Jews before they were dispersed across the state's frontiers into peripheral "development towns" that both proletarianized them and put them on the front lines as human buffers.[5] The camp form in this case exceeded the settler-native binary and, at least in part, shaped the internal racist class divisions of

Israeli society. Colonized Palestine, then, was, and to a large degree remains "an extensive laboratory of camps" (Katz 2017a, 2). For Palestinians, encampment—as dispossession's accomplice—has cast a decisively long and stubborn shadow over their lives.

Even in this short account, we can see how this fungibility in camp and colony forms relied on a circulation of expertise and knowledge across imperial terrains. Ann Stoler has tracked the overlapping contours of camp and colony forms and the concepts congealed around them, tracing the commensurabilities between them and the political logics they sustain to argue that "the colony and the camp are both containments, enclosures, and unsettled encampments that are more closely allied than we may have imagined" (2016, 77). She reads one mid-nineteenth-century French work (a five-volume study on *colonies argicoles*) not because it became a widely cited document (it did not), but because of the kinships it calls forth. And so, she tracks a litany of forms: agricultural colonies, penal colonies, resettlement camps, detention camps, island military bases, camps refitted as sites for colonial settlers, and failed settler colonies militarized with soldiers as settlers, which were all connected nodes in an imperial network; these were all connected, however, through mutation, not correspondence, and filiation, not fixity. Camp and colony are in a "deadly embrace" from the start: "a conjoined conceptual matrix, twin formations that give rise to social deformation with different effects," borrowing and blending essential features of their protective and coercive architecture "until they are strategically and violently torn apart" (2016, 78). In the colonization of Palestine, this is clear enough in the brief inventory we just ran through.

Yet what I'm arguing here is that the entanglement of the Palestinian refugee camp and the Israeli settler colony is of a different order altogether. The entanglement is not just about the filial borrowing and blending of forms in a joint conceptual matrix, or just another example of a "common camp" (Katz 2017b), one node among many in Israel's territorial transformation and demographic manipulation. Rather, the entanglement goes to the particularity of Zionism as a *settler* project, defined both by its own (now rising) immanent contradictions and—above all—by the long century of Palestinian struggle it has always been responding to. Here, the "deadly embrace" of (refugee) camp and (settler) colony does not belong to the order of kinship per se, but to the structural and historical oppositions of settler-native struggle; it belongs to the political necessity at the core of Zionism's project that Zangwill so directly squares up to, and its ongoing incompletion and frustration—the necessity of removal.

"The Refugee Camp Ambushes Me Anywhere, Any Moment"

The Palestinian refugee camp has its own status in this encounter, one that goes directly to the temporal contradictions and impasses of the colonial struggle here. There is a centrality, often contradictory and overdetermined but always urgent to the Palestinian camp question that is not hard to gauge. The refugee camps were the direct outcome of the near-total devastation of Palestinian lifeworlds and their forms of inhabitation in what came to be named and commemorated as the *Nakba*. The camp was not simply the *imaginary* opposite of the propertied settlement Zionism came to build; it was also the engendered *material* effect of the destruction of the rural and urban geographies Zionism encountered.

Between 1947 and 1949, and especially in the six months between March and September of 1948, almost 800,000 people (nearly two-thirds of the native population of Palestine) were expelled from their homes, some 530 villages destroyed, and eleven urban neighborhoods depopulated (Pappe 2007), with close to seventy documented massacres punctuating and shaping the waves of expulsion and flight (Abd al-Jawad 2007). Of the 370 new settlement towns that Israel would build in a frenzy of construction in its first decade of existence (1948–58), 350 were located on the lands of the depopulated villages, often directly on the same sites. The historiographical record is, by now, well established, even if forms of denial stubbornly persist and archival censorship and erasure, if anything, increase.[6] That increase seems only to confirm the state order's vulnerability to historical narrative and the collapse not only of its historical myths but also of the collective forms of repression that made them possible. In fact, today in Israeli society, denialism seems, if anything, a receding psycho-affective mechanism that constantly gives up and succumbs to the jouissance of an open affirmation of the violence that not only "had to be done," and may need to be done again, but that was good and right. Today, denial and affirmation come together, almost concurrently, often in the same conversation, such that you can easily be confronted with statements that insist both that "the *Nakba* never happened" and that, unless you're careful, "a second *Nakba* is coming."

After periods, often months and sometimes years, of wandering between villages, caves, disused buildings, or the open, many expelled Palestinians found themselves seeking refuge and relief in concentrated sites serviced by one or another charity organization, often in old military barracks or in previous encampments and temporary built sites, like Ottoman-era khans or caravanserai. An ad hoc United Nations (UN) body, the United Nations Relief for Palestine Refugees (UNRPR), coordinated aid and relief activity in these camps in the immediate aftermath of the expulsion.

At the tail end of 1949, with political negotiations at a standstill, the UN established an expressly instituted organization, the United Nations Relief and Works Agency (UNRWA), referred to colloquially and tellingly simply as "the Agency" (*al-wikala*), which took over the administration of these camps and the provision of services within them. Today, these same sites make up the majority of the fifty-eight recognized refugee camps in Gaza, the West Bank, Syria, Lebanon, and Jordan, most of them established in the years between 1948 and 1950 (though with a significant number, six, established in Jordan after the 1967 war produced another round of Palestinian refugees, most of them twice displaced). The camps range in population size from small formations housing roughly 2,000 to sprawling urbanized forms with some 200,000 people. In these camps live 1.5 million people (out of about 4 million registered Palestinian refugees), inhabitants from the majority of the depopulated villages and cities, still largely clustered according to their place of origin. They have never been allowed to return to their homes and, save the very few who managed despite grave risk to spirit themselves back onto their land, none has returned.

The camps, in the simplest terms, both contain and shelter those displaced bodies expelled but not allowed to return. They emerged as the inevitable, but also almost incidental, technical-humanitarian measure in place until a political solution or, as the terminology felicitously has it, a "settlement" might be reached. In other words, the camps emerged as the spatial effect of the engineered *political* irresolvability of the question of Palestine. The surplus population created in the establishment of the Jewish State could not be allowed to return, nor would the neighboring Arab states allow for their permanent resettlement, something the vast majority of them vociferously rejected in any case, and still do.

What came to be known in the West as "the Arab refugee problem" remains to this day, of course, *the* most intractable point of contention in the struggle over Palestine. For official Israel—in its racial self-organization—the return of the refugees is the single most threatening eventuality.[7] And so, unlike almost any other recent peace accord, negotiation here a priori precludes the possibility of any substantial return or repatriation.[8] What this book shows is that this "problem" is entangled with and often even exceeded by the question of the camps.

Since their establishment, the camps have incited quite different, often contradictory, but always urgent and stark responses in political practice and discourse. For the imperially backed regional state system, with Israel firmly established as one of its geopolitical poles, the camps hold in place displaced bodies that cannot be left to wander and move across borders; *but* equally, the camps came to be seen as obstacles to the final resettlement of the refugees across the border (and the effective liquidation of the "refugee problem") and as such sites of a distinct unsettledness, of potential movement. The camps are at once guarantors of stability in the region *and* an obstacle to peace: sites to be maintained as places of relief until a "solution" is found, or sites that need to be undone precisely for such a "solution" to be reached.

For UN administrators the camps were, for a long time, seen as overcrowded, vice-ridden, demoralizing spaces that eventually came to interrupt the imperative of work-based rehabilitation and the restoration of refugees to productive life. But, at the same time, for these same administrators, the planning and regulation of the built spaces of the camps came to be the primary instruments for both the provision of services and the construction of durable authority and the disciplining of the refugee-inhabitant. For Palestinian liberationist politics, the tension had been equally stark. The camps were carceral spaces of immobilization that paternalized and domesticated those in its ward. They were understood, by the earliest Palestinian political forces, explicitly as depoliticizing devices of racist and colonial institutions like the Agency; in producing this humanitarian statelessness of Palestinian subjects removed from historical time, camps were something to be overcome and left. At the same time, as temporary spaces that reinforced the openness of a *political* question, and blocked a permanent resettlement, the camps came to be seen as "way stations" that tacitly kept certain claims to return open. As such, they were political spaces to be defended and held on to, so much so that to be forced to leave a camp would be as bad as the *Nakba* or might even be worse, because it would mean being twice displaced and would also finalize the closure of the possibility of recovering what was lost in the original dispossession. For the Israeli colonial order, the camps did the work of keeping the displaced away from the state's borders and out of the territory it claimed; at the same time colonial officials came to see the camps as incubators of a dangerous "consciousness of the temporary," as the very material form of an ongoing land claim that threatened the settler order. The perceptions are at odds even within a single political formation, yet a sharp, even foreboding, sense of political-temporal consequence is consistent across the board.

The Palestinian refugee camp, then, weighs heavily on the archives. And yet it remains this slightly curious, overdetermined object of thought and practice that everyone initially agreed was to be but a passing temporary phenomenon. For Euro-American UNRWA administrators, the camps would eventually cease to exist, when the refugee problem was resolved through work-based rehabilitation in the 1950s and 1960s. For Palestinian revolutionaries, the camps were to be transformed into insurgent bases of revolutionary movement and eventually disappear through the redemptive politics of return. For Israeli officials, the camps were to be eventually undone through demolition or municipal integration in ways that would finally resolve the refugee problem and normalize settler time.

Nobody *really* wants the camp, nobody even wants the word *camp*, and yet it remains strangely resistant to the various forces of opposition it is up against, with an unexpected topological elasticity and a stubborn persistence. The camps have changed morphologically, infrastructurally, architecturally, demographically, socioeconomically, even jurisdictionally, but remain camps. Even the name, as we will see, stubbornly refuses to fade away, refuses to be divested from its object. And not for lack of trying. Almost everyone tried to change the name, as though, short of the transformation or destruction of the object, the very word *camp* becomes a problem, a liability, a nuisance, but also an opportunity for a shortcut, a quick fix. But not only is getting rid of the name sometimes not possible without getting rid of the object, names themselves, often even more than their objects, can prove stubborn in their persistence.

Yet, as we shall see, Agency administrators would spend months if not years haggling over what to rename the camps so as to delimit the organization's liability and responsibility over them (while maintaining an ambiguous form of authority): "settlements," "living quarters," "towns," "encampments" (as if that gets very far) all came and went as suggestions, until they realized "camp" wasn't going to budge. They spent a few years disassociating themselves by typing the word *camp* in scare quotes, before this pretense was eventually also dropped and *camp* remained *camp*. Palestinian revolutionaries, always careful about terminology, saw "bases" (*mu'askarat*) of militants or returnees rather than camps of refugees, and more than once at the height of the Revolution proclaimed the end of the "camp," sometimes in quite heavy-handed, almost awkward, style: "And the first wave of militants graduated from the training bases of the camps—sorry, of the barracks, for there is no longer a camp and there never again will be" (Badir 1969, 1). If the Agency thought it could get rid of the name and keep the thing, then the Israeli State understood that its plans stood a much better chance if both name and thing were eliminated altogether. In camp demolition schemes, after camps were to be leveled and refugees relocated, it was essential that they be housed in "towns," not "camps." Israeli planners feared, and these fears were to a large extent realized, that the new built environments they constructed for refugees, regardless of their level of planning and appearance of permanence, or their jurisdictional incorporation, would, one day, also become "camps." That is, not only would the object refuse to be divested of its name, but this name would claim new objects as well. Where UNRWA officials succumbed to a kind of nominalism and thought changing names would be enough, Israeli officials succumbed to a brute materialism and thought improvement or demolition would be enough. Yet camps remain camps because what is at stake is a question of neither language nor matter, but of the politics that courses between them; that is, camps remain camps as long as the political events that produced them remain historically open.

For every political force that faced it, the Palestinian camp was understood as a constitutive apparatus in its own right. The figurations may radically differ (refugee, huckster, returnee, militant, revolutionary, terrorist, rejectionist), but their causal relation to the camp is constant. UNRWA administrators worried about the camps' squalid environments and its "breadlines" breeding a "professional refugee mentality"—an abject figure of self-pity but also trickery and deceit. Palestinian revolutionaries, likewise, saw camp life producing a static, dejected, dependent figure of refugeehood and sought to transform the camps not only into "launching pads" that would "sprout" mobile revolutionaries, but also into communes that would revolutionize social relations, freeing women of traditional gender roles, freeing working classes from elite domination, and freeing youth of the conservative hierarchy of their elders. Israeli politicians saw the camps incubate a "consciousness of exile" and a subject of refusal; in the mid-1970s, when the camps were being politically mobilized, an Israeli diplomat fretted to one UN administrator—in a striking sentence—that the camps are seeing "the political evolution of the Palestinian refugees into Palestinians."[9]

Beneath this spoken discourse, there are the marked silences and absences, the *unsaid* that the camp indexes. For Palestinians, a sense of unspoken guilt, even shame, surrounds the fact that, despite the proclamations of unity and the symbolic place of pride the camp has in the national-liberationist economy of signs, the camps have paid and continue to pay a higher price. We know that there, in those stacked, almost beautifully fragile, and meticulously overdecorated houses, which most Palestinians will not even visit in the course of a lifetime, the poorest of the poor will pay with life and limb before anyone else. More recently, in the postrevolutionary period of "state building," this shame or guilt has been in some places overtaken by, or more likely displaced into, a classed, almost racialized, contempt for "camp people" (*mukhayyamjiya*) that also barely speaks its name, hiding behind appeals to law and order, or cleanliness and civility. This contempt, it needs saying, has a real material class basis: the camps as spaces of a militant urban poor incite fear in an insecure and entirely dependent Palestinian bourgeoisie and political elite that see their fragile class gains within a colonial economy perennially threatened by the camp's unwillingness to forgo insurgency.

For Palestinians, there is something at once hypersymbolic and unrepresentable about the camp. It has a kind of *totemic* presence in the Palestinian cosmos—emblematic but necessarily mystified, present often only at a certain repressed distance, and bound up with originary guilt. "The camp," writes Sharif Elmusa, "is a zone of exile in the Palestinian mind" (2012, 35). Difficult to talk about, heavy with pathos, and strangely absent from Palestinian poetry, the camp as a symbolic transit station remains the opposite of home (which can only ever be Palestine), and its present can never lead to a future (which can only ever be the camp's reversal). For Elmusa, a poet and scholar who grew up in Nuʿayma Camp outside Jericho, camp inhabitants have to navigate the marks of camp life alongside these silences and omissions: "It takes a reservoir of inner freedom and self-confidence for those who stay, or even those who leave, to heal the laceration of living in that flawed quarter" (35). And even then, the camp never leaves you: "Memories flash in unexpected ways, shake me into acknowledging them, and let me go. The refugee camp ambushes me anywhere, any moment" (28). The camp is Elmusa's "portable absence."

For much of Israeli political order, the camps, just as much as if not more than the remains of the depopulated Palestinian villages and cities, are experienced as anxiogenic sources of vague but imminent threat. The pathology with which the camps are imagined not only indexes but also hides or obscures the actual sources of this anxiety. It is easier no doubt to see only festering hovels of subhuman rage, the "crammed, stench-ridden ... shanty-towns of squalor and fundamentalist hatred," as one occupying solider put it (Ben-Tal 1991); it is easier to reassure oneself with the smug comfort of supremacy and see nothing but "infrastructures of terror." It is easier, that is, than admitting that one's own sense of home, one's very place in the world, was and remains contingent on stopping the inhabitants of those "shanty-towns of squalor" from ever returning home. It is easier than recognizing that Israeli political order—arguably Israeli political subjectivity itself—rests on the violence of the continued displacement of these very "refugees," a violence that is not just this subjectivity's enabling condition but its very substance. And *that* is the reason the bulldozers, tanks, cartographers, and urban planners descend on the camp with such persistent force. The camp indexes both the ongoing unsayability and necessity of the foundational violence that is still the condition of possibility for a Jewish State in Palestine; it is a reminder of the always-unfinished work of repression.

Here, the camp is a window onto the political unconscious. And coming to terms with all this, with the said and unsaid that the camp indexes, with what ties the camp form here to its seemingly inseparable double, the colony, demands thinking through the politics of time and temporality more closely: time not as historical context or periodization, or even as a political technology, but as itself the—at once clear and obscure—object of struggle between settler conquest and anticolonial refusal.

Settlerness, or The Time of Unsettlement

What is it about settler colonialism that makes it so unstable a political formation? Why is it that, even centuries after their foundational events, settler states seem so often stricken with a malaise and enmity that continuously open up "old" wounds and pose existential anxieties anew? Why has settler colonialism risen to the surface of our present, again, as a global problem? Today, we are told the settler colonial ethos has been globalized: the political language of besiegement and the permanent war-footing so definitive of settler colonialism are no longer confined to settler colonies proper, but now shape securitized politics right across the West (Hage 2016). Settler colonialism persists in our ostensibly postcolonial world and seems to proliferate along new axes and in new forms, dredging up questions of unfinished pasts wherever it goes.

Time itself in settler states seems like a charged and also particularly fateful political question. Both colonial settlement and the intransigence of anticolonial refusal keep time an object of political contestation. Colonial settlement is, after all, as much about the conquest and foundation of new time as it is about land; it depends on the creation of new foundations that wipe the slate before them, on both immutable racial myths of origin that exclusivize historicity ("the return to history," "manifest destiny") *and* new temporal beginnings that mark the start of civilizational and sovereign time ("making the desert bloom," "the birthday of a new world," settler declarations of independence). Frantz Fanon understood this as sharply as anyone in the anticolonial tradition: "The colonist," he told us, "makes history. His life is an epic, an odyssey. He is invested with the very beginning: 'We made this land'" (2005, 14). Opposite the colonist are those who are listless and petrified, consumed not by history but by static "custom."

Yet if "the colonist makes history and he knows it," as Fanon (2005, 15) insisted, the colonist also somehow feels that history's vulnerability. The challenge of time here, of unfinished pasts in the present, cannot simply be met in narrative or the writing of an epic. In a footnote to an essay about the transformation of Buenos Aires, Jorge Luis Borges wrote that "only new nations have a past" (1984, 42).[10] Borges, looking at the city in the 1920s through its layers of centuries of colonial-capitalist change, felt a heightened sense of time in conquest "so indecisive" that it constantly demanded renewal (such that his grandfather in the nineteenth century was still fighting the sixteenth century's wars of conquest). And though he doesn't say as much, we can also read this heightened sense of time, despite Borges's own attachments, in the "New World's" *precarity of achievement*. It's here, not in Granada (standing in for something like the Old World's taken-for-granted historicity), that Borges felt the "passage of time"; it's in the settler colonial "new republics" that time "moves more boldly" (42), and, I would add, looms more ominously. If the figurative settler seems obsessively fixated on stories with clear beginnings and ends (Simone 2020), then this has as much to do with the unsettled temporalities of conquest as it does with the narrative demands of new nations.

In turn, surviving and resisting settler colonization is about refusing temporal orders as much as it is about clinging to what's left of geography. In fact, the two are inextricably linked, native geography/land itself remaining the very basis of another parallel but incommensurate time, beyond or beneath the project of settlement—the time beneath the concrete. To insist on Palestine, for example, as this viable, still-existing, recoverable place is to insist on not only what is beneath the forests and housing complexes of colonial erasure, but what is beneath their present as well: that is, beneath the temporal order that settlement both relies on and constitutes. This Palestine is as much a when as it is a where. For so much of Palestinian life, then, the challenge has been to fashion practices of inhabitation and collective self-formation that produce distinctly Palestinian experiences of time beyond the temporality of settler sovereignty. I mean time here both in the sense of temporality—that is, the images, signs, embodied experiences, practices, rhythms that are constitutive of a sense of an age or moment (Mbembe 2001)—and time in its historical character as the organization of a relationship between past, present, and future.

There is, of course, nothing neutral about these terms.[11] In *Beyond Settler Time*, Mark Rifkin opens with a concise statement that speaks to the dilemma of thinking through time in settler colonial contexts: "Native peoples occupy a double bind within dominant settler reckonings of time. Either they are consigned to the past, or they are inserted into a present defined on non-native terms" (2019, vii). In turn, the need to assert Indigenous being-in-time, to insist on the coevalness and presentness of native peoples, always risks taking the temporal frames of settler governance for granted (Rifkin 2019). For Palestinians, as much as any other colonized peoples, these challenges and dilemmas were and remain formidable. Like so many movements for decolonization, the Palestinian struggle has moved between temporal inclusion and temporal alterity. We can see this for example in the Palestinian Revolution of the 1960s and 1970s that seemed to embody these dilemmas right to its end. The Revolution was, on the one hand, a bid to enter universal history through that history's privileged form (revolution) and as such normalize and include a self-determining Palestinian nation-state as a historical entity just like any other. On the other hand, it was the antistatist making of a new revolutionary and anticolonial Palestinian time that could *not* be assimilated into the historical present of the global national order—a time against history.¹²

Time has long loomed large over the Palestinian condition: a condition that Palestinians have come to understand through a set of distinctly spatiotemporal images and concepts, such as siege (*al-hisar*), waiting (*al-intithar*), exile (*al-hijra*), the temporary (*al-muwaqat*), deferral (*al-ta꜉jil*), and, above all, return (*al-'awda*). For all the dominance of the spatial turn and political geography in Palestine studies, the politics of time and temporality has recently come into its own. Edward Said ([1979] 1992) was early (or maybe the rest of us are just late) when he conceptualized Palestinianness as a state of temporal impasse, defined by the impossibility of its present. Now that we've caught up, we have compelling takes on the Palestinian condition as defined by the ruptures, twists, and emptiness of "checkpoint time" (Tawil-Souri 2017); the waiting and "stolen time" of closure (Peteet 2016); the perpetual present of "post-revolutionary time" (Abourahme 2016); or the fractured time of "internal severance" (*inqisam*) (Mor 2024). Israel's occupation has itself been understood as a state of "permanent temporariness" (Azoulay and Ophir 2009): a regime of endless, repressive "conflict management" that seeks neither solution nor decision but "buys time" and profits from deferral and abeyance in a style that draws on wider colonial histories of rule. And, of course, much has been written on Zionism's ideological formations as they relate to a fairly crude instrumental treatment of mythico-historical time: the negation of exile, the return to history, and so on (Raz-Krakotzkin 2013). Here, however, I am interested, in more pointed terms, in time as the *object* of political struggle.

My argument that the camp allows us to read the struggle in Palestine as a struggle over time demands bringing the temporal more explicitly into our readings of the settler colonial. But it also demands doing so in ways that exceed the limits of settler colonial studies. Though Palestine has functioned historically as the constitutive exclusion of the very field of (post)colonial studies, the question of Palestine has today become privileged terrain in the field of settler colonial studies (and not only for good reason but with good effect).¹³ What might be thought of as a second wave of settler colonial studies in the early 2000s has opened up a field of comparative thought and political solidarity. And though the reception of this work tends to elide an earlier Palestinian moment in colonial critique in the 1960s and 1970s, it has nonetheless de-exceptionalized the question of Palestine, taking it out of the quarantine that Zionism's claims to uniqueness had imposed on it.

This, of course, is one of the principal gains of a settler colonial analytic. Namely, it demolishes the claim of singularity every settler project depends on. That is, it insists that the interaction with the dispossessed *is* the very history of who the settlers collectively are; there is no history of the institutions and ideologies of settler societies that is not simultaneously a history of settler-native relations (Piterberg 2008). Which is to say, just like any other settler colony, there is never anything extrinsic in Palestine about the struggle with native presence; there is no "Arab Question" in Israeli society that might be bracketed and examined, recognized, even conceded to and redressed, apart from the wider political and social structures. One of the effects of comparative settler colonial studies as an emergent field of critical scholarship was precisely to challenge this fundamental conceit of hegemonic settler narratives that says they are defined by some national or civilizational essence—what defines settler nations first and foremost is the interaction with those they have dispossessed.

At the center of this turn was Patrick Wolfe's 2006 article that would go on to become something of a foundational text. For Wolfe, the key term in thinking the settler colonial was, of course, *elimination*. Elimination is settler colonialism's organizing principle with race as its organizing grammar. Settler colonies are, or become, organized around the logic of elimination because the historical conditions that are large-scale colonial settlement have, when it comes to existing native populations, tended to demand *land* more than they demand *labor*. In other words, settler colonies are a kind of threshold at which colonial politics and native-settler relations cease to be *primarily* organized around the exploitation of surplus value from Indigenous labor. "Territoriality is settler colonialism's specific, irreducible element" (2006, 388). In this article Wolfe gave us perhaps the most paradigmatic characterization of settler colonial invasion as "a structure, not an event" (388).[14] It is a statement that has become emblematic—and suffered all the associated consequences.

The massive gains of settler colonial studies notwithstanding, critiques of it have been compelling in their own right.[15] There is a tendency in this second wave to displace histories and critiques of capital, and too often, settler colonialism appears like a roving ideal type disassociated from the entangled histories of primitive accumulation, proletarianization, private property, and enslavement that gave us capitalism as a world system. The focus on elimination can obscure both settler colonialism's history as a class project—a project that not only mitigated class conflict in the metropolitan world but also shaped dependent class formations in colonized societies—as well as the persistent reliance of settler capital on the (super)exploitation of colonized people's labor (Englert 2020) in differentially valued forms of labor and life (Clarno 2017). South Africa, for example, often conspicuously missing from Wolfe's purview, was defined by the simultaneity of elimination and exploitation, or more precisely, exploitation *as* elimination (Kelley 2017).

This critique can hold for Palestine too. The Zionist project was undoubtedly founded on its ability to exclude Palestinian labor, on its ability to conquer both labor and land in what would relatively quickly become a "pure" type settler colony (Shafir 1996). But its separation from Palestinian labor has never been as seamless as it seems. Large sections of Israeli capital remain wholly dependent on the exploitation of racialized Palestinian labor and skill, most obviously in the construction sector— dispossessed Palestinians have quite literally built Israel (Ben Zeev 2020, 2021; Ross 2019). But beyond all this, *value* has always been generated from disposable Palestinian life alongside a logic of elimination, without necessary recourse to either formal exploitation or wage labor. The racialization of the Palestinians (as indolent, itinerant, idle), like the racialization of colonized peoples in any settler colony, is after all, the very basis of *all* value, because it is what renders native life removable and, as such, land and labor commodifiable. This same dispossessed life in Palestine has today become the laboratory target of an Israeli arms and security industry that sells its technology as "field tested" and constitutes a larger per capita share of the economy than ever before, as well as a larger share of total exports than any other country on earth (Hever 2018). In their maimed, disabled, debilitated, and killed bodies, Palestinians are part of speculative value generation on a global scale (Puar 2017). If the persistence of primitive accumulation at the heart of global capitalism demonstrates anything, it is that disposability is not antithetical to value but increasingly its very condition of possibility (Tadiar 2022). What I mean to point to here is the multiplicity of vying logics at play that might be missed with an overemphasis on elimination. Palestinians are absolutely slated for and subject to elimination as a collective, and yet they are *not* external to the generation of value by any means.

The earlier Marxist accounts of Palestinian scholar-activists—in what should be thought of as the (forgotten) first wave of settler colonial studies

—were arguably more adept at thinking about the tensions and synergies between elimination and exploitation, locating Zionist settler colonialism as an inseparable historical part of wider European imperialism and the capitalist world system (Sayegh 1965; Jabbour 1970; Kayyali 1977; Abdo 1991). In his 1965 text, published as the first monograph of the Palestine Research Center he helped found, Fayez Sayegh, for example, was not only among the first to identify Zionism as a settler colonial project founded on "racial elimination" (preempting aspects of Wolfe's much better-known essay by decades), but he also insisted on its ongoing connections to Euro-American capitalism in the region in a way we often lose sight of today. Settler colonial studies has never been a roving, prefab category "applied" (or "misapplied," as some have it) to Palestine and Zionism: it was grounded knowledge that emerged from the terrain of Palestinian struggle itself.

If all this weren't enough, there is too the uneasy tension between settler colonial and Native studies. There is a sense that settler colonial studies has tended to obscure the importance of precolonial lifeworlds and cosmologies as well as their endurance beyond the rupture of colonization; that it misses an account of the Indigenous and Black "earth-worlds" that settler colonialism could not have survived without—that worldmaking gift turned into conquest (Gill 2023). Even at its most critical, settler colonial studies has a habit of displacing the question of Indigeneity (Kauanui 2016), and as a narrative form it too easily ends up overemphasizing the "triumph" or "success" of settler replacement (Barakat 2017).

Many of these critiques seem to meet at what is seen as the mistake of isolating settler colonialism as a *type* from what then becomes "franchise" or "metropole" colonialism. Stoler, always apprehensive of the ability of hard typologies to make sense of what she has so consistently shown to be the patchworked, contingent, and contested nature of colonial history, tells us her reservation around settler colonialism "has less to do with the political concept itself than with the fact that it is often invoked as an ontological state rather than a fractious historical condition" (2016, 60). Settler colonialism, she insists, is but one "protracted moment in colonial statecraft" (60), appearing and receding in colonizing projects across the board as failed visions for the settlement of European colonists come and go; countless colonial governments, she reminds us, sought at one point or another to move European populations into the colonies, only to flounder, lag, or change course.

This is all fairly well rehearsed at this stage. What I want to get at here is how we might come to terms with what settler colonial politics does—in terms of opening a field of temporal struggle—without getting too bogged down in just what it is or isn't. If settler colonialism is, we can agree, not a unique type, then the question is what terms and concepts can parse this "fractious historical condition"—from which there does not seem to be any going back and which never seems to finish. Even if we rightly don't subscribe to a hard distinction between metropole and settler colonies, the protracted moment of settlement cum replacement seems at least to mean a shift in a colony's order of priorities and, I would argue, in its temporal dynamics.[16]

How then can we come to terms not with settler colonialism per se but with what we might call *settlerness*? I don't mean settlerness as a quality that might distinguish settler colonial situations from colonial situations.[17] I use settlerness as a concept and in the form of a nominalized adjective, instead, to describe a political mode of existence that can appear anywhere large-scale colonial replacement occurs. The condition of settlerness might intersect with extraction, exploitation, elimination, and replacement but is not entirely reducible to any single one. By settlerness I mean the way by which the recursive but endless task of dispossession-settlement both forms its own political imperative and is shaped by anticolonial refusal in ways that open up temporal contradictions. Settlerness describes both the project's dynamism *and* its inertia; it's a way of getting at this mixture of territorial expansiveness and a frequent sense of besiegement, even an unsettledness. Settlerness describes life in the shade of an uneasy domination. It describes a form of restless inhabitation, *because to describe things as still settler is to describe things that are not only stunted and unresolved but defined in large part by their opposition.*

I take the condition of settlerness, at least in Palestine, then, to be ultimately a kind of *dynamic stuckness*—a way of coming to terms with the mixture of unsettledness and expansiveness that defines the encounter here. In other words, it's a way of describing the political-temporal conditions of an expansive and powerful settler project but one that, faced with persistent refusal, is unable to overcome or move beyond its foundational violence and "naturalize" the ongoing dispossession in stable liberal regimes of property and civil law. And, so, I think of settlerness not as the opposite of Indigeneity but as the effect of struggle or anticolonial *refusal*. That is, here at least, this stuckness is as much the effect of the persistence of Palestinian forms of refusal as it is the effect of Zionism's immanent contradictions. The openness of the time of dispossession is double. Dispossession is not simply ongoing; in a very real way, the struggle *against* dispossession also stops it from becoming a mere administrative routine, technical legality, or fait accompli. It's the struggle that keeps dispossession in Palestine reliant on orders and magnitudes of explosive violence that belie or foreclose claims to "transition," "legitimacy," "success," or "normalcy." Israel's temporal impasse as a settler project isn't a failure. It's a defeat.

Settlerness is a concept, then, immanent to the terrain of social struggle, and it has its own direct equivalent in Arabic in *al-istitaniyya*. This is often used as a straightforward qualifying adjective, as in *al-isti'mar al-istitani* (settler colonialism) or *al-buʕar al-istitaniyya*, the ad hoc settlement encampments (mainly in the West Bank), somewhat euphemized in English as "outposts." And it's also present linguistically in the fact that Palestinians identify *al-istitan* (settlement) as the principal threat they face, with *mustawtinin* (settlers) (and not just *mustaʻmirin* or colonists) as their principal antagonists. But it can also be thought of and used more expansively as a concept drawn from existing Palestinian political practices as they act on the knot between time and settlement—practices in which there's an implicit refusal to consider the settler-state project and dispossession as anything more than temporary. The stealth cultivation of native wildlife and agriculture, the many furtive and open practices of return, the lived relationship to ruined and vanquished villages, the defense of the refugee camps, the rebuilding of demolished built structures, the entire ethos of steadfastness (*sumud*)—all of these are also temporal practices that refuse consignment to the finished past or inclusion in the settler historical present. They *refuse* closure, and as such what they refuse is precisely the transition beyond settlerness and its conflictual openness. The persistence of Palestinian life is measured in this refusal of resolution, in its insistence on the irresolution of the present. The secret of its power is not in any decisive finality but in keeping things unsettled and open.

Refusal is not just the disavowal of settler time; it is also the creation of a *temporal distance* that allows the colonized to know themselves on their own terms and in their own time: a distance that allows you to hold on to a set of truths that seem utterly implausible in the present but that you nonetheless know to be true. Refusal is rebuilding a village over two hundred times after it's been demolished and knowing perfectly well that it will be demolished again; refusal is living in the midst of a settler state that is massively built-up and urbanized, technologically advanced, globally integrated, and still *never* wavering in your belief that it is fundamentally temporary.[18] Audra Simpson writes of refusal as the political stance of those "supposedly sequestered in the past" (2017, 23) that pushes up on the present; it impinges on time as both demand (of a future otherwise) and reminder (of the ongoing work of dispossession, of what has not passed). "In living and knowing themselves as such, they [the Indigenous] pose a demand upon the newness of the present, as well as a knotty reminder of something else" (22). And so, for Simpson, refusal is a *puncturing* of the settler present that comes from "the interruptive capacity of Indigenous political life" (22). What I'm calling settlerness is the name of the uneven and unresolved time produced by this puncturing interruption.

In short, I take settlerness here to be this dynamic but unsettled, expansive but stuck, temporal condition shaped by the collision of the force of settlement with the sheer persistence of Indigenous refusal. There is simply no coming to terms with the colonial encounter in Palestine without an assessment of not only its coloniality but also its settlerness and the refusals from which it has been shaped. Without this, there is no way to understand the Zionist project's mixture of confidence in ongoing territorial conquests and land grabs, on the one hand, and its constant anxieties of recognition, on the other. Or to square a nuclear-armed state's formidable military power with its fear of "de-legitimization." Or to understand the Israeli State's frustrated attempts to organize and portray the dispossession of homes and land as a "real estate dispute," that is, as a legally contained and arbitrated dispute between two symmetrical parties subject to a single, given, and final property regime, and why this gets so vociferously rejected by Palestinians.[19] All these lines of contact are shaped by the open historical moment of conquest, by the struggle between the forces that seek to close this moment in time through law and property and those that refuse this moment any kind of closure.

Settlerness moves us away from debates about just *what* settler colonialism is and instead opens up a space to think about *how* settler politics and anticolonial refusals constitute a field of struggle shaped around time. It allows us to locate—with anticolonial struggle—the settler state's points of strategic vulnerability precisely in questions of permanence and endurance. If the camp, as I've been arguing, is a site from which to "read" the colonial struggle here, it's because it politically exists exactly at the point of temporal impasse that is settlerness. All of this demands we think through the politics of temporality more consistently. As much as land and race are the central concepts in settler colonial studies, it's clear, as I've been arguing, that once mass replacement becomes this almost irreversible imperative in a colonial project, it has its own particular temporal significance. The best engagements with Wolfe's emblematic characterization of settler colonial invasion as "structure, not event" all emphasize its temporal purchase, that this structure is "ongoing" (Simpson 2016, 440), "a system of relations in time and across time" (Gniadek 2017), and "endures Indigeneity" (Kauanui 2016).

But more than the ongoingness of settler invasion, what I want to get to here is the sharp temporal *impasse* of the settler project in Palestine. If settler invasion is a structure, it is a structure, as Lorenzo Veracini rightly notes, with a "specific end point" (2011a, 3). Veracini might veer into a hard typology of the settler colonial that isn't always helpful, but he is spot on in pointing out that the settler colonial moment "is characterised by a persistent drive to ultimately supersede the conditions of its operation" (3). The settler colony seeks its own self-supersession; *it seeks to achieve itself in the settler ceasing to be settler*. In other words, settler colonial moments ultimately seek to move toward—even if they never accomplish—the elimination of the native and the nativization of the settler.[20] Staying in a state of settlerness and temporal irresolution is a foundational problem.

To speak of this temporal tendency is not to posit a failure/success binary, or a comparative stagism in settler movements—none of them ever achieve self-supersession. The end point of nativization is, as I argue later in the book, a vanishing horizon; dispossession is not a "done deal" anywhere in the settler world (Kauanui 2016). But the drive toward "completion" and supersession is very real. And it's here that we can read the temporal impasse of settlerness *from* the refugee camps. Grant Farred, in an article called "The Unsettler," writes that the settler represents a form of "domestication," intent on "rooting" itself "against the temporal force of history, as it were, into the land," so as "to become integral to and at home in the land" (2008, 797). The imagery of rooting that Farred appropriates from settler repertoires brings together the bundled settler concerns about the possession and cultivation of land and self in forms of property and the temporal-historical dilemmas of colonial settlement.[21] Rooting is a getting to the depth of the land that is also an attempt at getting to the depth of the past, such that "expropriation becomes—through time—renarrativized as historic affiliation with the land" (797). To achieve this the settler has to overcome and surpass the lived past. "The indigene, like the land, must be temporally marked so that the passing of native time (the 'time before history') might be noted in order that it be surpassed by—and passed into if the project 'succeeds'—the modernity of colonialism" (798).

We can concretize this in Palestine by thinking about the importance of agricultural settlement in Zionism's early history both as a means of land dispossession and as an expression, much like the archaeological fever that so grips the project (Abu El-Haj 2002), of the desire to root and nativize the settler by reaching into the depths of land and inscribing itself into its past. But it's just as palpable in the architecture and housing projects.[22] We've come to recognize how much Zionism stands out, even among the "settler international," as a distinctly spatial project, or as Zvi Efrat has it, "a peculiarly deviceful architectural movement" (2018, 14). But we are less attuned to just how much this responds to the temporal anxieties and imperatives of settlerness.

Consider for a moment Israel's National Plan of 1950. Drawn up just two years after the establishment of the state by "Israel's foremost master planner" (Efrat 2018, 8), Arieh Sharon, this key strategic document was to be an outline for the comprehensive physical planning of the whole country.[23] It was to guide the publicly funded building sprees of the decisive decades of Israeli statehood in the 1950s and 1960s, in which a staggering thirty new towns and over four hundred rural settlements were constructed. What's immediately noticeable about it as a textual object is how laden it is with an explicit sense of urgency and purpose. In it, Sharon begins by identifying the particular challenges that "determine planning in Israel and dictate its objectives," going on to state that "three factors impose a unique character of planning in Israel. They are: land, people, time" (cited in Efrat 2018, 73). This is a striking—even uncanny—reworking of the threefold knot of modern sovereignty: land, people, state. Whether Sharon intended it or not as his own gloss on sovereignty is not really important. What's important is how, in this decisive strategic mandate—arguably one of the state's foundational texts—time stands in for the state; or, better yet, time "imposes" itself on the state, as it takes the state's place and threatens the very viability of the emergent state. Time is what has to be overcome for the state to take place. For Sharon, it was "urgently necessary" to treble the population and treble the urban and agricultural settlements within a few years if the state project was to have any chance of success. Time imposes an urgency that both compels and threatens the very viability of planning; it stalks this settler project from the very start.

What Sharon's plan missed, of course, is that no amount of construction or settlement can on its own close the temporal challenges of the state's foundational violence and dispossession. This is one gap that concrete just can't plug. The threatening urgency of time, which has only grown in the meantime, both drives forward the construction spree that is the Israeli project and at once, somehow, undermines even the most concrete of structures with a sense of instability and impermanence. There simply is no passing of the "time before history." Settlerness is a condition of protracted irresolution because settler replacement, as Farred reminds us, is an infinitely incomplete and incompletable project. Time, in its intimate relation with "place of origin," keeps the settler a settler, and the time of dispossession never passes. "Settlement," writes Farred, "marks a kind of infinity because it represents, due to its foundational violence, the time that will not pass—and cannot be passed—away" and, rather than become a given historical category, "the settler is, by virtue of the deracination it has enforced, the bearer of a fatal temporality" (2008, 799).[24]

Even among settler states Israel stands out in its temporal irresolution. Not because it is less "successful" or "complete" than other settler colonies but because it's more stuck. Stuck with a native population that makes up about half of its subject population that it can neither absorb nor (yet) fully eliminate, and stuck with a blunt set of political instruments that obstruct the normalization of its political order: formal apartheid and the legal distinction between citizenship and nationality, military occupation, states of siege, large-scale warfare, severe restrictions on the freedom of movement, and, perhaps most tellingly, systemic extra-legal and discretionary settler violence. Even the move to market- and capital-based forms of management is stunted, not least around land where dispossession is unable to transform it into a fungible private property relation, with over 90 percent of all land still held by the state or public bodies and administered by the Israel Lands Authority. There is no possible "transition" here to a set of liberal-procedural instruments and the politics of recognition and apology that might begin to look, at least on the surface, like some kind of historical resolution and transition. So, Israel remains reliant on open frontiers in orders of violence on a magnitude that set it apart. I return to this in chapter 4, but for now I just want to emphasize the temporal stakes of all this: Israel is a violently unsettled and unfinished project.

This is where one has to locate the entanglement of refugee camp and settler colony in Palestine. My argument is that the camp sits not only at the intersection of the most critical biopolitical sites of the settler colonial—the colonized body and its movements, land and its possession in regimes of property and state ownership—but also, and perhaps even more consequentially, at the point of their temporal (ir)resolution in a definite and stable form. Camp and colony are entangled from the start, coproduced in the double movement of dispossession and replacement, unsettlement and settlement, unhoming and homing; they are twinned but inversed topologies entangled in the temporal struggle between unfinished past (of the settler colony) and projected future (of the liberal postcolony).

Territorial Zionism both imagined its conquest as a civilizing, metropolitan, and engineering enterprise that faced, at best, encamped nomads, *and* at the same time, in a kind of performative engenderment, produced the Palestinian refugee camp, through dispossession and expulsion, as the settler colony's irreducible *foil* (foil in the sense of an antithesis or contrast, of connected characters in a story that expose one another's qualities, and foil also in the sense of that which frustrates or thwarts). If the camp is not just the result of the originary dispossession but is also, in its very material endurance, part of what keeps that very moment of dispossession unfinished and unresolved, then it is both the effect *of* and an interruption *to* colonial settlement. It keeps open the foundational violence that the settler colony needs to render into a past, even a wrongful past if need be, in which "mistakes" were made, but a past nonetheless that can be separated as extrinsic from the present project. Instead, the camps as placeholders for the vanquished geographies of Palestine, for the "time before history," persist as a set of claims to not only a pre-settler past but also a post-settler future. The camp doesn't simply mark this time: the camp *is*—in a very material sense, beneath its concrete—the time that will not and cannot pass. By keeping this past unfinished, and the question of return open, the camp sits at the heart of the temporal impasse that is settlerness. The camp, in one sense, keeps the settler colony, a settler colony. And in doing so it keeps the future open as an undetermined object of struggle.

The Camp Archive

What follows is neither an anthropology of encamped Palestinian refugees nor an urban sociology of one or more Palestinian camps (for both, we have many strong examples).[25] Rather I seek to read colonial politics in Palestine *through* the camp. That is, I attempt to locate a point of insight into the question of Palestine, into the project of settlement and the anticolonial struggle, into the means of their imperial and international management, in the very archival history of the Palestinian refugee camp. And in doing so I seek to ask how taking the camp as political object can open up ways for us to think through some of our political concepts *from* Palestine. What I am interested in, then, is the camp as a political object of practice and thought, and what we learn if we track it as such across the archives; if we follow the ways in which the camps have been conceived, constructed, regulated, planned, improved, policed, targeted, destroyed, defended, but also how they have been refused, disavowed, feared, revered, and celebrated. As such, "the camp" moves, necessarily and constantly, between noun and concept, object and figure; between a singular and definite article, *the* camp—by which I mean the generic and conceptual understanding of the Palestinian refugee camp as a unitary abstraction, often removed from the thing/entity it is thought to refer to (much like in the statement we opened with here)—and between the plural actuality of Palestinian refugee and other camp forms, camps. The camp in this work is a heuristic device, a way of seeing the whole and seeing it differently. In other words, the camp is an epistemic point of view that allows us to read global relations of forces in what otherwise appear as local sites. It is an archival pathway, an object to track and follow, and, as such, a method of reading the global political history of the question of Palestine and what this question, read through the lens of its camps, might tell us about our own historical present.

If there is an archival intervention here, it is not one of retracing a historical past. Nor is it one of inclusion. I don't seek to argue for the archival status of documents/objects in a revised account of the past—far from it. If anything, the history of our camps allows for a critique of archival authority not by uncovering something that wasn't known; the colonial records have long been betrayed by the open "archives" of colonial society and Palestinians have never stopped narrating their history to anyone who would listen. The critique instead comes in exceeding the limits of the archival; I use official archives heavily (the Israel State Archive,

UNRWA's central records, the US National Archives and Records Administration), but bringing the camp to the surface of appearance *across* sources is a way of both getting past the absences of these archives and at the same time avoiding the risk of getting caught in their internal citational logics. In reading across archival documents, texts, novels, visual artifacts, newspapers and print media, and personal papers, I use the camp-as-object to construct a different composite picture of the present. In short, if there is an archival intervention here then it seeks to create and contribute to an archive *of* the camps. It is not a complete repository, but a "shared place" that marks not only "the incompleteness of the past" (Azoulay 2016), but the irresolution of the present, the persistence of struggle: not archives as records of the past, but archiv*ing* as the active politics of a present-continuous (Hochberg 2021).

This book is organized conceptually and historically. Each chapter deals primarily with one single archive and, across a historical period, tracks the place of the camp in it as a political object of thought and practice. In turn, each chapter revolves around a single political concept, read *from* the camp: technomorality, authority, revolution, negation. Time and inhabitation are two conceptual through lines that cut across and string the chapters together.

Chapter 1 is a prehistory of the UN's Palestinian camp regime. It draws on the papers of the former director of the Tennessee Valley Authority (TVA), Gordon R. Clapp, whose recommendations established the camp regime in 1949. Almost every history of the camps or UNRWA starts from Clapp's report, but not a single one consults his papers or considers the wider histories and connections his role entailed and brought forth. By contrast, through the figure of Clapp, I show that the Palestinian camp regime emerged not in a strictly humanitarian but in a techno-imperial moment in global history that sought to put displaced "idle" refugees back to work. To really understand the logics of what would become a permanently interim camp regime, we have to understand the racializing presuppositions that Clapp and his team brought to Palestine from the US South. And I argue that we can better apprehend these presuppositions and their combination of technical mastery, racial figuration, and normativity in what I call *technomorality*. Read from the camps, via the long shadow of the South and in the wake of decolonization, the hidden content of the technocratic appears not only as depoliticization, or the triumph of instrumental reason, but also as repackaged racial world formation. The technical is an imperial alibi.

Chapter 2 looks at the place of the camp in the regime Clapp inaugurated and is written from UNRWA's archives. It unpacks the Agency's early planning efforts (1950–69) to formalize and spatially regulate the camps, before following the archival record around a moment of crisis that posed a foundational challenge to the Agency—the Cairo Agreement of 1969 in which the Palestine Liberation Organization (PLO) entered and assumed control of Lebanon's camps. The chapter argues that once the work projects that Clapp envisaged failed to take off, UNRWA's primary means of authority was in the regulation of the built environment itself, in domesticating the refugee as inhabitant. But in this history, the camps went from being the basis of the Agency's authority to the very sites at which that authority broke down. Camps should be seen not simply as legal artifacts but as built objects. In ways that presage the managerial turn, *authority* emerges in this history neither as something vested in popular mandate ("the will of the people") nor an inherited and continued historical foundation, but as the stuff of technical competence (what the Agency calls "administrative authority"), decoupling authority from sovereignty and exposing the former not as the opposite of force but as one half of its antinomian pairing.

Chapter 3 studies the camp from the perspective of the Palestinian Revolution in the period between 1968 and 1982. Turning to literary forms, it argues that the Revolution was defined by the historical dilemma of forming a militant subject from the encamped refugee; only a transformation of the camps that reversed their operative logic from confinement to movement could guarantee the popular-mass base necessary for revolutionary insurrection and the creation of a new historical time. But, where political discourse mediated the camp as an object to be transformed into the means of its own overcoming, literary narratives came undone at precisely this point, registering an irresolvable tension, in their very form, between life and politics. The chapter takes on three novels of the revolutionary period (by Ghassan Kanafani, Rashad Abu Shawir, and Yayha Yakhlif) to show that just at the point where the camp should be overcome in the protagonist's journey toward militancy the very narrative drive itself comes unstuck. Camp form and novel form are entangled. From this tension, the Palestinian *Revolution* appears as an event less about state capture or transition and more about an open-ended mode of subject formation, a becoming revolutionary.

Chapter 4 examines the place of the Palestinian refugee camp in Israeli politics. It relies mainly on documents from the Israel State Archives relating to the series of plans, developed after the 1967 occupation of the West Bank and Gaza, to completely undo the camps and resettle their inhabitants. I frame this chapter around one central question: Why do the camps themselves appear as such sources of political anxiety for Israeli officials? Here, I argue that Israeli state politics carried a deep abiding anxiety about political claims carried in the very temporality of the camps as interim placeholders for the originary villages of their refugee inhabitants. It was the camps themselves more than refugeehood that manifested what was repeatedly called by Israeli commentators a "consciousness of the temporary." Tracing the place of the camps in Israeli governmental plans illustrates, I argue, how settler politics demands the work of *negation*—the refutation of that which is not entirely repressible and its rendering in negative form. The push to undo the camps should be understood as part of the wider negational drive to "confirm" that there is no longer a place called Palestine, that there is nothing in fact to return to. Negation, as distinct from (if related to) denial, appears beyond the strictly psychoanalytic, as a mechanism by which settler politics acts—both reflexively and causatively—on anticolonial counterclaims.

The coda is written almost as a stand-alone piece in its own right; it doesn't so much wrap up the book as take flight along some of the conceptual lines the book forged. And it does so in a more explicitly global frame: What does it mean to read the global border crisis from the long colonial arc of Palestinian encampment? At stake in such a reading, at stake in a world of mass encampment is the question of inhabitation. Inhabitation, I argue, is perhaps *the* political question of our time. In camps, inhabitation, and not citizenship or rights, has become the basis of both political control *and* contestation. Thinking through inhabitation as a concept allows us both to recognize the enduring colonial terms of the border/climate crisis and to approach the political stakes of migrant/refugee struggle. A politics of inhabitation is one name for the life-making practices of the global dispossessed.

1 THE CAMP, INEVITABLE

TECHNOMORALITY AND RACIALIZATION IN THE PREHISTORY OF THE CAMP REGIME

Beginnings

"The end we know all too well; what we don't know is the beginning." That was Mahmud Darwish's (2002) beguilingly simple turn of phrase regarding the inevitable "drying up" of all human beings and his habit of starting new poetic works out of older ones. Yet I'm also tempted to read this a little obliquely, in a way I think Darwish is at least toying with, as a kind of sideways reflection on the Palestinian question itself—the end, one way or another, seems obvious enough: what we're really still missing is the beginning.

Some beginnings impose themselves with the full force of origin (1948 is not just a calendric year or even a point in historical time). Other beginnings are less obvious. Gordon Rufus Clapp, a name almost synonymous with the Tennessee Valley Authority (TVA), where he spent twenty-one of his short fifty-eight years, seems a curious and distant place to begin a story about the Palestinian refugee camp. And yet if any one person marks a productive starting point, it is this soft-spoken, red-haired, faithfully modern American public servant; this administrator-intellectual, of a kind perhaps extinct today, who seemed just as much at ease quoting Emerson and Tolstoy in articles on public administration, or talking about dialectics in a piece on dam building, as he was overseeing great public works projects. He lived and worked in the space between the *worldly* mastery of the technoscience of engineering and development, and the *otherworldly* spiritual, Christian ethics of virtue and duty, and his metaphors and images speak so readily to this entanglement: "people are rebuilt," "ideas are fertilized," "brains are tapped"; there are "adventures in faith and works," an insistence on "the tensile strength of faith" (Clapp 1947). "Gordon Clapp," wrote one contemporary, "was a man who preached what he practiced"; his words "restate the sermons he lived as an administrator" (Case 1964, 91).

Clapp inaugurated the Palestinian camp regime. Roughly midway through his tenure as TVA chairman, in the summer of 1949, he found himself thrust into the thick of the arbitration of the question of Palestine, as head of what was called the Economic Survey Mission for the Middle East, or what came to be known, more regularly, simply as the Clapp mission. Clapp's report in November 1949 provided the terms of reference for what would a few months later become the United Nations Relief and Works Agency (UNRWA), which would build and administer the camps. Every history of the Palestinian camp regime and UNRWA begins with Clapp and his mission as backdrop. But not one, to my knowledge, takes it very seriously or stops to consider its larger effects, let alone makes use of Clapp's personal papers or the archival records of the mission.

Yet we can't understand how the camp regime came to be what it is, or how it came to be part of the international order's devices for the temporary management of the question of Palestine, without Clapp, or without what Clapp brought with him. My primary claim here is that the Palestinian camp regime emerged not in a strictly humanitarian but in a techno-imperial moment in global history that sought to put displaced "idle" refugees back to work. Clapp via the TVA, I argue, brought to Palestine from a segregated US South distinctly racializing logics that figured displaced Palestinian bodies as idle, pitiful, threatening in their very movement, unprepared for self-determination, and in need of the corrective effects of work—all of which found an almost natural affinity in the architectural form that is the camp. Rather than signal the ascendancy of a humanitarian moment in global politics, the refugee camp regime indexed a postwar world being shaped around racial regimes of work and separation. And in this, it drew, however indirectly, on the long-entwined histories of dispossession, landlessness, work, and encampment. People deracinated from their land are never instantly proletarianized; they are subject to movement control, confinement, forced settlement, and disciplinary force. This, after all, has been one of the earliest logics of the modern camp form. And it should have surprised nobody that Clapp's regime, intent on rehabilitating and settling the dispossessed through corrective work, would end up in long-term encampment. Long-term camps weren't planned, they weren't even desired, but they became all but inevitable.

Reading this moment from the camps, I argue, also helps us read part of what is at stake in the postwar technocratic push to reorder the world. Read from the camps and via the long shadow of the US South, the hidden content of the technocratic appears not only as depoliticization, or the triumph of instrumental reason, but also as racial world formation. In other words, the technical was the alibi for a certain extension of the colonial ordering of the world. In an age of emergent decolonization and anticolonial nationalism, the technocratic moment *allowed* for ongoing racial world formation in ways that appeared nonpolitical and in line with the consensus around self-determination. To put it declaratively, the technocratic *is* a racialized refashioning of the world and its subjects around work, self-improvement, hierarchy, and moral betterment: one that takes shape through a mixture of technical mastery, racial figuration, and normative injunction—this is what I call *racialized technomorality*. This history, in short, pushes us to rethink the technical as a political concept.

The Administrative Technics of the Tragic Interim

So how did Gordon Clapp come to play the central role he did in this story? How did an official whose experience was strictly limited to the technical administration of a planning agency in the South, a man who studiously avoided and professed ignorance of what he called "politics," come to find himself in the middle of the arbitration of the fallout of one of the century's starkest colonial wars in a region he readily admitted knowing close to nothing about? How did the TVA, of all organizations, come to be seen as the right site of expertise with which to manage a political crisis of dispossession and displacement? The connections are not obvious at first glance.

The Clapp mission, I argue, was nothing more or less than an effect of the closure of *politics* as a frame of redress. It was an effect of Israel's successful translation of the racial-demographic imperatives and anxieties of settlerness into the language of technical capacity. And to trace this we have to start with the Lausanne Conference of 1949. In the wake of the 1948 war and the ethnic cleansing of Palestine, the question of the expelled Palestinians, or the "refugees," quickly became the central issue of contention. In December 1948, the United Nations (UN) had passed General Assembly Resolution 194 calling for the repatriation of the refugees and establishing the UN Conciliation Commission on Palestine (UNCCP), which was tasked with "facilitating a peaceful settlement between the parties to the Palestine dispute." After armistice agreements were signed in early 1949, the UNCCP convened the Lausanne Conference, which ran from April to September 1949, and was dominated by the refugee question.

Lausanne is widely considered a diplomatic failure (as is generally the tenure of the UNCCP), but that is to ignore the legacies of Lausanne, one of which is the Clapp mission and the camp regime. Lausanne was not just about the arbitration between competing political positions—it was about the clash between intentionally incommensurate frameworks. That is, at stake from the start was not the respective rightness or justness of a position, but the very *framing* and *bounding* of the matter at hand and thus the very *instruments* that might redress it.

The Palestinian and Arab states representatives, and the refugee delegates, on the whole, approached the refugee question as the stuff of political deliberation: what were the rights of those displaced, who was at fault for injury, what were the means of redress, and so on. The Israeli state delegates didn't necessarily contest the *content* of the claims, and had a weak case in disputing the *causes*, but they shifted the *frame*. It wasn't strictly the "what" they contested, but the "how."

The "refugees" were recognized by the Israelis only as a great human *tragedy*—a word that comes up again and again. Tragedy, of course, is something fated, blameless, and fundamentally unavoidable or inevitable; it has no conscious subject. Here is the white South African Michael Comay, who would play a leading role in establishing Israel's Ministry of Foreign Affairs, writing to the UNCCP in 1949, just before the start of the

Lausanne Conference: "During the war and the Arab exodus, the basis of their [the refugees'] economic life *crumbled away*. Movable property which was not taken away with them *has disappeared*. Livestock *has been slaughtered or sold*. Thousands of town and village dwellings *have been destroyed* in the course of the fighting, or in order to deny their use to enemy forces, regular or irregular."[1] Notice, and this will come up again, as it does in so many of the archival documents of the colonial world, how the grammatical voice is often passive (Piterberg 2001). In a reversal of conventional sentence structure, the syntax here sees verbs regularly end sentences (rendering some of them intransitive), and objects (economic life, property, villages) occupy the position of the grammatical subjects. There is no "agent" in the semantic sense at all: things just "crumble away," or "disappear," or end up "hav[ing] been destroyed." The present perfect tense only reinforces the sense of consequentiality of this immediate past to the present.

These were "tragic" events for which no one was clearly responsible, and the victims were entirely accidental. The refugees were not politically targeted any more than they were politically liable. Even, or especially, in victimhood it was important to remove any markings of political identity. Palestinians were rendered rightless not as a result of their political actions or thoughts, which would have made them victims of persecution (and political exiles); they were, on the contrary, innocents, geographic accidents—in other words, nothing but human beings. "Innocence," Hannah Arendt says of the stateless, "in the sense of complete lack of responsibility, was the mark of their rightlessness as it was the seal of their loss of political status" (1973, 294). The question, then, was never about persecution or its redress through justice, because a party at fault was never established here; "Israel was the victim, not the author, of the war which caused this tragedy," as another, even more well-known, white South African–Israeli diplomat put it.[2] It was about a humanitarian solution to a humanitarian problem, understood here as the immediate, practical steps needed to keep helpless people alive. And in this sense, as Israeli prime minister David Ben-Gurion would, in a meeting in April 1949, tell the commission, "Israel would never forget the humanitarian side of the question" (UNCCP 1949f). Indeed not.

Comay's letter to the UNCCP has the benefit of making clear the distinction between politics and pragmatism, or, between, as he has it, a historical analysis of conditions and a speedy solution to mass misery. He writes, "The Conciliation Commission is not called upon to analyse the historical conditions of the Arab refugee problem, but to find a solution for it—and to find it speedily, for the mass misery of the refugees has only been temporarily mitigated by international relief."[3] Establishing "historical conditions" might lead to the political stakes of accountability, establishing fault and means of redress; finding speedy "solutions," on the other hand, is the stuff of practical or technical intervention.

This precisely was the effect of the Israeli position at Lausanne: not only diffusing accountability in the language of tragedy and the protohumanitarianism of "suffering" and "misery" but also shifting to a technical and practical frame of intervention. Israeli officials did not just indefinitely defer "the refugee question" by pegging it to the vanishing point of a final, comprehensive peace solution: they also reoriented and reframed it. What appeared to and was articulated by Arab states as a self-evident issue of "humanity, rights and justice" was constantly reconfigured by Israel as subject to considerations of "practicality," "security and economy," "absorptive capacity," and "implementability" (UNCCP 1949e). Not only were the numbers of refugees disputed, as well as the validity of their claims, but the practical conditions of repatriation as an objective physical obstacle were consistently and constantly marshaled. That General Assembly Resolution 194 stipulated that the refugees should be permitted to return "at the earliest practicable date" would prove fateful: the word "practicable" was dissected, emphasized, almost always italicized in writing, to become a conditional clause in its own right. The Israeli Ministry of Foreign Affairs would frame this in terms of an economic impossibility, insisting on "the absence of an economic basis for 'Arab return'" and repatriation's "incompatibility with present realities" (UNCCP 1949c). The language is, as ever, abrupt and final: "Today, an Arab economy in that sense does no more exist.... The clock cannot be put back" (UNCCP 1949c).[4]

Nor was it only the Israelis who eventually framed the issues as such. The Senate Foreign Relations Committee report that authorized US financial assistance to the newly established UNRWA put it like this: "The situation was such that as a practical matter it was soon politically and economically impossible for the Arabs who had fled Jewish Palestine to return to their former homes."[5] The unspoken logic of racial separation simply becomes the stuff of practicality. The actual content of a notion of justice as repatriation/return is not actually contested but circumvented precisely *as* a notion that meets the objective immovability of material *reality*. Ideas break on the shore of things.

This rendering of the stakes as a practical, operational issue meant that a technical frame that might act on the immediate present became increasingly central. The pressure achieved its aims. In its second progress report, the UNCCP would effectively pause political negotiation in stating that neither repatriation nor resettlement "could be carried out without a considerable amount of preparatory work of a technical-nature" (UNCCP 1949e). No actual form of justification or analysis accompanies this claim; its basis is taken for granted.

The technical became the dominant *primary* frame. Any consideration of notions of "justice" or "rights" would now have to follow the technical work and its determination of the possible. The exact number of actual refugees who had "fled" and their places of origin, previous occupations, and means of subsistence would all have to be determined, as would how many and which refugees would prefer to be repatriated, and which would prefer to be resettled, as well as the practicable methods for the payment of compensation for the loss of property and how it would be valued. All of this would need, naturally enough, a "technical committee." And so in June 1949 the Technical Committee on Refugees was constituted and sent out to set up shop in Jerusalem. It came back with an inconclusive report that contained among other things one of the first proposals for work-relief as a way of boosting morale, as well as a mixed Arab and Israeli working group on property compensation (UNCCP 1949d). Needless to say, none of this ever really got off the ground, and the technical committee was dissolved, but not before the committee could recommend that its work be outsourced to external consultants. The stage was set almost perfectly for Clapp and the TVA.

The very terms of reference handed down to the Clapp mission in August 1949 formalize a certain boundary around the scope of its technical concerns and what must remain beyond them. The mission was instructed to "examine the economic situation in countries affected by the recent hostilities" and recommend an integrated program "to enable the Governments concerned to further such measures and development programmes as are required to overcome economic dislocations created by the hostilities" (UNCCP 1949b). This somewhat strange conjunction, "economic dislocation" (of which the refugees were said to be the "main manifestation"), is meant very clearly to circumscribe the terms of action. If to dislocate is to "put out of place," then, by this logic, what were out of place were not the political subjects of a national territorial order, but rather working and productive arrangements that seemed to stand in for a kind of social totality. Their redress would in turn require an *economic* re-localization. As such, a strange third term, "economic integration," appears in between what were the two accepted "solutions" to refugees, repatriation or resettlement. What we have come to call the dispossession of land was to be understood, at least for now, as a disjuncture between place and productivity, a series of geoeconomic effects.

Clapp and his three deputies assembled in Lausanne and by September 12 were in Beirut to begin work. Within one week of being appointed, Clapp was, in the appropriate parlance, "dispatched to the field." After they arrived, the work of the mission was divided into four working groups: agricultural development, engineering development, refugee problems, and financial and economic affairs. Each group was headed by "a general consultant around whom were grouped several experts (special consultants)."[6] The rest of the staff was made up of the principal secretary and his team of junior economists and statisticians. It's probably predictable that the first obstacle the Clapp mission perceived was the absence of statistical and quantitative data. True to its name, the mission demonstrated a palpable will to survey. The final report began with the observation that the Middle East was so bereft of reliable data "even on basic climatic conditions" that it required a whole host of advanced technical surveys—"the prerequisite for executing any development scheme" (UNCCP 1949a). The mission itself was pressed for time and could only scratch the surface, but it devoted most of its time anyway to preliminary surveying. One of the largest undertakings it took was a financial survey of the states involved—the balance of payments, fiscal policy, and budgetary conditions were all assessed.

The survey and the need for objective quantitative data extended, of course, to the refugees themselves.[7] An overriding concern of the Clapp mission was to determine both an accurate number of *legitimate* refugees and a surveying of their "general characteristics." While the mission conceded that no exact figure was possible, it still endeavored to reach a figure that was as "realistic" as possible. This meant that in opposition to the ration lists that the voluntary agencies had been using in their interaction with people on the ground, an abstract and objective calculation of some kind was in order. In the end, the calculation didn't add up to much because no real census was possible. Instead they ended up relying on a fairly blunt piece of arithmetic: subtracting the number of non-Jews in Israel as of May 1949 (taken from the first Israel Statistical Review) from the number of non-Jews in Mandate Palestine as of December 1947 (based on "population estimates by villages and religion" [UNCCP 1949a]), while allowing for natural increase. Because refugeehood here was to be defined by a measurement of neediness, they subtracted from this figure those displaced people *not* in immediate need of relief (derived from another estimate of those in gainful employment). So much for technical accuracy.

The surveying did not stop there, however, because the "general characteristics of refugees" had to be determined: average size of family, employability (the able-bodied had to be sifted from the unable, those able to undertake heavy labor from those that are not, and so on), and existing skills all had to be quantified. The surveying was absolutely rife with gendered assumptions about the lines of separation between work and social reproduction, indexed in terms like "employability" and the "able-bodied." The instrument of the survey looms so large in the mission's work that the vast majority of the two reports would be dedicated either to findings from surveys or to outlines and rationales for proposed surveys. The types of surveys that the final report goes on to propose are dizzying: cartographic surveys, soil surveys, land tenure surveys, meteorology and climatic surveys, subsoil water surveys, natural disaster surveys, agriculture and animal husbandry surveys, geological surveys, transportation surveys, statistical surveys, and, of course, administrative reform surveys.

This, then, was the domain proper of the Clapp mission as produced by Lausanne: the tangible, the objective, the countable, the surveyable. The prevalence of surveying here shouldn't be surprising. The survey was, after all, as Timothy Mitchell (2002) demonstrated, a pillar of colonial statecraft that sought to fashion discrete and geographically bounded objects called "national economies" in the late nineteenth and early twentieth centuries, first in the colonial world and then back in the metropoles. And Clapp, steeped in the social science assumptions of his day around aggregated national wealth, saw his mission as contributing to the forward march of "economic progress" in the region—one that would simply need surveys. But the survey instrument is also historically bound to land dispossession and race. Brenna Bhandar's (2018, 46) genealogy of the property form showed us how in colonial Ireland the cadastral survey functioned as an instrument of abstraction that set up the calculable and measurable value of people and land into a single quantified matrix—an instrument deeply tied to emergent racial taxonomies. With Clapp, the survey transformed the refugees into a fungible, quantified, and governable metric that was to be but one part of the larger accounting that would constitute the "national economies" of emergent states. And though it didn't survey the land that had already been dispossessed, it took that dispossession for granted by abstracting and constructing the dispossessed not as bearers of territorial-political rights, but as forms of potential value expressed as differing bodily capacities for physical labor.

After the surveying was done, Clapp and his team had to move to the trickier stuff of recommendations. If anyone was doubtful which way the wind was blowing, the interim report, published in November 1949, made things very clear. The report starts by putting to one side any talk of what were generally considered to be the only two viable options for refugees, repatriation or resettlement; these "simply underscored the bitterness" in the area, and addressing them "requires political decisions outside the competence of the Economic Survey Mission" (UNCCP 1949b). The politics are anyway muddled, confusing, intractable. "One thing, however, is clear. Rather than remain objects of charity, the refugees who are idle must have an opportunity to go to work where they are now: work which increases the productive capacity of the countries in which they have found refuge" (UNCCP 1949b).

Nor was there to be any large-scale mega-development projects or some Marshall Plan for the Middle East. The final report a month later in December 1949 would make clear that Clapp's conclusion on that front was consistent with the principle of social evolutionism: "You are not ready." As one *Herald Tribune* article put it, "The United States sought to disabuse the dreamers by telling them that there would be no overnight transformations, that the road to better economic and social status for a have-not country was a long and difficult one requiring diligence and patience and enterprise on the part of the beneficiary."[8] I. F. Stone, the radical journalist whose own writing career straddled both New Deal politics and a troubled, and ultimately fractured, relationship with Zionism, was, as always, a little more willing to call it like it was: "The final report is a bitterly disappointing anti-climax...an indecent joke." "Its flatulent flavor," he wrote, "may be sampled from its conclusions."[9] Those conclusions, he was correct, didn't amount to very much beyond a paternalist pep-talk: "It adds insult to disappointment to have the Commission read the peoples of the Middle East a sanctimonious sermon about helping 'those who have the will to help themselves.'" Preempting these conclusions, the interim report had already recommended a modest works program consisting of a series of work-relief projects around roadbuilding, afforestation, terracing, and water management that might begin to rehabilitate refugees into self-supporting individuals. Refugees understood as *idle* were to be met with *work* understood as remedial—perhaps the most classic pairing in the annals of liberal colonialism.

To this end, the mission—in what was really its only lasting impact—recommended the establishment of a new agency that would administer the relief and public works program. On December 8, 1949, some three weeks after the submission of the interim report, General Assembly Resolution 302 (IV) established UNRWA. UNRWA would receive from the interim report two meager terms of reference: the first instructed the Agency "to carry out in collaboration with local governments the direct relief and works programmes as recommended by the Economic Survey Mission"; the second instructed it essentially to begin its own self-dissolution by preparing for the time when international assistance for relief and works projects would no longer be available. The Agency was, in 1950, supposed to last all of two years.

It is easy to see how far we got from the stuff of political arbitration. Rather than establish a mechanism for adjudicating between antagonists and their claims, establishing injury and fault, and restoring rights or redressing injustice, the UNCCP ends up instead bequeathing an administrative regime of work defined by its externality to politics. What had begun with decidedly technical wrangling about practicalities and exact numbers, meant as the "*preparatory* work" for a future political "settlement," ends up becoming a regime of interim management that has no end in sight, an administrative apparatus of the meantime.

The TVA and Lineages of Race

Coming to terms with the effects of the Economic Survey Mission requires thinking more closely about what Clapp via the TVA brought with him to Palestine. In the postwar period, and especially after President Harry Truman's Point Four speech and program effectively crowned "technical assistance" as the pillar of US foreign policy, the TVA emerged not just as a model but as a *vehicle* for American-led (but *not* American-financed) modernization. It would be a crucial cog in the two-fronted global offensive against Soviet communism and anticolonial nationalism. TVA-led technical intervention (or what later simply became development) in the Global South was to be a kind of "hydraulic containment in the name of economic development" (Rook 2004, 66), building dams and planning regions so as to check Soviet influence on the one hand, but also ensure the flow of strategic resources and minerals on the other. This is a well-known story. What I want to underline for now, and which gets less attention in the scholarship, is how much the TVA abroad (and Clapp in his own right) was not just this great machine of technocratic restructuring; it was also a vector of racial and normative force, taking shape in cultural rather than biological terms, particularly around terms central to modernization: habit, work, idleness, custom, morality.

At one general level, this was all internal to modernization theory and practice. That is, modernization itself was premised on the central image of a global evolutionary sequence by which the nonwhite world might be lifted out of backwardness if only "traditional" customs, habits, practices, and institutions were removed and replaced with the technical mastery that was the modern condition. The sharing of technical mastery—for which the TVA became *the* name—in itself confirmed the notion of a global racial hierarchy. Or, as David Ekbladh had it in his book on the TVA abroad, "the capacity of westerners to master technology validated cultural chauvinism" (2009, 31)—it was both means and justification.

But at a more particular level this mixture (of the racial, technical, and normative) was internal to the context and work of the TVA in the South itself, a region seen explicitly as "backward" (Clapp's word) and inhabited by a majority rural, poor population, both Black and white, seen as in need of improvement. The region was, like so much of what would become the continental United States, seized and conquered at least in part through large infrastructure projects. Before we even get to Clapp and the TVA, then, there is the long settler colonial history of technopolitics—not least of all in dams. Dam building, after all, had long been an instrument of displacement and settler expansion; as late as 1944 the best lands of the Oceti Sakowin people, more than 550 square miles, had been flooded by dams built by the US Army Corps of Engineers in the Missouri River basin. The Pick-Sloan Plan, as it was known, flooded seven Native reservations, destroying more Indigenous land than any public works project in US history—"a twentieth-century Indigenous apocalypse" (Estes 2019, 121).

The shadow of race and conquest, then, hung over the TVA from the start. And it would not be one the organization was able to escape. On the contrary, despite its lofty global aims and its active courting of postcolonial elites (who would often awkwardly stay in the segregated Farragut Hotel in Knoxville, Tennessee), or the deadening neutral technical language it claimed positioned it outside of politics, the TVA was actively enmeshed in the reproduction of racial order in the US South. That is, for all the liberal idealism and alleged embarrassment that Jim Crow generated for the likes of Clapp and his predecessor, David Lilienthal, the TVA didn't just adjust to the fact of segregation in the South, it created what has rightly been called "racialized landscapes" (Alderman and Brown 2011). It didn't just work around the order of segregation; it, perforce, perpetuated and expanded it in everything from its employment practices and regional planning, to its land expropriations and population displacements, and to its housing policies and projects, going so far as to build an all-white segregated town in Norris, Tennessee.

In this light—and for our purposes here—it's key to keep in mind the wider historical-geographic conjuncture from which the TVA emerged. For Black life in the valley basin, disproportionately impoverished by the Depression and besieged by the revanchist rollback of brief political freedoms in racist violence and segregation, it was hoped, writes Nancy Grant, that the coming of the TVA would bring not only jobs "but a rebirth in spirit" (1990, 16). The TVA was meant to uplift the whole region, irrespective of race, but "no group had more to gain than blacks living in the valley" (17). In these terms, the TVA can be seen as the economic, technical, or developmental reorientation of Reconstruction; it was meant to put not just the region but the country itself back in its progressive historical arc, just through a different set of terms and instruments. What Reconstruction failed to do politically, the TVA as part of FDR's New Deal would achieve economically. In other words, with regard to Black collective life, the TVA's mission in the South can be read in part as the technicized redirection of the political promise of Reconstruction, just as the Clapp mission was the technicized effect of the closure of politics as mode of redress in the colonization of Palestine. If secure voting rights and genuine political equality were too hard to achieve, good-paying jobs and regional planning would mitigate the racial disparity in other ways.

Yet this was more than simply a redirection of Reconstruction: it was also its political evacuation, if not fundamental inversion. That is, it was as the NAACP charged in 1935, a "Lily-White Reconstruction" (Lily-White referring to the anti-Black movement within the Republican Party at the end of the nineteenth century). For the NAACP, which published two reports in *The Crisis* denouncing what it called "the Jim Crow tactics of the

TVA," this was an anti-Black Reconstruction (Davis 1935). That means it wasn't just the displacement of politics into economics, it was also the *inversion* of the promise of Reconstruction: instead of a program of radical political equality, the rebirth of Reconstruction as TVA-led development saw racial hierarchy strengthened, not weakened, *but* crucially obscured or hidden in the technical or developmental effects of things like (the very uneven) employment of Black workers, the inclusion of Black women in the labor force, the improvement in living standards, the electrification of Black towns and neighborhoods, and so on. To those familiar with the endless management of Palestinian (and wider) colonial history, this is akin to what gets dubbed "economic peace"—the use of partial material uplift to maintain racial domination.

These were charges, it's safe to say, that the TVA could not really deal with. For the TVA, the problem in the South was a "backwardness" born out of the mismanagement of resources and the idleness of workers. Their response to questions about racial inequity was to defer to a social evolutionism, in which Black people were not quite ready for self-sufficiency but would (in line with modernization theory) eventually get their turn *if* they worked hard enough. When Clapp in the Middle East insisted that the region was not ready for modernization and chided Palestinian refugees who he said would be helped only if they "have the will to help themselves," he was echoing the first TVA chairman, Arthur Morgan, who retorted to the NAACP in 1936 that "Blacks had to create their own opportunities" (cited in Grant 1990, 38).[10]

If this all sounds familiar, that's because it is. In 2019 the United States presented the latest iteration in a long line of technocratic plans for colonial management in Palestine in the "Peace to Prosperity" document, or what came to be known as the Kushner Plan. In language strikingly close to that of the Clapp mission, the plan concluded that the "unsolvable political situation" required a deferral of "political issues" to be dealt with at a "later date" in favor of creating the "economic pre-conditions" of peace. By *all* standards, Clapp was an infinitely more intelligent and decent human being than Jared Kushner (Clapp at least had the decency to avoid parasitic real estate capital and smarmy self-promotion), but there's no escaping the continuities. Much like Clapp did, Kushner channeled a set of racial and managerial logics to bring together Palestine and the United States. In 2019, while presenting the "peace plan," he effectively stated that the Palestinians were not ready for self-government: "The hope is that they, over time, will become capable of governing."[11] A mere year later, during the Black-led George Floyd uprising (then the largest uprising in American history), and faced with criticism of his father-in-law's administration, Kushner insisted that Black Americans have to want to help themselves: "But he [Trump] can't want them to be successful more than they want to be successful."[12] I'm not suggesting that in the complex of American imperial racism the Black and Palestinian questions pose the same kind of challenge. But I *am* saying that from the Clapp mission right through to this day, racialized figurations of Palestinians as undeveloped subjects not ready for self-governance and in need of work as a corrective remain *inflected* by American colonialism's own long histories of anti-Black and anti-Native racisms, and in the later paternalistic style of its management of racial hierarchy.

Idleness, Work, and the Subject of Self-Improvement

This history of the TVA in the US South came to define the Clapp mission: with the conceptual coupling of idleness and work. Going through Clapp's papers from the mission, it becomes clear that the Palestinian refugees are apprehended, in line with a long tradition in colonial discourse (one that goes back right to the colonization of the Americas), as at once too mobile and too idle; they either move too much or too little.

In one register, the refugees are seen as threateningly mobile and unmoored. A distinct border anxiety animates the response. The interim report begins, in a section entitled simply "The Problem," by setting the scene of this pre-camp world: "Their [refugees'] plight is the aftermath of an armed struggle between Arabs and Israelis.... Abandoning their homes and villages, their fields and orange groves, their shops and benches, they fled to nearby Arab lands. Tens of thousands are in temporary camps; some are in caves; the majority have found shelter in Arab towns and villages, in mosques, churches, monasteries, schools and abandoned buildings" (UNCCP 1949b).

The voice in this passage becomes active only as "refugees" become the grammatical subjects of their own displacement, as they "abandon" and "flee." Nonetheless, this abiding sense of great movement was not wrong. This intervallic world—after the expulsion but before the camp regime—was not only diffuse but fundamentally unsettled. Narratives and oral histories recount a constant movement of families and sometimes entire villages from one Palestinian village to another, until it itself is attacked, or from one host village across the border to another, until hospitality begins to run thin, or from one site of temporary encampment to another until weather conditions or lack of resources prove too difficult.[13] At face value, this unmoored period might seem akin to what Vilém Flusser calls "the wandering in the void" that is the second stage of expulsion, between the act of being expelled and the final stage of "being beached somewhere" (2003, 25).

Yet more than some kind of meaningless or void "wandering," the risk for incipient border regimes was that this movement might turn purposeful. Not only were most people not confined to camps or resettled, but they were also constantly moving or roaming across borders and, in many cases, at great risk, "smuggling" themselves back into Palestine, especially into the Galilee. We know that tens of thousands of people refused the wandering and expulsion and crossed back. In his epic novel of Palestinian exile, *Gate of the Sun*, Elias Khoury writes of what Palestinians called "return fever," a psychic condition that gripped Palestinians in Lebanon in this period (2006, 60). We also know that the Israeli State declared a "War on Infiltration" in 1949 with its border police shooting dead a thousand people that year alone, a figure that would rise to five thousand by 1956.

The threat and reality of people seeping back across the border was a constant source of angst. Yosef Weitz, the head of the settlement department of the Jewish National Fund and the head of the Transfer Committee, known for his leading role in the depopulation of Palestine (Morris 1986), would write in 1949 to Moshe Sharett, the foreign minister, recounting his nightmares of "long convoys of returning refugees and ... no one to help" (cited in Masalha 2003, 77). "Every day our people meet acquaintances who were formerly absent now walking about in complete freedom and also returning step by step to their villages.... Refugees are returning! Nor does our government offer any policy to prevent the infiltration.... The reins have been loosed, and the Arab in his cunning has already sensed this and knows to draw the conclusions he wishes" (cited in Masalha 2003, 78). This anxiety was particularly animated, for obvious reasons, among the Zionist leadership. But the fledgling and mutually jealous Arab states that bordered Israel (all of whom had only taken bordered form as nation-states very recently in the mid-1940s) had their own concerns about border movement. The refugees were a threateningly mobile and unsettled mass.

At the same time, the refugees were cast as stagnant, torpid, and dangerously idle, posing a risk to themselves and others. This figuration of idleness is marked everywhere: the interim report starts with Clapp describing the refugees as "a vast body of idle manpower" (UNCCP 1949B); State Department reports would use the same language, and so too would the voluntary and religious organizations that Clapp met with before going to the region. In fact, in the records the words *idle* or *idleness* appear with regularity and seem to summon a self-obvious risk that most involved understood implicitly.

This risk was understood in a distinctly moral register. That is, idleness posed a distinct moral risk, indexed in the prevalence of a word that often accompanied it, *demoralization*. Idleness was seen as producing a demoralization both in the sense of a loss of hope and confidence and also in the older sense of a corruption of morals. To be idle, then, was to be a risk to yourself and others, to the very moral fabric of community. Idleness, destitution, demoralization, dolefulness—this was the mixture of pity and suspicion that defined this economy of sentiments. The refugees were seen, much like refugees are still seen to this day, as a nondescript mass of people that was destitute but dangerous, idle but unsettled, demoralized but corrupting.

In one sense, this should come as no surprise. For figures like Clapp, steeped in high-modernist conceits of human mastery, idleness was a key mediating term that brought together the technical taming of nature on the one hand and society on the other. In fact, idleness is here a key mediating term that brings together, in almost classically racial terms, *untamed* nature and *undisciplined* bodies; to master or domesticate nature with the efficient use of laboring bodies was to temper the wasteful and dangerous idleness that lurks in both. So, Clapp, for example, would write of river technology, "Today the Tennessee neither destroys nor sinks into idleness" (Clapp 1947, 59), instead, writing elsewhere, that it has been turned into a "source of obedient human benefits" (Clapp 1948b, 183).

Within this framing, work emerged as the operative principle of the proposed regime. Idleness was understood as something connected to custom, or what Clapp called, in almost classically paternalistic terms, "the habit of inertia" (UNCCP 1949b). This habit in turn would require, as it had always done in early liberal moral psychologies, the proper application of a trained will. It would need a *will* to self-improve. Work, or a return to productive life, would furnish precisely that.[14]

The interim report laid this out in practical terms: "The only immediate constructive step in sight is to give the refugees an opportunity to work where they are now" (UNCCP 1949b). Part of the emphasis on work is drawn clearly from Clapp's wider career as a New Deal administrator. The image of the breadline, for one, that he invokes in more than one place indexes a historical consciousness no doubt shaped in part by the Great Depression. "This programme," he said to a small audience in Beirut at the start of his mission, "needs projects that will put men to work instead of keeping them at the bread-line; projects that will require manpower, that will offer idle men a chance to work, to work for pay, to buy and make things they need."[15]

Yet there was something much more fundamental about work than simply a restoration of purchasing power. Clapp himself gets at this quite readily in more than one place; in the interim report he wrote that policy will grow out of "an understanding of *the value of work* as a chance to earn and restore self-respect" (UNCCP 1949b, emphasis added). What I want to emphasize here is how much work was understood in terms of the transformation, or what was called the rehabilitation, of subjects. The task was not just putting the refugees to work in ways that would shore up what was being constructed as the object of "national economy," or even in ways that would proletarianize and thus emplace the dispossessed—this was all relevant—but it was just as much about the transformation of the refugee/dispossessed subject, reaching a kind of interiority or essence: a kind of Protestant corrective, if you will. The very frequency in the records of the usage of the prefix *self-* (self-respect, self-improvement, self-esteem, self-help, self-support) is, of course, telling—not only is the responsibility shifted onto what is posited as the individual, but we are dealing with the individual qua individual, in the very thing that makes you an individual or a self. To anyone familiar with the place of work in carceral and colonial history, this should come as no surprise.

Work would act on the refugee at a formative level. The Senate Foreign Relations Committee, for example, wrote that "work and the interest stimulated by the nature of the works projects will go far to change the outlook of many of these people."[16] Ekbladh saw this impulse to reach interiority at the heart of the TVA's entire developmental mandate abroad, which was always a modernization of the mind: "Individuals, as part of this larger process, had to incorporate modern outlooks on intimate levels for the process to proceed and succeed" (2009, 5). Yet I want to argue that more than an "outlook" was at stake here. The moral or normative force, entangled as it is here with racial presuppositions, marks something more primary, more basic, maybe even more ontological. In political-theoretical terms, what's at stake in the emergent work-camp regime is a kind of racially differentiated subject formation. When Michel Foucault recounted the operative principles of the incipient penal-disciplinary forms of the late nineteenth century (of which the camp, despite Foucault's reticence to really include it in his purview, was an integral part), he listed isolation and work as the most important; both were tools of carceral transformation that targeted the link between conscience and body in ways that exceeded precisely what we might think of as outlook: "A profound submission rather than superficial training, a change of morality rather than of attitude" (1995, 278). Work "is intrinsically useful, not as activity of production, but by virtue of the effect it has on the human mechanism" (242).

For the Clapp mission, work, then, was not really about a collective integration into something like a labor force—the horizon, if anything, was *work without workers*—but about a moral corrective of individualized subjects prefigured as almost naturally idle. Again, Clapp himself furnishes the best example of the stakes. When, in a meeting with religious and voluntary organizations in Washington, DC, before he flies out to the region, one of the representatives of the Society of Friends urged him to keep in mind that at stake is the very "morale and self-respect of those receiving the dole," Clapp responded, with a phrase that goes to the heart of the issue. He insisted that he would not forget the importance of "the constructive salvage and rebuilding of people"—giving us this perfectly apt notion of an engineered, built construction of subjects that is also a form of moral salvation.[17]

Clapp's intervention, dragging with it all the assumptions and all the baggage of the TVA's place in the segregated South, from the very start, understood itself as something that sought out the moral depths of thoroughly racialized refugee subjects seen as not ready for self-determination, dangerously wandering across borders, raked with the habits and customs of idleness, and in need of the morally corrective effects of work. I'm not claiming this was the only force shaping the UNRWA's eventual regime. For one, the racial thought at the heart of the Mandate system—entirely premised on a logic of wardship and the evolutionary notion that societies in the region were not yet ready for self-government—also shaped the wider institutional environment in which the Agency emerged. But Clapp and the TVA, and their experience in the US South, were a direct tributary. Clapp bridges and connects, then, these two moments in two different but *entangled* settler orders and brings into relief a consistency in both the *figurations* of racialized subjects and the technomoral *devices* of their depoliticizing and rehabilitative management. The camp is but one of these devices.

Genealogies of Encampment: Dispossession and Humanitarianism

So how do we get to all-but-permanent encampment from this? The Clapp mission, after all, had no interest in the maintenance of existing camps, let alone in their expansion or formalization. The terms of reference that Clapp handed down to UNRWA made no mention of camps whatsoever. The camps for Clapp were simply to be temporary stepping-stones for a return to work and permanent resettlement, present here in the thinly veiled euphemism of "economic integration." They were to be done away with as quickly as relief was. And yet the explicit imperatives of the mission we've just gone through—to transform naturally work-shy and dangerously idle roaming populations into moral subjects *of* work—lead almost seamlessly to the camp form. For these are precisely the logics that governed camp regimes in colonial history from the very start. Any colonial genealogy of the camp form will take us to these logics and by extension to a history of dispossession (much more than the history of humanitarianism per se). The Palestinian camps were somehow at once incidental and inevitable.

This history of the entwinement of relief and work (and its reliance on the idiom of idleness) is entirely continuous with the history of dispossession. Idleness, after all, is a category that, for all its theological Christian roots, comes into its own in the European and then colonial history of enclosure and land expropriation. We can see these exact logics at work in some of the earliest architectural predecessors of the camp form as they emerge as strategic responses to primitive accumulation. For example (and here I'm drawing on Andrew Herscher's [2017] architectural history of the camp form, and Aidan Forth's [2017] history of camps in late British imperialism), we see them when we go back to the history of incipient capitalism in England, in sites like the parish prisons or, later, the workhouses and poorhouses, before these too gave way to the more forceful technologies of labor colonies and work camps.[18] Here too the language of idleness was central. And here too the spatial removal and confinement in camp forms of the landless and impoverished—those who refused to be proletarianized—were seen as the basis for *both* their rehabilitation as workers and their forced resettlement. Karl Marx's striking counternarrative of primitive accumulation is as much an account of the place of movement and confinement in the emergence of capitalist social relations as much as anything else.

We see similar logics too, infamously, in many of India's famine camps in the late nineteenth century, where the ideological work of race allowed for a much more comprehensive level of control that, again, pegged relief to residence in the camp and work. And here too work wasn't economically productive, but punitive and didactic: "the senseless shifting of stones from one pile to another" (Forth 2017, 29). When the Clapp mission understood its main imperative to be moving refugees off ration rolls and into waged work as a form of rehabilitation, it effectively reproduced a long-standing principle in the administration of camps and relief from Britain to India. "From nineteenth-century Victorian England to the present," Herscher writes, "the ambition of relief is the restoration of its recipient to wage labor" (2017, 81). In this sense, the mission was completely in line with a tradition of liberal colonialism that, as Barbara Arneil (2012) has shown us, relied on figurations of idleness and custom in its use of labor and work colonies that would form industrious and rational citizens both in Britain (in what she terms "domestic colonies") and abroad.

In a historical lineage that takes us closer still to Clapp and the TVA, we also see this combination of logics in the so-called contraband camps of the US South—sites of encampment set up by the Union army during the Civil War to house and put to work freed and escaping Black slaves deemed "contrabands of war." This happened after over half a million slaves upped and left the South—in what W. E. B. Du Bois famously called the "general strike of the enslaved" ([1935] 2013) that dealt the decisive blow to plantation slavery—to which the US government responded by issuing the First Confiscation Act of 1861, which deemed the self-emancipated, and now mobile Black bodies, property of the US government. Here too the application of relief that would be gradually replaced by work in sites of encampment was seen as the right corrective both to idleness and to the anxiogenic effects of the unregulated assembly and movement of Black bodies.[19]

The logics (the written and unwritten rules) that have shaped the camp form are inseparable from this global history of colonial dispossession and racialization. Insofar as dispossession produces landless surplus people that cannot be left to move freely, it so often precedes the emergence of the camp form. Dispossession, racialization, and encampment quite simply have a coconstitutive history. And this history of dispossession primed both the terrain Clapp emerged on in the US South and the terrain on which he made a fateful turn in Palestine.

For all its particularities (and there are many), the Palestinian refugee camp was meant to be a device to achieve what so many other camps had tried to do: transforming a dispossessed landless people into a disciplined, resettled source of labor. All these camp and proto-camp forms held those who had been displaced or dispossessed and provided them with relief only insofar as they might be rehabilitated and held in place through work. In all of these cases, the camp is seen—along the carceral continuum it is indissociably a part of—as a transformative device. Camps, like prisons, have thrived on the basis that they are capable of fundamentally changing, or "rehabilitating," those in their ward. As Forth nicely has it, the secret of the camp's endurance is that it rests squarely on modernity's basic premise: that humanity is pliable (2017, 10).

Very similar logics would congeal in UNRWA's early camp regime. Here too, at least initially, relief was tied to residence in the camps and work. And the camp regime was designed to counter idleness and demoralization by rehabilitating its inhabitants. And though the work projects themselves were something of a complete failure, the logics behind them endured. Yes, there would be no transformation of the refugees into a regional labor force as a means of mass resettlement; instead, segregated super-exploitation and precarious underemployment remain the order of the day. And it's true that the mass work projects never really absorbed a large number of refugees (only twelve thousand in 1952), were incredibly inefficient (costing as much as five times as relief), failed in their main objective (never eliminating the need for relief, with ration-entitled refugees growing on average by twenty-five thousand per year), and, most decisively, were wholly refused by the vast majority of refugees.[20] *But the logics around idleness and rehabilitation would make their way into the vast governmental complex that was UNRWA's camp regime, in everything from public hygiene to education. In fact, a fairly fungible notion of rehabilitation would become the cornerstone.*[21]

Maybe most effectively, these logics also made their way into the planning of the built environment, and part of what I call a politics of inhabitation, the governing of the refugees *as* camp inhabitants. For one—in a striking echo of the logic of the workhouse—it meant maintaining the camps at a level of livability that wouldn't draw people away from labor markets. The Agency resisted replacing tents with built structures until 1952, and when they did turn to solid built structures, these were meant to meet only the minimal requirements of shelter; the records show that the engineers were explicitly instructed to make sure the camps didn't reach or exceed the standards of neighboring towns and villages, lest the refugees see this life as an alternative to work.

Seen in this wider arc of dispossession and encampment, the Palestinian camps have to be read beyond the humanitarianism we associate with the postwar refugee regime. That is, the story that we often hear of a global response to the horrors of the Second World War and the minority question taking shape in a drive to create a regime of asylum and protection, which sees the camp form—somewhat uncomfortably, even scandalously, but decisively—transformed into a technology of refuge and protection, care and relief, is somewhat belied by the Palestinian case.

I don't mean here at all to draw a hard line between the histories of dispossession and humanitarianism. As we've seen, the Palestinian refugee "problem" was often described as "humanitarian" and was actively framed as such precisely to foreclose political redress to dispossession. And if humanitarianism is both a moral economy of sentiments combining emotion and reason, affect and value, *and* an aesthetic that lends itself to the tonality of tragedy and for which the proper emotional response is compassion (Fassin 2011), then it was clearly present in the Clapp mission. And it's worth noting that humanitarianism as a form of government has always been defined by its own constitutive entwinement of care and violence not entirely separable from the technocratic turn.

Yet there is almost nothing in the founding documents that talks of the inalienable, natural rights of the refugees or the necessity of their protection. It's not that humanitarianism is innocent of the history of encampment and dispossession; this history just exceeds the history of humanitarianism (Herscher 2017). Take the words of Clapp's deputy, Sir Desmond Morton, who, when insisting on the need to move to works programs, said—with a contempt for relief that befits a scion of the English upper classes—that it is "better to spend money on works of permanent value than on merely keeping profitless refugees alive."[22] Now, humanitarianism and keeping refugees alive is subject to its own calculative rationalities (we might call them triage), but this patently is not the language of a humanitarian.

It is worth bearing in mind that the regime established for Palestinians took shape a good two years before the UN's Refugee Convention of 1951 was even ratified; the humanitarian complex that formalized a legal status of refugeehood around protection from violence had not yet really taken off. In the Palestinian case, refugeehood was not a legal status but an operational one defined around necessity and livelihood. "For working purposes, the Agency has decided that *a refugee is a needy person*, who, as a result of the war in Palestine, has lost his home and his means of livelihood" (UNRWA 1950, emphasis added). Compare this with the UN's 1951 Refugee Convention that defines a refugee as a person who "owing to a well-founded fear of being persecuted for reasons of race, religion, nationality, membership of a particular social group or political opinion" crosses an international boundary and is unwilling to return. They may both remove collective forms of life from politics, but they do so through different mechanisms, and arguably with different consequences.

In the shadow of the geopolitical accommodation of the Israeli settler imperative of "no return," the Palestinian camp regime emerges, then, at the historical intersection of, on the one hand, this long colonial history of dispossession and encampment as it encounters, on the other, a technocratic postwar development machine and its rehabilitative "will to work." This intersection is exemplified by the TVA itself; to put it more declaratively, the TVA, at least in one sense, *is* an effect of this very intersection.

Technomorality

To read the camp regime in this wider history is also to open up the space to read this history *from* the camps. As seen from the camps, part of what this history shows, I argue, is how technocratic development is entangled with the racial reordering of a restive and revolutionary non-Western world around the imperative of work. In other words, the prehistory of the camp regime not only helps us locate the question of Palestine in this wider historical conjuncture but also helps us read at least part of what is at stake in the postwar technocratic push to reorder the world in the image of the TVA. Namely, it helps us recognize how the technocratic refashioning of the non-Western world and its subjects always carried with it these racialized and normative presuppositions around idleness, habit, the will to work, rehabilitation—this is what I've called racialized technomorality. Rather than the violence of high-modernist order signaling the separation between technical and moral rationality, as one important reading goes (Bauman 1989), with Clapp, technomorality marks the imbrication of the technical and the moral in the domination and rescue—the "constructive salvage"—of racialized subjects not quite ready for self-government.

The camps, then, can be seen as a kind of seismic space that registers—in a particularly extreme and stripped-down form—the logics of the (counter)worldmaking project that is technocratic development. Refugee camps may seem far from the techno-aesthetic sublime we associate with postwar science and the mega-engineering projects of TVA-led technocracy. But that is to miss the *political* logic that undergirds this turn. Insofar as they are spaces of nonpolitical management, camps are distilled sites of technical administration. What this history does, then, is force us to rethink what travels under the name, the technical; in particular, what gets smuggled or hidden in appeals to technicism/the technical. In other words, what is the technical as power's alibi?

Genealogies of the technical can throw up a wide variety of lines to trace. In a political-theoretical mode, we could trace it back to the emergence of liberal governmentality as a distinctly *self-limiting* mode of rule, as Patrick Joyce (2003) does: a history of English municipal incorporation, which sees a split between politics and administration, with the latter emerging as a self-regulating sphere in part achieved by the performance of statistics and social knowledge as neutral and objective. Or we could locate one line in the repressed paradigm of economic theology as Giorgio Agamben (2009) does, tracing the technical to the Trinitarian dogma and the split between the being or substance of God, which is one, and his *oikonomia*, or his administration, which is triple: a split that Agamben says gives us, for the first time in history, "a pure activity of governance devoid of any foundation in being" (2009, 11), a kind of administration-without-substance. Or we could go even farther back, as Hannah Arendt (2000) does, and locate one beginning in Plato's attempts to find the basis of rule in neither persuasion nor force but an authority that stems precisely from the hierarchy of technical competence.

At one level the specific genealogy doesn't really matter all that much. What comes up consistently across these readings is the technical as both cause and effect of *separation*. If the technical remains a slippery concept, it is in part because it is difficult to give it stable positive content. It seems to be most consistently defined, or definable, in negative, by its separations. The technical, crudely put, is the nonpolitical. There is nothing "science-y" per se about what the technical does. In its political effect, as technocracy, the technical is not strictly about know-how, skill, or expertise (though these very well may be part of the picture and are often the performative basis of its self-boundedness).

Nor is the political effect of the technical fully captured by secular rationalization, or the ascendance of an instrumental rationality that seemed in postwar high modernism to signal the final victory of human mastery over the natural and social world. This was certainly part of Clapp's Saint-Simonian vision of the world pacified and nature dominated through scientific arrangement and technical administration. "Technical development," as Mitchell points out, "portrayed the world as passive, as nature to be overcome or material resources to be developed" (2002, 51). All of this is relevant. But for the world to be constructed as passive and for nature to be mastered, they first had to be separated from the stuff of human contention and popular petition, from the whole world of human unpredictability and mutuality that is politics. The technical is also, and more specifically, about the separation between itself and what it bounds as "politics." And the technical expert or technician is they who stand and operate at a separated distance from the world on which they act. This was, in this story, as we've just seen, precisely the effect of the recourse to the technical at the Lausanne Conference in 1949.

This separation with politics was salient and very real for Clapp, taking form in what he called—taking the technical back to its etymological connections with craft—"the art of administration." For Clapp, who wrote extensively on the subject, administration was "a public instrument whereby democratic society might be more completely realized," *but* this meant "separating political from administrative facts" and resisting, as he had it, the victory of "political judgment" over "administrative recommendation" (Clapp 1948a, 169). Authority here is divested from personage, office, or the relation of force (what is understood in negative as politics) and instead vested in administrative objectivity or what Clapp calls "the authority of knowledge" (1948a, 169)—a performative neutrality that enacts the very separation it names. As we'll see in chapter 2, it's precisely this form of an authority that the UNRWA comes to realize and affirm in what it called "administrative authority" (presaging, in my view, the much wider technomanagerial logic that sees authority stripped of any relation to sovereignty).

In this separation, technical administration eschews politics as the stuff of rights-bearing subjects bound by a social contract to law and sovereign power—all of this is bracketed or separated; instead, we are much closer to the objectified world of administration-as-government, to the regulation of population (and *not* "the people") as a set of optimizable variables, to what Henri de Saint-Simon on the cusp of the nineteenth century declared modern society would be about—the transition "from the government of men to the administration of things" (cited in Rabinow 1995, 30). In truth this statement is somewhat misleading, because government itself as a political technique only emerges *within* this transition. In fact, Clapp—who called himself a physiocrat—reproduced many of the tenets that Foucault identified as emerging with the paradigm of government in the physiocratic European state of the mid-eighteenth century. For Clapp, administration, as *the* supreme public instrument, was about bringing ideas, things, and men harmoniously together; it is, he writes, "a discipline of methods by which men's minds and energies *organize and arrange things in rational interrelationships* with a high degree of mathematical precision and *reliable prediction* in the setting of time and space" (1948a, 174, emphasis added). This is an effective, if slightly idiosyncratic, summation of many of the operative principles of the technique we call government: predictability and the calculable, the arrangement of things, the environment or milieu as the point of intervention. In contrast to sovereign technologies of power, Foucault tells us, "government does not refer to the territory in any way: one governs things" (2009, 96). Or, to be more precise, he adds, in language that takes us closer to Clapp's emphasis on "interrelationships," one governs "a sort of complex of men and things," which is to say "men in the relationships, bonds, and complex involvements with things" (96).

In the colonial scene in Palestine that Clapp was thrust into, this separation of technical administration from representative or rights-based notions of politics takes on a much sharper edge, in part because it productively intersects with older colonial rationalities that exceed the genealogies of government/administration we find in people like Foucault. After all, the rationale that colonized subjects were not ready for self-government and should be governed as wards is arguably as old as the European colonial enterprise itself. It's been progressively, if discontinuously, articulated as a central pillar of colonial rationality all the way from Francisco de Vitoria's tentative and almost self-rebuking use of it as a title for Spanish conquest in the Americas in the middle of the sixteenth century, to Lord Cromer's bullish and baldly stated use of this logic in a well-known essay, "The Government of Subject Races," at the start of the twentieth century. In one sense, what Clapp's mission navigated and reformed is little more than this old tension of proto-liberal or liberal imperialism. Colonialism has always been a kind of administration without politics.

Yet Clapp's mission takes place at a historical moment when emergent anticolonial nationalism and decolonization movements posed a challenge that could not be brushed aside with the same brazen appeals to social evolutionary hierarchy. The Mandate system of trusteeship in the region—perhaps the last major form of imperial domination organized explicitly around the unreadiness of colonized peoples for self-government—was reaching its terminal end; the 1940s saw a steady spate of Arab states gain postcolonial independence. The Clapp mission, like the TVA's global role writ large, shows how, in the postwar period, the old wardship or trusteeship rationale for domination had to hide in appeals to ostensibly disinterested and neutral (which is to say, nonpolitical) technical expertise. We can read, then, technical assistance here historically, at the midcentury conjuncture of anticolonial nationalisms and the modernization project, as an attempt to globally repackage or translate racial-colonial hierarchy that was decisively on the wane. And in this sense technical assistance was entirely complementary with the extension of the self-determination principle in its Wilsonian variety. In other words, the technical and technical assistance emerged as a way of maintaining hierarchy beyond "politics"—that is, a way of governing explicitly racialized subject populations, of unevenly integrating newly independent countries into the global economy, of restricting the sovereignty of new postcolonial states, of maintaining control over resource and mineral extraction, of globalizing a disciplinary will to work *without* an explicit appeal to domination, when direct colonial control was quickly becoming unsustainable. This, at its core, was exactly what the TVA abroad was about. The technical is an imperial alibi.[23]

Part of the challenge of this history and, for that matter, part of the wider challenge that the long shadow of global mass encampment casts on our world is to figure out *not* how to give positive content to something like the technical, but how to sustain a rigorous critique of the separations it both depends on and enacts. To talk about something like racialized technomorality is not to define the technical but to insist on making these separations visible. It is a way of both conceptually refusing the separations and insisting on seeing the work of racialization, dispossession, and violence that has long lurked at the heart of seemingly innocuous terms and practices like the technical.

Clapp wasn't entirely unaware of the separations or displacements his mission and its recommendations rested on. Going through his papers gives a sense of Clapp as a fairly sensitive man, modest and aware of his own limits. He was, however, entirely conditioned by the instruments and paradigms he lived and worked in. In a long private letter (nine typed pages in length) to the editor of *The Progressive*, written in April 1950, some four months after his mission came to an end, Clapp strikes a reflective and sober tone. Yes, he concedes, the criticism is correct that his mission and the work-relief program it proposed "doesn't come to grips with the basic problem confronting the Arab refugees."[24] And, yes, "if justice be the sole measure on this question, [he'd] side with the Arabs.... From the standpoint of abstract justice, it does seem logical that the refugees ought to be permitted to return to their homes in Israel's part of Palestine, but the problem is not quite that simple."[25] Reality, he effectively tells us, is less forgiving, and the question required a certain distance from notions like "justice."

Clapp responded through the terms handed down to him by the UNCCP, with the only tools he and the TVA really knew. "I had to fight," he wrote, "the same temptation to indulge in an emotional revel of passing judgement." Instead of emotion and judgment, Clapp wanted to apply some administrative pragmatism. After all, he writes, "The Middle East doesn't need people to interpret its defeatism; it needs people who can look hard until they find the place to apply a little realistic optimism and mobilize a few people to capitalize on the opportunities that are there to do something."[26] Something had to be done beyond the politics. The separations for Clapp are present but hardly worth interrogating. That in this case they would lead fairly seamlessly to the camp form—*the* space of separation—doesn't seem to come up for him in any meaningful way. And yet when a generation of encamped Palestinians rose up in organized refusal, their first target was precisely the camp regime as an instrument of separation, removed from politics and history. One of the first things organized political groups called for rejecting was the "Point Four programs" and "technical assistance": "For the ships and planes do not scare us, the technical assistance and the dollars do not seduce us" (*al-Thaʕr* 1955). It was they who would begin the actual work of moving out from under and removing Clapp's long shadow, and it was they who would go on to teach us that any refusal of colonial wardship begins in refusing our separation from politics.

2 THE CAMP, FORMALIZED

AUTHORITY AND THE BUILT IN THE MANAGEMENT OF THE INTERIM

Between the Built and the Political

What makes a camp, a camp? Or, better, how do camps do what they actually do? And how is encampment not just resisted but redirected? What if anything does all this have to do with the built? In other words, do camps have built histories? If so, what are the politics of these histories? That we have long relied on a theoretical construct of camps, forged in reflection on the midcentury crucible of European catastrophe, as legal structures defined by above all their juridico-political status is by now well established. As are much of this model's shortcomings: from its Eurocentrism and elision of colonial and racial histories of the camp form to its effective bracketing of questions of built or architectural history. The critiques are compelling, and I don't intend to rehash them here.[1] What I want to point to now is how, beyond or beneath statelessness and exception, what camps do and what kinds of uses they can be put to, by their administrators *or* their inhabitants, revolve quite simply around struggles over the uses of built space. If camps are historically defined by a series of political antinomies—care and control, relief and work, humanitarianism and genocide—then it has as much to do with spatial as legal structure.

For the administrative agency Clapp bequeathed this was no different, and the camp regime's defining tensions ran precisely along the fault line between the built and the political. In 1950, the newly formed United Nations Relief and Works Agency (UNRWA) assumed control of a series of encampments spread out across five separate national jurisdictions and a broad topographic range, from urban formations at the heart of cities to isolated rural sites. These camps would become the international order's principal means of managing a threateningly mobile surplus population in a drawn-out present that was safely humanitarian-developmental. At the same time, in bringing the refugees together spatially, camps were a constant source of risk for mass politicization and mobilization. This after all is historically one of the defining features of the camp's double quality: *both* a prophylactic device for managing the threat of revolt, by confining and "rehabilitating" the "dangerous classes" (and their various analogues), and at the same time, in massing suspect bodies together in proximity and high density, at least potentially, a "breeding ground" for precisely such revolt.

From the start it was around the use of space and the built environment that this tension or double quality would become sharpest and most consequential. For the Palestinian refugees, construction was politically double-edged: it opened up questions of permanence and the threat of plans for resettlement, but eventually, and conversely, it also played a role in the insistence on not being (twice) displaced from the camp, and thus on return.[2] From the outset there was a fairly widespread stance of both refusing permanent settlement in the camp *and* refusing to be moved to housing outside the camp. Almost any account of early camp life is replete with stories of the refugees burning tents, uprooting trees, smashing new constructions, and demonstrating outside UNRWA offices at the slightest whiff of news about housing projects. Refugees tended to resist being moved to other locations or sites of encampment, and where they were forced to do so, they always protested and bemoaned not only the immediate hardships but also the political costs of being that much farther away from Palestine.

In one of Fawaz Turki's many memoirs, which are full of images of his childhood in Bourj al-Barajneh Camp in Beirut, he recounts a story from the late 1950s about a prominent Palestinian woman in the camp, who would go on to lose six sons, two daughters, and her husband in battle—an almost unimaginable scale of loss that became generalized in the Palestinian condition. As news begins to filter into the camp that UNRWA has just begun mass shelter construction, she addresses a gathering of Palestinian women around a water pump and makes a stand that was paradigmatic of a certain refusal of resettlement housing projects: "O sisters, I swear to you by the blood of our fallen patriots that I will not hammer one nail in a wall while we are outside Palestine. We shall build only when we return to our land. There we shall build!" (1988, 39).

For the Agency and the host states, construction and building were also fraught with tension and risk. In the camps, inhabitation itself became a political problematic, one that cut right through to the political temporality of encampment. All the host states established fully fledged institutional bodies solely tasked with the refugees and the camps.[3] All of these bodies kept, and still keep, a parallel population registry of refugees, issue various types of documents, and register births and deaths (often setting up closely controlled and assigned "local" committees of refugees to do their bidding). But what they did most assiduously was regulate construction. In the 1960s in Lebanon, for example, it was said that it was easier to smuggle guns than cement into the camps. And the ubiquity of zinc or tin roofing in the early decades, always hot in the summer and always cold in the winter, came to mark not only the temporariness of this form of inhabitation but also the vindictive nature of authority as it took shape through the built environment.

The struggle over the question of Palestine was here not just a struggle over the camps. It was more precisely a struggle over what kind of spatial/built practices—and therefore politics—the camps could support. Alongside the refusal of housing projects (exemplified by Turki's account of the woman issuing her warning by the water pump) was the refugee insistence on being able to build without fear of reprisal or loss of political claims (to return). When revolutionaries from the Palestine Liberation Organization (PLO) assumed control of Lebanon's camps in 1969 (a key threshold I'll come back to in this chapter) they changed, as much as anything else, not just the political conditions but also the political *effects* of building. One impressionistic account by a member of a left-wing militant group described the change in the camps as such: "For in this camp, in which the sound of a nail being hammered into a tin roof was enough cause for interrogation and torture, it is no coincidence now to hear the sound of gunfire and slogans" (Badir 1969, 5). This impression confirms the fraught violence around the built as a matter of life and death—in which putting up a roof over one's head might have been enough to find oneself the victim of torture. It also establishes, by way of sonic analogy, the changing entangled relationship between the built and the political. With the Revolution, it's not simply that gunfire and slogans replaced the sound of nails, but more precisely that they changed the political conditions and effects of the latter; in other words, being able to hammer nails into tin without fear was both cause and effect of revolutionary gunfire and slogans, of a life worth living.

The excessive political consequentiality of something like tin roofing gives us a sense of how the regulation of space and the built environment had emerged as the backbone of the camp regime. For the Agency, which for so long saw itself as the correct authority in and over the camps, spatial regulation became the instrument not only of moral order but also of keeping the camps strictly nonpolitical and interim spaces, the means for rehabilitating the bodies in their ward so as to keep them on the right side of the life/politics separation. As its administrators saw it, UNRWA's very viability as an authority, and thus as an institutional entity at the heart of the drawn-out management of the struggle over Palestine, became entangled with the built environment and the regulation of construction. The indefinite and indeterminate status of the question of Palestine was not just reflected but itself took shape in the indefinite and indeterminate built environment of the camps. The camps physically and materially mediated the condition of *settlerness*, of the drawn-out unresolved status of the struggle with the colonial project.

This chapter takes up the camps as urban objects in the politics of temporariness. It focuses on the collisions with UNRWA and its interim management regime, but the background is always the wider temporal struggle with settler colonialism. Our histories of UNRWA, of which there are less than a handful, focus either on its unique organizational character (Buehrig 1971), its function as a diffuser of regional geopolitical tension (Viorst 1984), or, in the most attentive and comprehensive of accounts, on its inevitable enmeshment in politics, and its contradictory dual character as *both* a Palestinian organization and an instrument of "residual colonialism" at the same time (Schiff 1995). This fate was perhaps inescapable for an organization headed by a small class of Euro-American administrators, initially drawn from the ranks of either the recently disbanded or still active colonial civil service, but staffed by thousands of "local staff," overwhelmingly stateless Palestinian refugees (more than thirty thousand today). In all of these accounts, the Agency's focus on health and education services, after the collapse of large-scale resettlement in the 1960s and its turn to so-called human development, is taken as the core of its practice. Instead, I take up what is usually (incorrectly) considered the Agency's less essential domain: the regulation of the built environment of the camps, and its relation to a political concept that remains ill-defined, authority.

Tracking the camp as an object in UNRWA's practice shows how the camp as a malleable built and governable form became the basis of the management of Palestine's surplus population. But in producing a *form*—a discernible and bounded shape or arrangement that might regulate movement and organize time in a way that enables/disables capacity—the Agency's very fate became entangled with the camps. The Agency shaped the camps, but the camps in return shaped the Agency. Working primarily from UNRWA's archives, this chapter argues that the camp as an urban object of intervention became both the basis of UNRWA's exercise of something it called "administrative authority" *and* the site at which that authority broke down. This form of authority, which bears Clapp's imprint, indirectly prefigures the managerial authority of later forms of technocratic governance, as a nonpolitical form of administration that is, however, ultimately reliant on the very force it seeks to distinguish itself from.

In turn, I argue that we need to approach the camp not as a legal structure but as a built-urban object. That is, I argue that these camps were defined not by the *absence* of law or legal exception (as presumed in the still dominant juridico-political paradigm) but by the *excess* of regulation. It was in the planning, mapping, bounding, construction, and regulation of the camps that this agency based and exercised its normative claims to "authority." Here, the life/politics split took shape not around a zone of legal abandonment per se but around an excess of government, around the proliferation of proto-legal codes or regulations—blurring the very line between law and regulation—and the contestation of their authoritativeness. Encampment, as a regime, works through urban instruments, at the site and fact of inhabitation itself.

This chapter revolves around two historical moments that are at the core of my argument, and it opens up a series of questions about authority, the built, and the camp. The first is from the early 1950s when the Agency began to formalize the camps and decisively created a code of "camp regulations" that might both shape general behavioral norms and also form the basis of authority. The second revolves around a moment that throws this regime into sharp crisis. The Cairo Agreement of 1969–70 saw the officially sanctioned entrance of the PLO into Lebanon's camps, prompting a crisis for the UNRWA in which the nature of its camp administration would be severely examined and a host of foundational political and nominal anxieties would surface: What does it mean to administer a camp? How is it related to what we are as an institutional body? What is a camp anyway? And what happens if we just name these spaces something else? All this culminates in a limitation of legal liability through the disavowal of the Agency's role as an administrator of camps, moving, again in ways that presage the wider changes of the 1970s, from the government of *community* to the servicing of *individuals*, while keeping in effect, and this is the rub, their prerogative over the authorization of construction.

This history locates the Agency's understanding of its authority (as something grounded in the interim, technical, self-limited, and nonpolitical administration of space) in a wider emergent technocratic history. It allows us, in turn, to open up conceptual questions about authority and move the camp problematic out from under the shadow of the sovereignty concept. In these camps—where no one *really* wanted to be sovereign—the historical record poses much more of a question about authority rather than sovereignty. And precisely as such, this history resonates with the wider disjuncture of politics and representation in the technocratic or "post-political" age—an age itself increasingly defined by the emergence of the camp as a global instrument of "nonpolitical" government.

Material Thresholds, or "The Political Position of the Tent"

So, where does one start a built history of the Palestinian refugee camps? Perhaps the only point at which to start is in the recognition that this history emerges not only circumstantially, but also against the direct desires of those that would produce it. In short, the camps were an unwanted outcome. For the Clapp mission, the camps were to be a temporary mechanism of returning refugees to work. In the first two years of the Agency's existence, the camps were regarded with a kind of anti-urban, almost Victorian, apprehension about the density, overcrowdedness, elemental exposure, and perhaps above all *moral risk* that was the likely effect of bodies massed in what were decried as abnormal conditions. The very first annual report is awash with the wretched imagery of camp life: "leaky tents," "squalid barracks," a lack of privacy. And this perception of the environment combined with Orientalist racial figurations of "the Arab... a confirmed individualist" (UNRWA 1950, 8) to produce a distinctly anticamp imperative.[4]

This language, and the easy, almost automatic ascriptions of indolence and selfishness, would have been familiar to those involved in the Clapp mission. Except now it is not simply the "economic dislocation" and worklessness that are at fault, but the camps themselves, which seem to exert a determinate and corrupting force on moral fiber. "In the crowded and abnormal existence that the refugee leads, moral values tend to deteriorate" (UNRWA 1951, 11). Or, take, a year later, the conviction, expressed repeatedly in UNRWA's 1952 annual report, that the camp environment is tending to "create and reinforce a professional refugee mentality" (UNRWA 1952, 9). As a figure of trickery and deceit, the encamped "professional refugee" is a huckster of a kind, wretched and miserable but also cunning and sly, concealing deaths and even surreptitiously burying the dead or passing babies around to inflate numbers of births—"they are born in great numbers, and they die in lesser numbers" (6).

In these early stages, then, the camps appear as problematic spaces, to be done away with as quickly as possible. A program of "reintegration," essentially a codeword for resettlement, initiated in 1952, was in practice about getting rid of the camps and getting refugees away from "the deteriorating influence of camp life": "The essence of the new programme is the improvement of refugee living conditions and *the elimination of the need for camp life* and ration rolls" (UNRWA 1952, 13, emphasis added). So, the Agency would spend the first few years of its existence looking for ways to get bodies out of camps. A mixture of peri-urban (the Heineken Housing and Madaba projects outside Amman) and rural housing schemes ("model villages" in Qalqilya, Bardala, and 'Ayn 'Arik in the West Bank) were initiated in the early 1950s and continued right into the 1960s, many of which involved the obligatory award of legal land title as a precondition for the receipt of a housing unit.[5] At the same time, tens of millions of dollars were poured into two Tennessee Valley Authority–style mega-development projects that would have seen the majority, if not all, of the camps closed and some 200,000 refugees resettled in one fell swoop. But neither the Yarmuk-Jordan Valley Project nor the North Sinai Project, despite the millions spent, ever moved past proposals and feasibility studies.

In fact, year after year the Agency found that the camps grew at a steady pace. And yet, despite this, no plans were made to move beyond the tent landscapes of the early camps. It was only the combination of a particularly harsh winter in 1951–52, the fact that the Korean War had created a shortage of tents on the global market, and sustained pressure from "local staff" that forced the Agency's hand and pushed it into the mass construction game. In the end, putting up concrete brick shelters proved far cheaper than replacing canvas tents every couple of years. And so, in the early and mid-1950s the Agency embarked on a building program and began, for the first time, to etch out its own shelter policy.

Housing was progressively rolled out along three standardized models of single-family, single-room structures (figure 2.1). Practices varied, but generally each family was allotted a plot of land, on which a "shelter" made of four walls of hollow concrete blocks would be erected.[6] Roofing at this stage was mainly corrugated zinc or asbestos sheeting, but, depending on locale, the Agency "experimented with reeds, milk cartons, empty asphalt barrels, tiles and ceramics" (UNRWA 1951, 9). In addition, in many of the camps, families (now divided along a nuclear family demarcation) would be given a bag of cement and a single large tile, from which they could build a small outhouse above a pit latrine or septic tank (though public latrines remained a big and much-resented feature of camp life for decades). UNRWA's sanitation department sometimes emptied the pits, but more often than not they would fill up and another one would have to be dug. The scale was, for an ad hoc interim agency, fairly impressive. Between 1951 and 1955 some thirty thousand shelters were built in Gaza alone (Berg 2014). And in 1955 the UNRWA established its official "shelter program," which institutionalized the building and repair of housing units.

The construction of mass housing marks one of the first material-political thresholds the camp would breach—the movement from cloth tent to solid built structure. The Agency understood this as well as anybody else, and their first concern was political resistance to this "improvement." In a report, they tried to reassure those in their ward that "refugees use the facilities, live in decent shelter, and support themselves *without modification of the political position they had in the tent*, in the camp and on the ration line" (UNRWA 1952, 14, emphasis added).

The threshold, however, was not only in the built materiality of the camp. The Agency itself was changing. All of a sudden, the Agency was knee-deep in the housing game. And we know that building housing never comes alone: it creates a broad host of social, legal, and political entanglements. It raises questions of town planning, regulations, parceling and bordering, landownership (Feldman 2008, 143), and, perhaps above all—permanence. But it also expands the possibilities for control and government. The formalization of the camps (by which I mean both their demarcation as discernible bounded spaces *and* their regulation by a formal code of rules) may have not been part of the plan for the Agency, but once it became an unavoidable reality its political effectuality as a means of control became invaluable.

With the move to mass housing, the Agency turned almost inevitably, in the style of an extra-judicial form of power, to ordinances or regulations. One of the first such documents regulated admittance: "Camps administered by UNRWA are established for the sole purpose of accommodating ration recipient refugees who have been officially recognized by the Agency to be in need of shelter assistance."[7] To be admitted, refugees had to be found "needy" by the relevant area officer. The request had to be made in writing, and the officer was bound to "inspect" the current place of residence to determine the validity of said request. Admittance was then subject to "the acceptance of refugees to abide strictly to Camp Regulations, issued from time to time by UNRWA, and which will be conspicuously posted on camp Notice Boards for the attention of in-camp refugees."[8]

All camp refugees had to sign a copy of the camp regulations. These regulations function as something of a contractual relation between the refugee and the UNRWA; they declare a set of nonpolitical "rights" (access to water, latrines, shower-baths, medical services, access to education, and so on) and a series of "general responsibilities of refugees" ("adhere to the camp regulations and carry out legitimate instructions of the Camp Officer," "keep their dwelling and immediate surroundings clean," and "observe law and order"). Among the first things the regulations do is establish the Agency as a territorial authority by vesting it with the power of *eviction*. Absence without justification for more than six months; intermittent absence that confirms another residence outside the camp; repeatedly breaking camp rules; or being a threat to public security or public health are all enough to get you thrown out of the camp. But because the Agency is only capable of adjudicating the grounds for eviction, any "breach" of the camp regulations would see the camp leader inform local police, either at the camp police post or the nearest station, and "request the police authorities to take necessary corrective action."[9]

Aside from brief rules about public hygiene (that other hallmark of the urban governmental project), what is telling about the camp regulations is that the largest section, "Special Rules," relates overwhelmingly to control and regulation of the built environment. The first article of this section constitutes a hierarchical structure of authority around building: "Refugees wishing to erect constructions within a camp can only do so after the written authorization of the Camp Leader is obtained."[10] The second makes clear the recourse to law and order/policing in case of *contravention* (a word that will take on considerable significance): "All constructions carried out contrary to this regulation will be demolished and make the refugee liable to be evicted from the camp."[11]

The camp regulations also reinforced the Agency's peculiar custodianship over the camps by prohibiting the sale or rental of any constructed structures in the camps. Because the land either had been expropriated by national governments or was leased for a nominal fee and "given" to UNRWA, the camp regulations stated that "all construction thereon [the land] are therefore under the temporary jurisdiction of the Agency."[12] Under no circumstances can camp refugees sell huts or other constructions, whether erected by UNRWA or themselves, or sell the plot of land or lease or transfer either the premises or the land. All of this would be eventually skirted by camp inhabitants who, among other things, relied on and creatively used parallel systems of ownership and exchange that did not rely on formal title but instead used older, often Ottoman-era systems of sociolegal documentation (Alnajada 2023). But the significance of the regulations was not in their social efficacy; it was in how they shaped the Agency and the broader field of political struggle.

The regulations were the discursive basis of the Agency's authority. And yet very quickly after the regulations had gone into effect, administrators found that they lacked something even more fundamental: plans. The regulations, they discovered, were essentially contentless without plans as their basis. As one field engineer complained to his superiors, when police are summoned to demolish a structure, "The point which is invariably raised however is that there are no official plans on which to base our statements that contraventions have arisen."[13] No plan, no contravention; no contravention, no authority. Indeed, if regulatory norms are only substantiated in the moment of their transgression, then the very notion of a *contravention* needed, as a condition of its possibility, a plan to begin with.

By the early 1960s the Agency's field directors were exchanging a series of memos and telegrams around the possibilities of increasing control with more comprehensive planning. From Gaza, the call was for more planning, seen as necessary for "the continuity of development of camps (which in fact are assuming the aspects of small towns rather than camps) and *to their control and maintenance*."[14] From Jordan, the feeling was similar; planning is needed as part of "an operation we hope will give us more control over the population in our Camps."[15] By 1961, there seemed to be a consensus that they needed to find ways to "improve the conditions in existing camps and provide some 'town planning' standards for camp extensions and for new camps."[16]

Yet again one turn to practice opened up another. This time, no sooner had the Agency decided on planning that it found itself facing an even more basic or foundational problem: the boundary—where exactly the camps start and finish. Without a clearly bounded territorial space, planning was impossible and the operation of a distinct regulatory regime was useless. In Jordan the field director wrote, "We have a particular problem here in that the boundaries of some of our camps are not properly defined and marked, which is a pre-requisite for control of squatters and preparation of plans."[17] Moreover, even establishing basic demographic information and a quantitative measure of camp inhabitants needed boundaries: "Our camp population survey will be largely ineffective if we do not have the boundaries of our camps defined."[18] Defining the boundaries was a precondition for constituting a surveyable—and we should add, because it's precisely what's at stake, governable—population. Maps that were fully detailed and would show roads, installations, and the position of every shelter were deemed too expensive, but the go-ahead was given for surveying that would mark the camp boundaries and internal blocks (figure 2.2). The lines were drawn.

Planning Authority

Every practice of bordering is a practice of the establishment of definite identities. In something of a seminal essay on the subject, Étienne Balibar writes, "To mark out a border is, precisely, to define a territory, to delimit

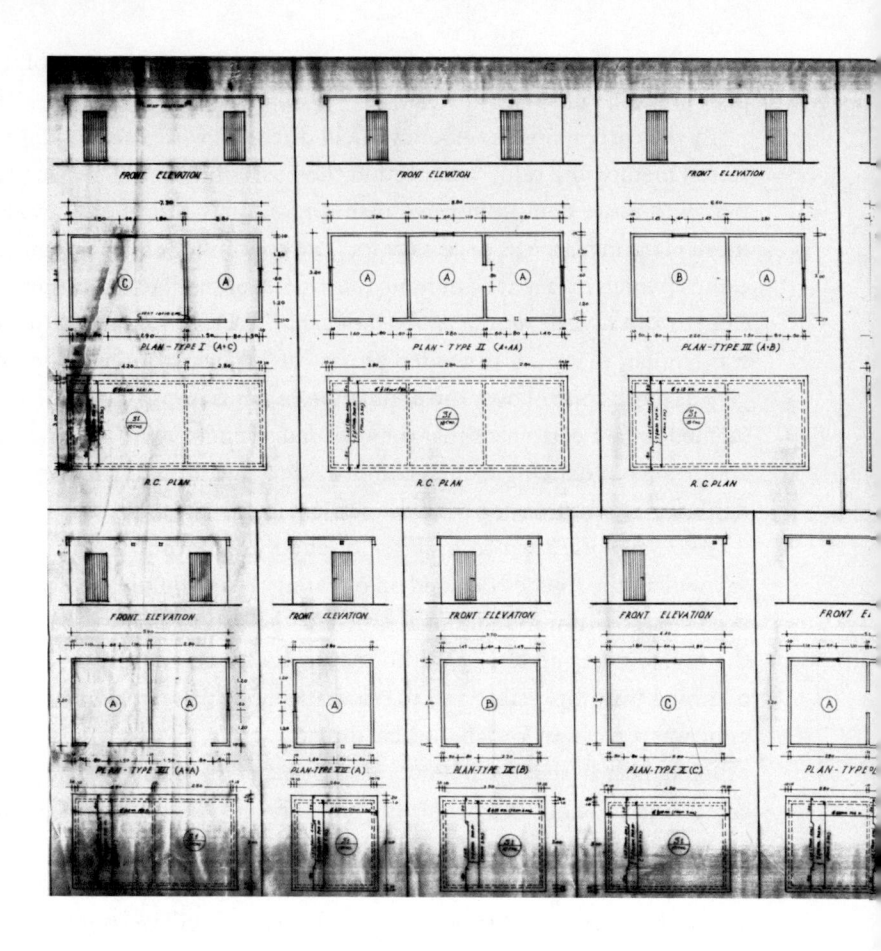

2.1 (*above*) Standard shelter units in three types (a, b, c), UNRWA Technical Division, circa 1952. UNRWA.

2.2 (*opposite*) Map showing topographical details and proposed shelter construction program for Deheishe Camp, in two-phase roll-out, 1955. UNRWA.

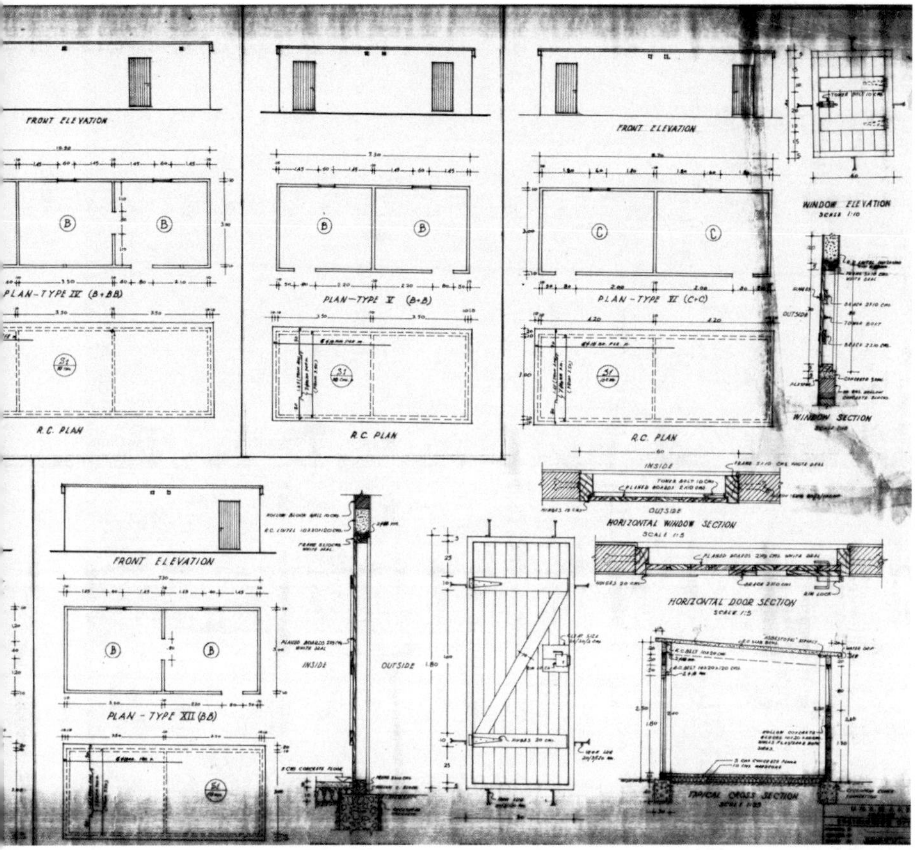
FRONT ELEVATION
PLAN-TYPE IV (B+BB)
R.C. PLAN
PLAN-TYPE V (B+B)
R.C. PLAN
FRONT ELEVATION
PLAN-TYPE VI (C+C)
R.C. PLAN
WINDOW ELEVATION
SCALE 1:10
OUTSIDE
WINDOW SECTION
INSIDE
OUTSIDE
HORIZONTAL WINDOW SECTION
SCALE 1:5
FRONT ELEVATION
PLAN - TYPE XII (BB)
INSIDE
OUTSIDE
HORIZONTAL DOOR SECTION
SCALE 1:5
TYPICAL CROSS SECTION
SCALE 1:20

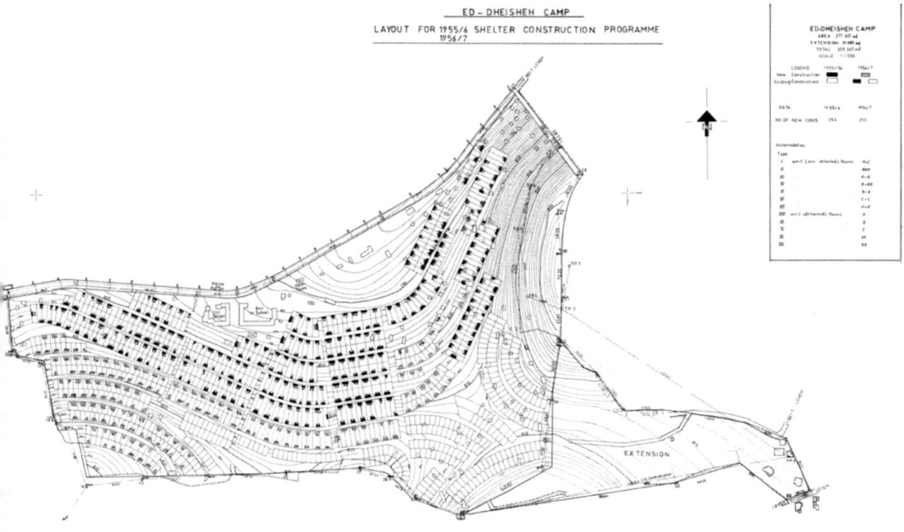
ED-DHEISHEH CAMP
LAYOUT FOR 1955/6 SHELTER CONSTRUCTION PROGRAMME
1956/7
ED-DHEISHEH CAMP
EXTENSION

2.3 and 2.4 Images of Deheishe Camp in 1950 and 1969 after the initial phase of shelter construction. UNRWA.

it, and to register the identity of that territory, or confer one upon it" (2002, 76). We can go a step further: defining and conferring an identity on an *inhabited* territory is to constitute, perforce, a kind of political community. In other words, it is a foundational act, one that usually either involves or presupposes a specific arrangement of territory, authority, and rights (Sassen 2008). Yet, here, this arrangement was neither national nor global nor strictly municipal in scale, but formed around the temporary nonpolitical administration of an exceptionally defined population and territory. Again, the production of space marked the threshold; mass construction and urban planning within a distinct bounded/bordered space took the Agency firmly into the more permanent plane of government. Indeed, it had itself established the conditions for recursive and indefinite governmental regulation of the built environment—planning produces control, but control demands constant planning in return.

Within the space of ten short years the Agency went from an organization actively trying to eliminate camp life to an organization operating overwhelmingly through the spatial regulation of camps. I want to emphasize two points at this stage. First, the Agency's very authority took shape through the regulation of the built environment. Sure, the Agency already had at its disposal a host of other disciplinary mechanisms for the government of bodies and behavior: schools and classrooms, vocational training centers, health clinics and doctors' offices, all of which were, of course, reinforced by the potential withholding of rations as punishment. *But* it was in the production of a built environment around housing where the Agency would substantiate a form of authority. For the Agency, governing a largely confined population that didn't partake in formal local labor markets (from which they were and remain largely excluded), the built environment became the primary instrument of order for controlling the refugee-inhabitant and keeping the camp a strictly nonpolitical and temporary space.

Second, in making it *the* indispensable site of its authority, the built became a fraught, highly charged, and contested domain of life; in short, it became *the* primary site of politics. UNRWA governed its subjects as inhabitants of a temporary space, and in turn these subjects contested the limits of this authority as inhabitants of a temporary space. I return in the coda to how we might think through these stakes of camp life, here and beyond, through a notion of the politics of inhabitation. For now, I want to flag how the built and construction emerge as overcharged sites of contestation. It is no wonder then that the crisis to come in 1970, which would take shape so explicitly around the camps themselves, would strike at the very core of what the Agency is and does.

"Get Out of the Camps Business"

All these tensions would surface in a moment of acute crisis in the final months of 1969. Against the backdrop of increasing militant organization, Lebanon's camps were in something of a state of revolt. What had started in Nahr al-Bared Camp outside Tripoli with the seizure of the camp's police station spread rapidly to other camps with the police and army being routed by armed and organized camp inhabitants. On November 2nd, under the brokership of Egyptian president Gamal Abdel Nasser, the PLO's Yasser Arafat reached an agreement with the head of the Lebanese army, General Emile Bustani. What came to be known as the Cairo Agreement established a set of governing principles for the presence of Palestinian guerrillas in Lebanon's camps. In effect, all sixteen camps in Lebanon were removed from the authority of the military intelligence apparatus, the Deuxième Bureau, and handed over to the PLO's Armed Struggle Command. On November 3, 1969, all of Lebanon's police officers were withdrawn from the camps. Literally overnight, the guerrillas moved in and the Lebanese state vanished.

The shockwaves sent through the ranks of the Agency's upper management were tremendous. Just days after press reports in Lebanon made public the details of the Agreement, UNRWA's (American) commissioner-general, Laurence Michelmore, made an initial statement to the UN Special Political Committee: "It appears that commandos have taken control of most of the UNRWA camps in Lebanon."[19] Michelmore was trying to steady the ship, but he knew he faced a critical conjuncture. A few days earlier, Frederick Dalziel Vreeland, of the United States Mission to the UN, had presented a statement in which he proposed (or implicitly threatened?), "UNRWA should get out the camp business, for there is nothing in its mandate requiring the Agency to operate camps." This, coming from a representative of the Agency's principal donor, caused a small firestorm. With American political pressure on one end and the PLO's "capture" of Lebanon's camps on the other, Michelmore kicked into action, immediately instructing his appointed deputies at the heads of the various departments (Education, Health, Relief and Social Services, Technical) in what was tellingly called "the General Cabinet," to start drawing up a substantive policy review on camps. In a handwritten memo that only mediated the sense of urgency, he requested "a statement of UNRWA activities in relation to camps—that is what do we mean when we say that UNRWA 'operates' or 'administers' refugee camps."[20]

At this stage, the archive marks a dense, even frenetic, exchange of documents and reports, indicating a prolonged and intense period of introspection and argumentation with a distinct tangible anxiety about just what the camps are and what "administrators" are doing in them. What kind of political liability does "administration" or "operation" entail? What form of authority do they produce? And what is it about a camp that opens up this can of worms anyway? For the Agency the issue was how to somehow restabilize the line it had drawn between a technical sphere of administration and spatial regulation, on the one hand, and a political sphere of liability/representation, on the other.

In January 1970, the UNRWA's influential director of relief services (and yet another American), R. L. Fisher, was tasked with formulating a policy response. He began to compose a report running for some sixteen pages, titled after Vreeland's injunction: "Get out of the camps business." This document, which would go through a series of drafts and comments, almost all of which are marked as confidential, would eventually become the basis of the Agency's policy position. Fisher started, as it were, from the top. What is a camp anyway? After all, in his memo, Michelmore himself had opted to initially respond to the crisis by questioning the very term *camp*; the term was misleading, he insisted, because it suggested people are confined: by contrast these camps "are like villages or particular areas within cities."[21] Michelmore was fudging things a fair bit, because the term also implied precisely the exceptionally bounded territory and types of regulatory control his Agency had just spent the last two decades putting together. But, nonetheless, the sense that the Agency had to reckon with the nature and political stakes of camps as distinct territorial spaces was clear.

Fisher's reply to his own rhetorical question was pragmatic and quintessentially authoritative—a camp is "what we recognize as an official camp, and for which therefore UNRWA has accepted some operational responsibility."[22] This in turn meant, to him, that the Agency provides some central administration, environmental sanitation, and shelter assistance and regulation of the built environment. These spatio-environmental practices, which critics wanted the Agency to halt, were "essential" to what the Agency does and could not really be relinquished without an abdication of its mandated responsibilities. It is not health, education, and relief services, which might easily be passed on to a host government. We might get rid of some nonessential functions, but what, Fisher asked, in a later draft, should be done with those "other functions [that] are quasi-governmental, e.g. the promulgation and enforcement of building and sanitation rules," and which have been the basis of order?[23]

For Fisher and the Agency, the camp question is foundational in a distinctly political sense. Camps were a historical necessity and fact. For refugees lacking everything, "the only possibility to survive with UN assistance, and to live like human beings, was to agglomerate into some sort of community or communities." Regardless of whether these "de facto communities" were encouraged or not, "their existence is both a fact and a human and practical necessity." And so too was some sort of administration: "No community can live (except in fiction books) in total anarchy."[24] And it's not that UNRWA appropriated power; in effect nobody wanted to deal with the camps. "As the only 'authority' on the spot, UNRWA, through its local officials, also acquired an ill-defined responsibility for peace and good order going beyond what, on a strict interpretation, might be regarded as essential for the provision of services but nevertheless inescapable in the circumstances."[25]

The problem, as Fisher saw it, was that the legal grounding of the Agency's authority and its limits were purposely and constitutively ambiguous. No one, it seemed, either desired or was capable of defining "the limits of the responsibilities of UNRWA as an 'administrative authority,' i.e. distinguish between administration of assistance and administration of the refugee communities."[26] This, he suggested, is because such a distinction would "seem fallacious." The Agency was explicitly mandated to "administer relief." But, Fisher argued, what is administering relief/aid if they cannot actually administer the camps? To do one in a camp is to do the other. Administering the camps was simply a prerequisite for the discharge of the Agency's mandate.[27] Fisher combined a distinct sense of moral responsibility with a pragmatic piece of biopolitical common sense—to count, register, feed, house, clothe, and medically treat a territorially bound group of people is necessarily, perforce, to govern them. The capacity to administer the camp, to order it spatially, was a responsibility born of what he calls a "moral obligation" to the "refugee-residents of the camps."[28]

In the earlier drafts, Fisher clearly wanted to resist any rollback of the Agency's authority. He was all for changing terms and names, but language was not the problem here. They could "unilaterally change the names" and the commissioner-general could "prohibit any reference to UNRWA 'administering' or 'operating' camps," he wrote, but whether they could "revise substantially" the Agency's function in the camps was much trickier and probably undesirable. To restrict the functions of Agency employees in camps to administration of assistance only "might well create a 'gap' of authority which could bring more harm than good.... It would be either futile or dangerous to try and, so to say, wash our hands of the administration of these camps."[29]

That the Agency's exercise of authority in camps was always bound to open up a legal-territorial aporia seemed, to Fisher, inevitable and effectively irresolvable.[30] In a second draft circulated in April, Fisher made it clear that the question of who was "in charge of" the camps *could not* really be answered—"I doubt that a precise legal, political or practical answer can be discovered."[31] Where UNRWA's "responsibilities" end and the government's begin was entirely unclear, and the confusion was "considerable." For two decades now, no actor seemed even remotely interested in resolving it. And for good reason, it seems, because some things, Fisher suggested, are better kept ambiguous: "While there are many good cases where 'the tail is wagging the dog' it is not obvious that, if we want to wag the dog at all, this would be the best tail to choose."[32]

When Fisher consulted some of the field relief directors as to how they interpret the Agency's action in operating or administering the camps, he got answers that largely reflected his own convictions. The host government deals with the security aspect of the camp, but "camp administration affecting the refugees is carried out in accordance with standing camp rules and regulations, which are made known to all the inhabitants of the camps."[33]

Yet though Fisher is forthright about the political implications of the Agency's spatial administration, he is keenly aware of the need, outwardly at least, to temper and limit them. With their back up against the wall, the Agency attempted to reestablish the boundary between politics and the technical, in part by concluding that what they practiced in the camps was a particular form of authority that they called *administrative authority*. With this, they attempted to clarify the demarcation—we don't do law and order, we're not liable for issues of security or representation, but we *are* the relevant authority on the ground and we *do* write the rules and regulations of the built environment. The Agency might be the only "authority on the spot," but it had to square that with the fact that law and order remained the responsibility of the sovereign state in which it operates: "The 'camps' are not 'extra-territorial' and UNRWA has no legislative or police power."[34] And yet it remains an authority of some kind, testifying, as it were, to both the relevance and difficulty of the distinction between authority and sovereignty (to which I shall return).

If the question that Fisher rhetorically asked is "*Should* the Agency get out of the camps?," then the answer was "Probably." But this, he rightly pointed out, has been what the Agency had been trying to do since its inception. *Can* they get out of the camps? "My estimate is that it is most doubtful that we can, except possibly over a period of years."[35] He should have forgone the subordinate clause altogether.

A Camp by Any Other Name

In 1970, as Fisher was circulating drafts of his report, the clamor to come to terms with what a camp actually is in a way that might mitigate political liability took on a distinctly nominal bent. It precipitated an ultimately failed attempt to find a terminological alternative to the word *camp*, an attempt that is noteworthy only because it underlines so effectively the irreducibly political-historical character of the camps. In the immediate months and years after the Cairo Agreement, in textual terms, one of the most striking things in the archival documents is how all of a sudden what seemed like a perfectly objective noun, *camp*, suddenly seemed so fraught with political and linguistic instability that it began to regularly appear in scare quotes, as if its very reality had to be cast in doubt.

Starting an extraordinary exchange around terminology, in April 1970, Fisher conceded that descriptively the word *camp* was not quite working: "Since 'camp' tends to denote a place that is temporary and tented, the term is not adequately descriptive of the established camps."[36] In principle a new term could be found, but was there an "alternative word or phrase" that was realistic and practicable? He suggested "settlement," "village," "town," "township," "quarter," and even "encampment." But none of these seemed to cut it. And his own hesitation was marked even as he posed alternatives; there is precedent to the word *camp*, he added, and the "political sensitivity" of making a change should probably mean the present term is retained. Moreover, he pointed out, the Arabic equivalent and "local usage" of *mukhayyam* was unlikely to change, no matter what the Agency did.

What the Agency had to drop definitely, all agreed, was the prefix UNRWA as in "UNRWA camps" or "UNRWA-administered camps," though Fisher liked the possibility of maintaining the term, where necessary, in "UNRWA-supervised camps."[37] Dropped too were the terms used for the Agency's camp-based employees, "camp administrator" or "camp leader," and though both "camp commandant" and "camp overseer" were toyed with, ultimately they settled on the more anodyne "camp services officer," like something out of tertiary industry but still, as will long be the case with the Agency, quietly but jealously holding on to its own authoritative prerogative in the term *officer*.

But by no means was this the end of the problem. By November 1970 the issue was still not settled. A confidential memo from the New York–based liaison office pushed back. Fisher's suggestions were decidedly insufficient. The deputy commissioner-general noted "the adverse effects on the UNRWA 'image' of the popular identification of UNRWA refugee camps with *fedayin* recruitment, training, domination, etc." and threw into the ring the term *sub-area*, with a *camp leader* instead becoming a *sub-area officer*. In the meantime, he urged, "let us stop distinguishing on our maps between numbers of refugees living inside and outside camps."[38]

But the issue proved sticky and more than a bit thorny. A month later Fisher replied to say that the terms *sub-area* and *sub-area officer* just didn't work. To his previous suggestions he added a few more. If the term *camp* had to go, then the term *refugee center* was best suited to replace it.[39] By the end of 1970 things were getting more than a little confused. The chief of the Public Information Office worried about what to do with the maps they regularly publish. The office head summed up the absurdity with a perfectly apposite observation: "I should be grateful for guidance on this camp question and particularly to know whether we may continue to identify camps as 'camps.'"[40] When, then, is a camp not a camp?

At the start of 1971, the Cabinet decided it needed help from its people on the ground as it were and reached out to all five field directors. The deputy commissioner-general, Sir John Rennie, put it baldly: they needed to switch to a terminology that would "discourage total identification of UNRWA with refugee camps." He threw the term *refugee community* into the ring.[41] But that too failed to stick.

The most unequivocal objections—and the terminal point of resistance—came from "local staff" in the occupied West Bank, the mainly Palestinian refugees who make up the vast majority of the Agency's workforce. Local staff found themselves, not for the first or last time, at complete odds with the almost exclusively Euro-American management. Here the argument shifted gears to cut straight to the politics of naming as it plays out with regard to not just the temporariness of camps, but what is understood, implicitly at least, as the political claims maintained in that very temporariness. "The word 'camp' denotes a temporary abode and in fact the present status of refugees is temporary, pending an acceptable solution to all concerned. The word 'community' suggests a status which is not temporary."[42] The language became almost antagonistic, pointing to violence in the proposed terminological change. The field health officer, Sharif Hussayni, writes, "I will not hide my greatest concern" at the proposal to "wipe out the name of Refugee Camp."[43] Wiping out the name, insofar as it was a threat to the interim character of the camps, appeared almost as grave an issue as wiping out the camps themselves. Refugees, Hussayni reminded his superiors, live in camps as "temporary residences in host countries pending implementation and redemption of their rights in their original homeland."[44] The head of the "Provisional Staff Committee" (effectively the union for West Bank "local staff" and a considerable player in its own right), likewise, insisted on "the transitory nature of livelihood in camps" which justifies the continued usage of the word. "No change in nomenclature should be effected."[45]

In these responses, what defines the camp in form *and* name is not only its temporariness or provisionality, but also what the Palestinian "local staff" recognized as its political interruption to the permanence of the status quo, to a de facto *settlement* in the broad sense of the word. The camp precisely in its campness, that is, its temporariness, keeps open a future not predetermined by the present. Or it stops the present simply becoming the future. This is why, in contrast to other built environments, the Palestinian camp remains temporary and transitory, no matter how built-up, planned, or durable it might become.

The deputy commissioner-general replied to assure local staff that nothing in terms of permanence was intended; the question remained a delimitation of responsibility. "Whatever is done about terminology it is desirable to avoid official statements that be read as implying that UNRWA 'administers' the camps in the sense that a government administers its territory."[46] Nonetheless, a Cabinet meeting on May 25 all but conceded defeat in getting rid of the name *camp*. The commissioner-general concluded that the Agency should continue to use the term "without giving unnecessary prominence to it." The title of camp leader would still have to change, as would the budgetary item "Camp Administration."[47] The title of camp services officer eventually sticks, though the translation into Arabic will be flexible; instead of the word *dabit*, a more accurate translation of "officer," the more corporate *mudir*, or manager, was selected.

The term *camp* didn't budge. But for a period, so fixated on terminology were the Agency's directors that they seemed to succumb to a kind of naive nominalism, the notion that underneath their names these objects might not be so real after all. They seemed convinced that by wishing away the word *camp* and by whisking away the title of "leader" or "administrator" and putting "services officer" in its place, the dilemmas of this self-limiting authority would be resolved. But the camp is no more a pseudo-object or realist illusion than it is a natural entity; its material existence exerts a level of political force and mediation that is neither reducible to discourse nor can be discursively undone.

A Short Balancing Act

All of this would culminate in an attempt to issue a clear policy directive, with the 1971 annual report stating, "It has not always been realized that UNRWA provides services in rather than administers 'camps' (in which only 40 percent of registered refugees live); that the 'camps' are not extra-territorial areas under United Nations jurisdiction; that the inhabitants are normally free to move in and out now, as in the past; and that the responsibility for the maintenance of law and order rests not with UNRWA, but with the Governments of the host countries."[48] The shift here saw "administration," with all the governmental obligations it entails, replaced with the emergent consumer-friendly language of "service provision." We might read this shift retrospectively today, in light of the wider political-economic restructuring of the 1970s, as going from responsibility to/over a *whole*, the *community* formed by the bounding of territorial space, to transactional relations with disaggregated *parts*, the servicing of *individuals*. As far as the Agency was concerned, a line was drawn in the sand.

Well, not quite. The impossibility that Fisher had pointed out in drawing a line between the administration of service and the administration of space had not gone anywhere. And the Agency's insistence on maintaining a form of regulatory authority over the built environment *while* limiting its political liability would prove a very hard tightrope walk to pull off. Ultimately, and tellingly, the Israeli military government upended the Agency's balancing act. Israel's occupation of the West Bank and Gaza in 1967 had effectively pitted the ambiguous authority of the Agency up against the ambiguous authority of the Israeli military government. This encounter was of two indeterminate and temporary forms of political power, both with partial claims to authority and no clear long-term judicial grounding (supranational administrative agency versus occupying military power). And it was an encounter that ended up taking conflictual shape precisely through a grapple around housing, and more precisely the authority to issue permits for housing construction: Who issues building permits? Who is obliged to request them? Who can demolish homes? Who is the legitimate authority over a temporary camp on occupied land?

The Israeli military occupation would eventually expose the gaping holes in the Agency's exercise of authority. But UNRWA opened the door. In a bid to maintain the standing of its regulations, the Agency had appealed to Israeli military public prosecutors and the penal code to enforce contraventions of its camp regulations. Across much of the 1970s, the Israeli army obliged and demolished houses and even imprisoned refugees who built inside the camps without UNRWA permits. But it didn't take long for the Israeli military bureaucracy to sense the opportunity and take it. As they widened their own house demolitions and building enforcement in the occupied territories, they also usurped UNRWA as the primary authority in the camps. In 1981, they not only decreed that all refugees themselves would have to apply for building permits from the military government, but also demanded that UNRWA would have to do the same when it sought to construct anything in the camps. This all but extinguished the diplomatic privileges and immunities that the Agency exercised in the domain of construction. And in hindsight, it's this erosion of immunities that began the Israeli state's slow but then accelerating assault on UNRWA, culminating today in a concerted effort to completely dismantle the Agency, and in particular to cripple its food distribution capacities in Gaza as part of a broader genocidal assault.

The Agency had anxiously appealed to Israeli officials in a bid to reaffirm its failing regulatory grip over the camps, only to find that "if you lie with the devil, you wake up in hell," or, as it's known in this story, the Central Planning Office of the Military Governorate of Judea and Samaria. And so just as it thought it had adequately worked out a grounding for its authority that was neither simply arbitrary nor legally liable for those in its ward, the collision with the Israeli military government reminded the Agency, and us all, that a political authority completely separated and external from force remains a theoretical fiction.

Authority('s) Remains

The notion of authority looms large yet ambiguously over this history. The word and its contestation and various permutations are, as we saw, all over the historical record, but in ways as unclear as they are pervasive. The Agency looked inward and articulated its role in terms of a pragmatic and necessary "administrative authority"; the Israeli military government would eventually question "the basis of this authority," in the name of their own (purportedly) authoritative hold over the territory itself. As we'll see in chapter 3, when Palestinian revolutionaries entered the camps, they too envisaged change in terms of authority, with absolute "popular authority" replacing "the authority of the administrative apparatus that was running the camps, UNRWA" (Sarhan 1975, 435). In this final section I turn in a more conceptual register to think through the question of authority, its separation here from sovereignty, and how this particular history helps us flesh out some of the wider stakes in the technocratic turn.

The ambiguity around authority in this story is by no means historically exceptional. If anything, it is symptomatic of the state of the concept of authority itself. "It is a curious fact," begins Alexandre Kojève, in one of the few direct theoretical engagements with the concept, "that the problem and notion of authority have been little studied" (2014, 1). Curious, because it is impossible, he adds, to even begin "to tackle political power or the structure of the state without knowing what authority is as such" (2014, 1). Just over a decade later, in 1954, Hannah Arendt would, in similar terms and, it must be said, with strikingly similar reactionary, even conservative, concerns, bemoan the same absence, but take it even further.[49] "Practically as well as theoretically," she writes, as though by way of response, "we are no longer in a position to know what authority really *is*" (Arendt 2000, 463). For both Kojève and Arendt the absence of a clear definition or the current impossibility of reaching one is symptomatic of authority's vanishing from the modern world. Another two decades later, in 1980, Richard Sennett would, in something like a social psychology of authority, reach a similar conclusion: the modern world is defined by the parting of ways between authority and legitimacy; authority remains but is unmoored from truth, and we subjects are left attracted to strong figures we simply do not believe to be legitimate.[50] All this leaves authority as concept more elliptical and elusive than ever. With the result that today, "Authority slips away as one tries to pin it down.... Unlike its syntagms of power, tyranny and injustice... authority is difficult to track, impossible to monitor, complicated to talk about. It stares down talk, dismissive of every effort to gain on it" (Ronnell 2012).

And yet authority not only remains but remains indispensable. It remains, Avital Ronnell (2012) tells us, "because authority is the most elusive of terms that inform relations, and yet no politics, no family, no pride of accomplishment can exist without it, according to the few thinkers who have donated their efforts to writing about or around it or its mystical foundation." Indeed, the work of the handful of modern theorists who take on authority directly is marked by the twinning of the diagnosis of its crisis or passing on the one hand, and the imperative of its salvage on the other. Unlike, say, sovereignty, which, where it has not been exposed as an ontological conceit, pernicious reification, or theological fairy-tale (Goldstone 2014; Walker 1996), is open to critical jettison (the embrace of postsovereign politics), authority is rarely, if ever, treated with the same dispensability. For its modern theorists, the script on authority is read at once as both eulogy and call—authority is dead, long live authority.

What, then, remains or is yet to be discovered of the content that is/was/might be held in place, however tentatively, by the concept? For these theorists, and the traditions they are mediating (Plato, Aristotle, Roman jurists, the Scholastics, Hegel, Freud, Weber, to name a few), authority is a highly normative concept. Authority is not force; when force is used, authority has failed. Authority is not persuasion; when persuasion through argument is used, authority is in abeyance (Arendt 2000, 463). Authority, if anything, is *legitimate compulsion*. Arendt writes, "The authoritarian relation between the one who commands and the one who obeys rests neither on common reason nor on the power of the one who commands; what they have in common is the hierarchy itself, whose rightness and legitimacy both recognize and where both have their predetermined stable place" (463).

Authority, then, compels without violence or reason. But it is also without occlusion or silence; it is the compulsion of open hierarchy itself, of the pre-givenness and naturalism of the division between ruled and ruler; it is the compulsion of the idea of the good, regardless of its content—not what Marx figured as the silent compulsion of economic power and the wage relation, but the vocal compulsion of accepted and recognized hierarchy. Authority, in other words, establishes relationality *prior* to command (Arendt 2000, 476). It is not the command itself that is authoritative, but the very relation from which it springs. And as such, authority is not only, as Sennett ([1980] 1993, 10) has it, "a bond between people who are unequal," it is a bond (in the double sense of the term) premised openly on that very inequality. Where authority is recognized, and its recognition for someone like Kojève is its very condition of possibility ("Authority and the 'recognition' of Authority are one and the same thing" [2014, 45]), it produces a voluntary and conscious renunciation of reaction, a willful foreclosure of resistance, what Sennett calls in similar prose (despite relying on entirely different texts and traditions) "a voluntary compliance" ([1980] 1993, 22).

In this sense of a naturalized inequality or hierarchy, authority has been closely associated with both the pre-political space of the family and the technical figure of the expert or master. In her discussion of Plato's search for a convincing argument for the transcendent authority of the philosopher-king, Arendt identifies at least one source of the technocratic turn in politics far earlier than most histories. In *The Republic*, Arendt argues, Plato's analogical turn to art and modeling (by which the Idea of the good can be used like a model or yardstick as the transcendent measure of human behavior) first introduces the figure of the craftsman or expert into politics: "Here the concept of the expert enters the realm of political action for the first time, and the statesman is understood to be competent to deal with human affairs in the same sense as the carpenter is competent to make furniture or the physician to heal the sick" (2000, 478).

It is instructive, then, that the exercise of the Agency's authority was so closely bound to architecture and construction. Of all our technicians, it is perhaps the architect or the engineer who most closely reproduces this facet of the craftsman in the primacy of modeling. In these terms, the Agency's exercise of what it called "administrative authority" involved an explicit example of the vesting of authority in the technical competence of its administrators—chiefly its town planners, architects, and engineers. What is at stake here is the grounding of the very facets of political authority itself (hierarchy, leadership, adjudication, mastery, discipline, anticipation, the right to rule) not in politics, and not simply outside politics in any transcendental source (God, the law, the good), but rather in the very stuff of spatial administration—in this case, administering the built environment of the camps. In other words, here, political authority *becomes* technical competence and takes shape through the shaping of the built environment.

This then is authority without foundation, authority entirely immanent to its own operation.[51] Questions of consent or the political future are entirely moot. But what the story of the Agency's rise and fall as an authoritative body tells us is that the grounding of authority in the administrative is itself also a highly normative if unstable practice. It is not that legitimacy is simply deferred but that it is—as in all technocratic captures of politics—reconfigured. Legitimacy here is anchored in what was considered the self-evident normative hierarchy between administrator/expert and inhabitant-refugee, in the very acts of regulating construction, providing shelter, establishing rules, operating infrastructure, ordering eviction and demolitions, or treating patients and educating children. That this relation was thought to have normative dimensions is made clear in the repeated appeals Agency staff make to their "moral obligations" to camp-based refugees and in the language of moral opprobrium that was used to talk about refugees "contravening" rules and regulations.[52]

Yet, for all the insistence on a practical and legitimate authority, the question of force was always at the surface. Regardless of whether and to what extent the Agency was *recognized* as an authority by encamped refugees (and this is very difficult to gauge and separate from fear of punishment), ultimately "administrative authority" was reliant on force in ways that entirely undermine its self-identification as an authority, at least in the Kojèvian/Arendtian sense. Or, conversely—and more accurately—this history might indicate that this very positing of an ideal "pure" type of authority without and in contradistinction to force is just that, an ideal type. In a critical return to this earlier midcentury grappling with the concept, Mladen Dolar writes that authority's enigma stems from precisely its status as threshold concept between violence and reason: "Authority is exerted at a point based in neither force nor reason, *yet not simply external to them either*" (2021, emphasis added). Eventually, the Agency's recourse to "administrative authority" only exposed the underbelly of force beneath it and, arguably, beneath all modern forms of authority. Authority and force here no longer appear as antipodean distinctions per se, but an antinomic pairing, united in opposition; in this sense, the concept in its pure state is a conceit, one that works precisely to obscure this codependency.[53]

Read in this light, the camps are not really about the sovereign exception per se. The Agency sought to shape the behavioral norms of its subjects and exercise an authority in the shaping and regulating of built form itself, in its very competence in shaping and administering forms and things. The sovereignty question, when it came up, was at best bracketed. Or in other words, what the Agency tried to uneasily articulate is a split between authority and sovereignty. It is *not* a sovereign territorial or extra-territorial power; that is, it is not responsible for law and order, it has no police power, it is not answerable to rights-bearing encamped subjects, nor is it responsible for their actions. But it *is* the relevant authority: it *can* write rules and regulations which *should* be respected; issue permits; adjudicate between competing spatial claims; evict inhabitants; and request and authorize demolitions; in fact, it alone has the technical competence to plan and regulate the built environment, and it is precisely from this competence that its authority springs. In this sense, UNRWA prefigures the interim but permanent character of the expert-led technocratic capture of politics and the steady fragmentation of sovereign space into zones of managerial authority, at all kinds of scales, not least of all in cities.

I do not mean to imply that there is a lesson as such in this history. We won't find any essence or truth of modern authority in the administration of Palestine's camps. But there are lateral-moving historical lines in this story that seem to presage wider movements in global politics after the 1970s and connect them to earlier colonial histories. We can see connections in our latest instantiation of indirect rule and native authority in the permanently interim Palestinian Authority (PA) itself, an asovereign but managerial administrative formation defined precisely as an "authority" (and *not* a state): one that is wholly reliant on a circumvention of national representational politics through market mechanisms and private capital (Rabie 2021). Or we can see connections with the "tutelary government" of indebted non-Western states by the IMF or the World Bank that might in effect cover a state's most crucial political functions beyond any local representative mechanisms—the sovereign debt crisis is a crisis *of* sovereignty first and foremost. Or, to take a different scale, we can see connections in the placing of entire bankrupt(ed) cities or towns into "receivership," "administration," or "emergency management." Indeed, the notion of "administrative authority" prefigures in one sense the rise of the manager as the new unelected sovereign in cities in receivership (Martin 2016)—a rise that blurs the very boundaries between sovereignty and management. In the United States, Detroit is the most paradigmatic example, but New York of 1975, bankrupted, financialized, and then fiscally disciplined through the introduction of unelected *authorities* over budgetary control, was perhaps the base form, one that would be multiplied many times over.

In one sense the notion of "administrative authority" prefigures the very *temporality* of our technocratic managerial moment. Sandro Mezzadra and Brett Neilson point out that austerity politics takes effect not in the (sovereign) time of decision but in the endless duration of (authoritative) management: "an indefinite prolongation of the time in which any decision might be made" (2013, 8) involving an expansion of micromanagement practices to ever-higher scales of governance. "Administrative authority," authority as read from camps, prefigures not only the unaccountable and occluded violence of the technocratic capture of politics but also its drawn-out and indefinite temporality. This temporality comes back full circle today to take clearest shape in mass encampment. It is, after all, in our camps that contemporary crisis is most clearly experienced *not* as a decisive break in time, but as entirely continuous with chronological time. If "crisis" today is as an indefinite temporality, then it's no surprise that it takes form in the mass proliferation of camps as spatial devices of temporal suspension. In one sense, camps *are* indefinite crisis management in spatial form. Insofar as the Palestinian camps were early forerunners of the technocratic closure of politics in a permanently interim time, their history of "administrative authority" carried at least one kernel of the contemporary mass encampment that shapes our world today.

3 THE CAMP, OVERCOME

REVOLUTION AND MOVEMENT IN
THE IMPOSSIBLE PRESENT

"Fugitives and Nothing More"

Yunis, the aging revolutionary militant in a coma (this is the 1990s, after all) who makes up one (silent) half of the (mono)dialogic structure of Elias Khoury's *Bab al-Shams* (1998), went by many names—Izz al-Din in the western sector, Abu Salim in the camp, Abu Ibrahim in 'Ayn al-Zaytun, Abu Salih on long-distance missions, and, simply, "the man" in Dayr al-Assad. With Yunis this was something more than the precautions of clandestine militancy or a weirdly excessive liking for *noms de guerre*. All these names were indeed his and thus also were all aliases. "All names are pseudonyms," his blind father, a Sufi sheikh, would say. "The only true name is Adam. God gave this name to man because the name and the thing named were one" (Khoury 2006, 118; in original, 1998, 94).[1] And yet with Yunis, it's not simply that thing and name get separated, but that the thing itself appears so multiple. He not only had many names but also lived many lives. His lack of a fixed proper name appears as nothing less than an effect of his refusal of confinement, fixity, even unitariness itself. This is the stuff of Yunis's heroism—not his military exploits or his serial love affairs but his very insistence on *movement*. The most important of these movements is perhaps also the most literal—his constant traversing of the deadly border between Lebanon and Israel, his continuous returns. In other words, what sets him apart is his refusal of emplacement, both nominal and physical, refusal of both the jurisdictional facts of sovereign states that is also necessarily his refusal not just of refugeehood but of the unitary identity and interiority of the national-legal subject itself.

Sure, Yunis lives (or lived, it's not clear) in 'Ayn al-Hilwah Camp, but he is neither bound nor defined by its stunting grip on life. The abjectness, the misery, the elemental exposure, the deadly *stillness* of camp life that would appear as such determinant and animate forces in Palestinian history are refused. With Yunis, the camp and its inescapable subject-position of the refugee are overcome with the only thing that can trump the strictures of a place of confinement, the only thing that can still open a future from its static present: physical movement. *Bab al-Shams* is at once a sweeping epic of the originary event of Palestinian displacement, *al-Nakba*, and a mediation on the impossibility of really telling this story. It is also a self-critical and at times cutting account of the Palestinian revolutionary struggle, a struggle itself that can be read as at once a struggle *for* movement and *of* narrative. And yet for all of Khoury's retrospective, sepia-toned grappling with the collapse of the Palestinian Revolution's figures of heroism and ideological certainties, Yunis's locomotional drive never loses its political, or indeed, romantic force.

Khoury's novel—episodic, digressive, taxingly long, and with no real plot to speak of—is structured around the stories that Khalil, Yunis's adopted or spiritual son, recounts night after night in a bid to wake his "father" from a coma. Early on in the book, he reminds Yunis, "As they were setting up tents that wind blows through from both sides, you told them, We're not refugees. We're fugitives and nothing more. We fight, and kill and are killed. But we're not refugees. You told the people that refugee means something shameful, and that the road to all the villages of the Galilee was open" (Khoury 1998, 20).[2] The fugitive, here, is the figurative inversion of the refugee. Both figures start with a constitutive movement, but where the refugee ends in the terminal limbo and stasis of a camp, the fugitive keeps moving, and moving with consequence. The fugitive returns life to *action* that is still consequential, if only in its illegality or transgression; it is a figure that kills and is killed, rather than simply subject to (equally lethal) waiting.[3] This is why the figure of the fugitive is interesting here, its flight is a consequential action—in the Arabic original, the word Khoury chooses is *farrun* from the verb *farra*, to flee, escape, or defect from the military, which has both the illegality or transgressiveness of the term *fugitive* but even more of a connotation of kinetic, bodily motion that is closer to the notion of a runaway.[4] Much like the figure of fugitivity in Black radical thought, the fugitive of Palestinian liberation also starts with a refusal to stay in their given place. The movement, then, is not a wandering but a flight from the law and, in this case, back into the realm of legal consequence. In short, it is politics, or, better still, it is politics-as-movement. What interests me here is how this politics-as-movement is enabled by the refusal of the camp, of the tent itself. Yunis hails people as they set up the tents because he senses the implications (implications that will grow only graver as the tents give way to concrete cinderblocks); you're not refugees, he tells them, because the road is still open, you can still go.[5]

I open here with this short reading of Khoury's novel because it goes to the heart of what I argue: that Palestinian revolutionary politics were in part defined by the historical-temporal dilemma that was the question of the camps, and that this dilemma—how to form a historical subject *of* movement from the encamped—became itself a problem of narrative. If revolution and narrative are both about the *movement* of time, and camps are essentially devices for the immobilization of time, then how does one stage and write a revolution from the camp?

In the late 1960s Yasser Arafat, who always had a knack for good showmanship, paraphrased Marx and Engels to declare, "We have nothing to lose but our tents!" (cited in Karaoglan 1969, 144). Here the tent, even more explicitly than with Yunis, became a synonym for a chain, an object of ensnarement, an impediment to movement, and, as such, something to be struggled against and removed. In keeping with a certain Marxist insight, Arafat was determined that what we might call, just for now, consciousness begins with a self-negation. For Marx and Engels, "the practical *movement*" of revolution is necessary not only as the transformative reorganization of social order but also, and necessarily so, as the very "alteration of men on a mass scale" (1998, 60, emphasis added). At least at this stage in their writing (1846), no revolutionary consciousness precedes revolution—it emerges immanently only in the revolution itself.[6] If, as they had it, a revolutionary class can "only in revolution succeed in ridding itself of all the muck of ages and become fitted to found society anew" (60), then for Palestinian militancy this muck (in often quite literal terms) wafted squarely from what were often referred to as the "camps of despair" (*mukhayyamat al-yaʾs*).

And yet the difference that Arafat's paraphrase enacts is quite critical—the chains in Marx's maxim are metaphors, but the tent is a literal material object. This presence of the camp at the very foreground of revolutionary, anticolonial thought was not incidental; it was a historical difference bound up with the very conception of a revolutionary class. Palestinians, the discourse often went, were not a class of workers and peasants, but a class of refugees (Qaddumi 1969, 102). Ours is a revolution, said Palestinian Liberation Organization (PLO) leader Salah Khalaf, different from other world revolutions because "the people, as is clear, are socially, politically and geographically dispersed" (Khalaf 1969, 69). The latency of a revolutionary historical subject lies precisely in the displacement itself, but only in its negation. Even among leftist and Marxist-Leninist currents of the movement, where these subject-positions, refugee/worker, overlapped (that is, where the revolutionary forces were articulated as the peasant and workers of the camps), the territorial predicament of the camps remained a constant. This was more than a tension between nationalist and socialist tendencies, or the national versus social questions in the revolutionary movement (a tension arguably as old as revolution itself).[7] It was the historical challenge of launching a revolution from the camps themselves. This requires not simply burning the "muck of the ages" in the fire of movement and action but the very reorientation of the camp as the means to do so (figure 3.1). "Launching bases or detention camps?" (*Qawʿid intilaq aw muʿaskarat iʿtiqal?*) asked Ghassan Kanafani in a 1969 *al-Hadaf* editorial, on the eve of the Cairo Agreement (which effectively handed Lebanon's camps over to the PLO)—on this, he insists, rests nothing less than "the very historical and fateful existence of the revolution."[8]

This chapter is concerned with the *place* of the camp in the Palestinian Revolution and in turn with the camp *as* a place. It argues that the Palestinian Revolution, which roughly lasted somewhere between 1960 and 1982, didn't just emerge as a popular mass movement *from* the refugee camps; in many respects it emerged *against* the camps as well. To become a popular mass movement, capable of reversing settler expulsion and not just interrupting but overturning settler time, the Revolution required nothing less than the transformation of the camps into the means of their

3.1 Muwaffaq Matter, 1981, PLO. "The genie is out," on the sixteenth anniversary of the launching of the Revolution. Palestine Poster Archive.

3.2 Ismail Shamout, 1974, Fatah. The refusal of humanitarian capture. The speech bubble says, "Our issue is national liberation, return, and self-determination." Palestine Poster Archive.

own undoing. So, the Revolution had to produce and police its own demarcation between life and politics. Where humanitarian-developmental technics produced an interim space of pure administration, a space of the work- or relief-based management of life and nothing more, the Revolution would do the exact opposite. The camp was to be the site of political renewal, a "launching base" not just for militancy but for a new *type* of revolutionary historical time. Among other things, this resistance to the domestications of the camp regime in a politics of renewal or rebirth pushed much of the liberation movement toward a kind of pure politics. That is, this politics of liberation-insurrection *stricto sensu* often, even in its socialist and leftist variations, ended up constructing a stark, almost Arendtian distinction between the social (or life) and the political: a separation between the satisfaction of basic bodily needs and livelihoods (often bracketed under the term "livelihood matters"—*qadaya ma'shiya*) and great words and deeds (almost always referred to as "militant action"—*al-'amal al-fida∻i*) (figure 3.2).[9] One can think of a broad set of dichotomies that undergirds this revolutionary thought: inaction/life/stillness/description versus action/politics/movement/narrative; what

98 CHAPTER THREE

sits between this disjuncture and what must be overcome to move from one side to the other is the camp.

Reading across three novels of the revolutionary period, I argue that literature heeds this insurrectionary call but also undermines it. On the one hand, in its generic conventions, narrative structures, and symbolic formations, it *mediates* the camp as nothing but the surficial expression of a (deeper) political totality, one that can only be reached in consciousness-producing and almost always masculine turns to insurgent militancy; these are novels that, in the tradition of realism, take narration-as-explanation very seriously. On the other hand, the camp, even at a symbolic level, cannot be kept on one side of the life/politics divide; it spills over constantly, appearing as an ambivalent and indeterminate space between place and nonplace and also as a site of affection and attachment, often taking on gendered-feminine qualities that both call into question traditional gender divisions and reinscribe their own set of gendered figurations. But more than this, the camp exerts a force on the very form of the revolutionary novel, shaping some of its formal attributes and acting as a *drag* on narrative in ways that seem to impede the plot. Just at the point where the camp should be overcome and disappear in the protagonist's journey toward militancy, it persists and the very narrative drive itself stutters. In other words, the very struggle to shape national form out of a coherent narrative form of revolutionary becoming within the novel comes up against the camp. Camp form and novel form are entangled.

Revolutionary Novelties

The Palestinian liberation movement started both in and against the camps. The discourse and aesthetics that emerged from this movement are marked, even defined, by this spatial particularity. The very first forms of Palestinian political organization after the 1948 War took shape in and around the camps and also emerged explicitly to counter the formalization of the camps as permanent settlements. As early as the start of the 1950s, activists who would go on to establish the Arab Nationalist Movement (ANM), the precursor to the Popular Front for the Liberation of Palestine (PFLP), began making their way into Lebanon's and Syria's camps, setting up cells, holding talks, and agitating against resettlement programs. They organized mass demonstrations, sabotaged public

3.3 Cover of the "With the Displaced" section of the weekly al-Thaᵓr, December 2, 1954.

works and housing projects, established cultural centers, and developed perhaps the first post-*Nakba* ideological platform and manifesto, one in which the United Nations Relief and Works Agency (UNRWA) was identified as a colonial institution. They also printed a weekly clandestine newspaper, *al-Thaᵓr*, that was distributed largely in the camps (often surreptitiously in UNRWA's schools) and addressed the encamped directly in a section called "With the Displaced" (*Maʿ al-nazibin*) (figure 3.3). We know from UNRWA records that the ANM were most likely the forces behind the successful prevention of a number of development projects, and they probably played a decisive role in UNRWA officially ditching large-scale resettlement programs altogether in 1962. And while the ANM never really developed its own cadre of armed militants or a serious guerrilla force, their insistence on the need to mobilize the encamped refugees in a militant organization that would refuse the camps as permanent settlements would be ideologically formative for the wider movement.

The Palestinian liberation movement changed rapidly in the 1960s, and this is where most accounts pick up the story. The narrative is by now well trodden. In 1965, Fatah, established in 1959 as a political party, launched its clandestine guerrilla operations under the name al-'Asifa. It was followed two years later by the PFLP announcing its foundation. In the meantime, the defeat of the 1967 War fatally weakened pan-Arab statist anticolonial nationalism and allowed the factions to seize control of the Egyptian-managed PLO, which emerged as a regional player. And then less than a year after the trauma of the 1967 War, the Battle of Karamah in 1968, where guerrillas stopped an advancing column of Israeli armor and inflicted heavy damage, became the catalyst for the explosion of the Palestinian guerrilla movement onto the political scene. This is retrospectively read as the start of the Palestinian Revolution and the point at which it begins to take shape as an experiment in mass mobilization, first in Jordan's and Syria's refugee camps and cities, and then (after both Jordan and Syria closed their borders to the revolutionaries) much more protractedly (and, in the end, tragically) in Lebanon, until the PLO is forced out in a full-scale Israeli invasion in 1982 that besieges Beirut, kills tens of thousands of civilians, and culminates in the brutal three-day massacre of mainly women and children in Sabra and Shatila Camps.

What is often missing from this narrative is both how central and how fraught the place of the camps was in all this. The armed struggle gets the most attention in this story. But it's easily forgotten that this struggle was inseparable from nothing less than the revolutionary creation of new space-time. And if one reads the political literature of this period closely, it is clear that the camps were paramount in all of this. Only the Revolution could liberate the camps, but, in turn, only the camps could achieve a genuine mass revolution and the radical changes in social relations such a revolution would require. What had begun as a classic example of *foco* guerrilla warfare had to pass through the camps to move to popular mobilization.

There was a tension here even at the level of political discourse. On the one hand, the camps became sites of *insurrection*, a dense network of insurgent bases that sought to liberate land in a futural politics of return; they were sites for the forward and outward physical movement of the revolutionary body, and both the descriptions and the visualizations of this period stage or figure the Palestinian body in the camps as one in perpetual kinetic movement (fighting, training, building)—the camp as a means to another end. On the other hand, the camps were spaces of *autonomy*, described at the time as becoming something like revolutionary communes in which life and sociality are transformed in the present; they were sites of experimentation in which all kinds of social relations (gendered, generational, religious) are upturned and replaced, and novel arrangements between governed and governing are implemented—the camp as an end in its own right.[10]

This same tension around the question of the camp marked the literature and aesthetics that this revolutionary moment produced. Here, I take up three literary texts that belong to a (Palestinian) genre we can think of as "revolutionary realism." I do so to argue that the camp stood against the twin struggle to shape a national form out of displacement, and a narrative form out of the novel. Both spatial forms—nation and novel—come up against the camp. The three novels considered here—Ghassan Kanafani's *Um Saad* (1969), Rashad Abu Shawir's *al-'Ushaq* (1974), and Yayha Yakhlif's *Tuffah al-Majanin* (1983)—are all self-consciously written as part of a revolutionary political moment. And they all, I argue, straddle, in often ambivalent ways, the divide between life and politics in the camp that the Revolution so uneasily negotiated. In historicist terms, these novels are all inconceivable outside the Revolution's transformation of the refugee camps. *Um Saad*, writes the novelist and literary critic Radwa 'Ashur, "carries" the very "excitatory pulse" (*al-nabd al-hamasi*) of the "unimaginable" achievement that was the "transformation of the refugee camps into popular bases for the armed revolution" (1977, 177). What is significant about all three writers is not simply that they were all activists in revolutionary parties, or that they all either lived or worked in the camps at some point in experiences that were often formative.[11] All that is important. But what I want to emphasize is that they wrote from within what everyone agreed was a revolutionary time—a time that was the very condition of their writing. This time was itself conceived differently, as futurally open and transformable, and to that end carried a historical challenge—forming a subject of militancy—to which the writing of these novelists rose.

My concern is neither with identifying the generic qualities of the revolutionary novel nor grappling with its literary history. I'm interested in what a reading of these novels says about the politics they so self-consciously sought to achieve (and what it betrays, provokes, indexes).

And before turning to the novels themselves, it is worth dwelling on this revolution-as-context a little further to get a sense of how the relation between politics and aesthetics was understood. The Palestinian Revolution produced a prodigious outpouring of art and writing about art, as well as institutional spaces for art—the Plastic Arts Union, the Palestine Film Unit, the Division of Artistic Education, the Union of Writers, and so on. This space attracted every avant-garde element in the region (and many from beyond), and it did so—and this is what stands out about this self-perception—in a way that involved a radical, decluttered, and uncomplicated correspondence between aesthetics and politics. It shared not only a common aesthetic and idiom with a much wider assemblage of anticolonial, Third World, and Tricontinental liberationist movements, but also the unperturbed confidence that any such aesthetic could only operate as such, as aesthetics, *because* it was political. One of the abiding slogans of the Revolution was a full-blown tautology: "Revolution is innovation; Innovation is revolution." Perhaps no one personified this ease of overlap more than Ghassan Kanafani—"You can't tell where Ghassan the revolutionary begins and where Ghassan the innovating artist ends." That was Mahmud Darwish writing Kanafani's obituary days after Kanafani and his thirteen-year-old niece were murdered by Israel in a booby-trapped car just outside Kanafani's Beirut home. Kanafani, says Darwish, "achieved the fantastic congruence (*tatabuq*) between two movements or two revolutions—the movement of revolutionary literature and revolutionary practice" (1972, 6).

In his introduction to Kanafani's collection of short stories, Egyptian novelist and critic Yusuf Idris argues that Kanafani wrote from a time before criticism had "drowned us in pits of debates about what art is and what art is not" (2010, 12). Writing from what had become in the late 1970s a deeply divided Arab literary scene, Idris charges that literature had been "ripped apart from life and liveliness, from struggle and politics," all so as to foreclose the possibility that someone can write from within a "cause" (14). The revolutionary cause here is not an ideology per se, but a shared and irrefutable awareness of one's own time, in its very particularity, or what Richard Greeman (1967) writing about Victor Serge, perhaps the twentieth century's greatest exemplar of a nondoctrinal revolutionary literature, simply calls a "historical imagination." The Revolution as historical imagination shaped not just the overlapping themes, or plot structures, but the very architecture of Serge's texts. Between politics and aesthetics, Greeman tells us, sits history.

I chose these three novels not because they stand out as brilliant pieces of writing in the Palestinian scene (there are better written novels, even by these novelists themselves—*Um Saad* some insist is Kanafani at his least compelling), but because they are so singularly *of* their time; they mark so clearly the imperatives of this historical-political aesthetic across the most intense decade in the revolutionary experiment (in fact, they bookend its historical span, the late 1960s to early 1980s). More specifically still, all three directly take up the experience of militancy—as fundamentally the experience of putting the body back into consequential physical movement—which forms the narrative journey of each story, as it plays out against the camps or camp life. And all three are exemplary in their overriding concern with the treatment of consciousness. "*Um Saad*," writes Muhammad Siddiq, "embodies the clearest and most comprehensive ideological treatment of the question of political consciousness not only in Kanafani's but perhaps in all Palestinian fiction" (1984, 50).

Um Saad is set in a camp and revolves around the eponymous character's conversation with the author-narrator. It follows the story of her son Saad as he joins the revolutionaries and ignites the consciousness of the camp. Like Maxim Gorky's short novel, *The Mother* (1906), it places an illiterate, working-class woman as the hidden protagonist; in both novels a son joins revolutionary forces but it is the working, toiling mother who stays behind that reflects the genuine change in consciousness. The novel culminates in a large-scale mobilization of the camp's youth, which sees even Saad's drunken and abusive father regain a measure of decency: "The rifle is like measles," Um Saad tells us, "it infects." *Al-'Ushaq* takes place in the two weeks between Egypt's decision to withdraw permission for United Nations (UN) forces to remain stationed at Sharm al-Shaykh and the end of the June 1967 War. It follows Mahmud, a young refugee in 'Ayn al-Sultan Camp outside Jericho, as he is released from jail; courts his beloved, Nada; witnesses the debacle of the war; and begins his clandestine cell's military operations with a raid on an Israeli patrol. *Tuffah al-Majanin*, set in an urban neighborhood that is an adjacent spillover of a camp, uses a first-person narrative as recounted from the perspective of a child whose daily life, previously centered around misadventures with his friend and his father's hapless and fruitless attempts to secure a rations card from the UNRWA, is interrupted by his militant uncle's return from Israeli jail. This return dramatically accelerates the plot, unraveling the little stability the family had but restoring the imperative of fighting, albeit somewhat ambivalently. Neither Kanafani nor Yakhlif provide any place-names or actual geographies in their texts, underlining the genericity and singularity of Palestinian experiences of camp life and displacement.

It is around their encounter between aesthetic and built form that I want to read these novels. They heed, quite self-consciously, what they perceive as the call of politics but that is not what sets them apart per se. This entire generation of Palestinian writers faced a political imperative that was total and totalizing. In the words of the poet and literary critic Salma Khadra Jayyusi, "There is no escape. For the writer to contemplate an orientation completely divorced from political life is to belie reality, to deny experience" (1992, 3). This was in part what set Palestinian literature itself apart from wider Arabic literature; for while it was part of and often led the various experiments in the Arabic literary scene in the second half of the twentieth century, Palestinian literature showed marked differences, "especially in the treatment of place and time, of tone and attitude, and in its particular involvement in the pervasive political issues" (2). There is a political immediacy, even an angst, shared with other "deterritorialized literatures" (67), that takes shape as a will to narrative, a drive to write a collective into visibility, to emerge, to appear, to overcome isolation, "to beat a path into the consciousness of others by simply telling the story over and over again" (68).[12]

This is all pertinent. But for the revolutionary novels I consider here, the historical conjuncture is not simply a will to narrative produced by displacement, but the metonymic capture of the entire condition of displacement in the camp form. It's not only that the camp is so apparent as the descriptive setting of these narratives, not only, that is, that so many of the novels and memoirs of this period have to start in or pass through the camp.[13] It is also how the very *conditions* of both this politics and writing were contingent on a reckoning with the stubborn object of thought and action that is the camp. Put differently, the struggle to shape political (national) form out of the confinement and fragmentation of the camp, while not homologous to, is certainly *mutually determined* by the struggle to shape a coherent narrative form of revolutionary becoming in the novel. *Both spatial forms—nation and novel—come up against the camp.*

Despite the stylistic differences between them (Kanafani, by contrast to others, writes at this stage in a much sparser, almost ascetic prose that eschews any kind of flourish, repetitiveness, or verbosity in dialogue), all three novels take up the camp and camp life but rely on a kind of social or socialist realism to mediate this life back into politics proper. Perhaps only with Yakhlif, writing at a slightly later conjuncture, and tellingly with a style that moves toward a kind of magical realism, do we begin to register the fading of the gloss of revolution. It's clear that by the late 1970s and early 1980s aesthetic and discursive figurations of heroism had started to badly fray. The ascendancy of the right-wing, oil-financed Gulf monarchies, Sadat's takeover in Egypt and the Camp David Accords, and the relentless viciousness of the Lebanese civil war (1976–92) and the 1982 Israeli siege of Beirut in particular meant that "it became impossible to endure the repeated national disasters with the same kind of bravado" (Jayyusi 1992, 56). Palestinian and Arab literature of the late 1970s and 1980s marks the losses of this period in a turn to inner psychology (over plot) and a narrative disintegration that registers the end of collective and future-oriented emancipatory vision, amounting for some to an entirely new form, a full-blown "aesthetic of defeat" (Abu-Manneh 2015).[14] Yakhlif's novel is not yet defeatist by any means but is already jaded, disenchanted, even a little cynical. Scenes are muted, food is slowly eaten in silence, and the return of the militant—broken, disheveled, forced into menial labor paving roads that literally stains and tars him ([1983] 2008, 75)—brings no clear line of flight, even if it does confirm the need to keep fighting. In one scene, written with an irreverent humor almost entirely absent from the other novels, children run down a street heartily repeating revolutionary slogans. "Down with colonialism!" they all shout, before one of them turns around to ask his friend, "And, what is colonialism?" (25).

And yet in one sense Yakhlif only heightens a tension already at work in the revolutionary novel itself, a tension that belies any simple sequential periodization in the Palestinian novel (realism to modernism, for example). Even at the height of their heroism, these novels are beset with a persistent melancholia and the fragmentary textuality we associate with modernism (though this, if we follow Fredric Jameson, might be as much a mark of their "realism" as anything else). I don't mean to downplay the literary shift that happened in the late 1970s once the revolutionary novel had exhausted its historical conditions. I only mean here to point to a tension already at work in these novels, one I contend had as much to do with the spatial conditions and contradictions (chiefly, encampment) in and from which this political aesthetic emerged, as it did any borrowed generic qualities of the novel form as it had emerged in Western Europe (the social realist novel, say), or for that matter any straightforward historicist periodization. Whether these conditions produced a political aesthetic we should think of as its own conception of realism is not really, at least for my purposes, that important.

The Impossible Present as Spatial Predicament

"The striking thing about Palestinian prose and prose fiction," wrote Edward Said, "is its formal instability. Our literature in a certain very narrow sense *is* the elusive, resistant reality it tries so often to represent" (1998, 38). Most literary criticism focuses on what is said, on the plot, on sociological or political meaning, but for Said, "it is the form that should be looked at." The struggle to achieve form "expresses the writer's efforts to construct a coherent sense, a narrative that might overcome *the almost metaphysical impossibility of representing the present*.... A typical Palestinian work will always be concerned with this peculiar problem" (38, emphasis added).

This "almost metaphysical impossibility," I want to counter, might not be that metaphysical at all. Said thinks of this predicament in temporal terms, but he himself relies on a set of spatial metaphors and images to do so. The Palestinian present is "bewildering" and "disorienting," a "maze of uncertainties" and "untidy overlappings" (Said 1998, 70). If that were not enough, Said's reading gets literally urban, if only by way of symbolic analogy: "Look at it [Palestinian life] with some sense of what it means to negotiate it. You will immediately see its symbolic analogue in any panoramic overview of contested sites such as Gaza or even Amman, where the patchwork of overbuilt and structureless dwellings offers little regard to symmetry, form or pattern" (70). There is much to take issue with here (the longing for pictorial order, the need for a vantage point from which to visually capture the symmetrical whole that betrays a highly modernist, perspectival prejudice in which the world is meaningful only insofar as it corresponds to its own image or plan). But what is significant is Said's recourse to spatial form to come to terms with this temporal impasse and its formal effects in prose fiction. Yet, more than analogy, this impasse was lived and corporeally experienced in the spatial forms that exile and displacement took. The Arab city of exile was one, but the exemplary or metonymic form was and remains the camp. The camp, I am arguing, *is the spatial form through which time itself is organized and represented in the revolutionary novels*.

Put differently, the difficulty in representing the present is at some points inextricable from the camp condition and the long shadow it cast over the entirety of the Palestinian experience. Fawaz Turki, writer, activist and camp inhabitant, in one of his many memoirs, describes camp life as the experience of the "vagaries of homelessness," in which "we existed not in the present tense, the tense of reality, but the future imperfect, when next year, next time, next speech, the wrongs will have been righted, the grievances removed, and our cause justified" (1972, 16).

The camp suspends time. Fawaz's strange grammatical tense, the future imperfect, "the will have been" that expresses something in the future that will have been past by the time you get to it (that is, the already-given future "pastness" of any possibility of justice, of grievances being righted), marks the static continuity of the condition of encampment, its temporal suspension, its immobility. "The camp," writes Samuel Weber in a succinct definition, "is a spatial device of immobilizing time" (2012, 9). The question, then, is not simply one of impoverishment and its vulnerabilities. The lifeworlds of the urban poor are, of course, themselves subject to the relentless barrage of risks and threats that impose a "tyranny of emergency" (Appadurai 2002, 30) and enclose the poor in a "perpetually intrusive, futureless present" (Perdigon 2015, 90). This is no doubt also true of the camps, but it is being physically immobilized *and* sundered from the historical time and geography of nationhood that here seems most decisively to close the future.

In revolutionary Palestinian literature, the camp was itself often the object that suspended historical time and, even as it provided a kind of relief and very real community, exposed those in its wards to various states of injury. In many instances, the camp comes to stand in for the whole, for the entirety of the Palestinian condition; it is an arrangement that brings together and concentrates all the insurmountable odds the Palestinians face into one miserable, paralyzing, ramshackle built structure. The entire breadth of the conspiracy seems funneled through the camp: the repressive Arab regimes and their police apparatuses; xenophobic host societies and their resentments; the resettlement projects and UN depoliticizing paternalism; Israeli military force, coming down hardest and first on the camps; traditional rural social structures that survived in deformed but even more pernicious shape; heat, cold, inclement weather, and environmental force. All this somehow came together in and through the camp. The stock imagery of camps almost always included things like wind-swept tents, overflowing sinkholes and latrines, and flooded muddy pathways. It included images of the precarity of this life, of the constant police and army raids and beatings, of the routine burial of infants who didn't make it through a cold night, and it included the corporeal markings of all this: bodies frail from chronic hunger and malnutrition or from toxic exposure; downward gazes and hunched backs; the sores, scabs, and scars of hands rough with cement and soil.

The encamped refugee body is always doubly marked: a classed, working, or toiling body, and also, in its encampment, a confined and exposed body. This mark is the mark *of* the camp. Statelessness or refugeehood alone does not suffice to cause it. The city-based exiles turned revolutionaries in Jabra Ibrahim Jabra's novels, for example, are of a different order altogether. Often successful professionals or intellectuals, they too are stateless refugees but their narrative journey toward militancy is the result of an inner psychological dislocation or unease that persists, despite their often seemingly smooth adjustment into Arab urban bourgeois life. The site and surface of contradictions is an idealized psyche, often burdened with the effects of (too much) self-reflection, not an inescapable spatial environment. What separates Kanafani's refugee hero from Jabra's intellectual hero is not statelessness, which they share, or even strictly class, but the camp. Siddiq notes that in comparison to Jabra's, Kanafani's revolutionaries "cultivate political consciousness of necessity, not choice" (1995, 97); the utter intolerability of material conditions is the *motivation* for the revolutionary subject. And the eventual realization that those conditions are determined elsewhere establishes lines of causality and the journey on which the revolutionary protagonist must set.

In *al-'Ushaq*, life in the camps is a constant drawn-out battle with the elements. Everything takes place under Jericho's "hellish sun," an atmospheric envelope of thick air, perspiring bodies, flash floods, sandstorms, and unbearable temperatures, with "scorching steam rising from the earth itself," oozing soft, hot asphalt beneath one's feet, and the transparent mirages and shadows that dance on the surface in dreamy sequences (1974, 181). The writing here takes a thickly descriptive tactile tone and slower pacing, marked by paragraph breaks to channel the slow density, hot stillness, and unstable ground of the desert camp. With Yakhlif, the exposure of camp life merges weather and authority into a contiguous force of pressure, one atmospheric totality. In scenes in the tent classroom of a UNRWA school, the harshness of the teacher overlaps with the harshness of the environment itself—in fact the former seems to follow from the latter, because the teacher can't stand the bodily effects of camp life, "the coughing, sniffling or smell of the camp's children" ([1983] 2008, 11). "The winds were shaking the sheet. The class had the sting of nails. I was shivering. And Badr al-'Ankabut was looking for an opening from which to escape" (11). Camp life is elemental life.

This mixture of exposure and injury with the "non-being" of statelessness renders the camp historically closed. In this literature, the camp in many senses *is* the suspended, ahistorical present. In *al-'Ushaq*, the camp first appears as the foil of its surrounding city, not just any city but (and with apologies to Ur) the ur-city, the oldest continuously inhabited city in the world, Jericho—a city that *is* history. The camp is surrounded by a sheer excess of historical and biblical significance: the ancient Canaanite Moon City (*Yareah*, meaning moon in Canaanite, and from which the Arabic *Ariha*, Jericho, is derived), the Mount of Temptation and its monastery, the architectural glory of the Umayyad-era city in Caliph Hisham's palace. All of this defines the camp negatively, by its externality to historical time. This temporal opposition is registered spatially and aesthetically in the opposition between stone and mud brick. More specifically, there is the very durability or longevity of built materiality: the timeless stone of the city against the ephemerality of the camp's mud houses and palm roofs. The visual differences are stark: "stone, so particular in the sharpness of its color," renders the city and surrounding mountains a shimmering bronze or golden yellow, alive with color, while the camp appears in the dullness of the monochrome gray-brown of its mud walls and tin-sheet roofs.

Removed from the sequential movement of historical time, the movement of the urban proper, the camp becomes a site of endless *waiting*. Abu Shawir's camp dwellers are repeatedly analogized with the waiting monks on the Mount of Temptation—parallel forms of madness. Paralyzed by caution ("Time is treacherous" [1974, 48], Mahmud's mother warns him) and immobilized by the camp, the refugees too enter messianic time. In Yakhlif's novel, the narrator's father is at first too proud to register as a refugee before backtracking later in his penurious life, and he whittles most of his time away waiting for a rations card from the Agency—which itself appears, just as much as any god, a remote, otherworldly, and indifferent sovereign power, one to which the hapless must also genuflect and petition with no guarantees. "And as such my father again began writing appeals to gain a rations card. But he kept waiting without result" (38).

Where the Concrete Is Never in the Concrete

Although the camp might *appear* as continuous with timelessness and statelessness, it is, for these novels, the effect, not the cause of the removal from historical time. These novels, then, seek to uncover what is beneath the camp, the concrete political totality underpinning it. Where the camp is analogized to other spaces it's treated in a way so as to get to its concrete essence. As a space of terminal waiting, a space of killing time, the camp, almost inevitably, emerges as a prison, with camp time as prison time. Across these and other novels, the camp appears in an analogical or synecdochic relation with the prison, substituting for or standing in as one part of a larger prison whole. One of the few actual spaces that appears with any regularity in all the novels is the camp's prison. In fact, the opening sequences of all three novels are either set in or reference prison and prison guards. Most UNRWA camps had by the 1960s dedicated police stations and prisons. As we saw in chapter 2, the Agency as a regulatory force depended on these sites of coercion to substantiate its own claims to authority.

In *Um Saad* the correspondence between prison and camp becomes total. Its story begins with a young man, Saad, in prison after being caught on his way to join the resistance. His mother, Um Saad, recounts that he was presented with a chance to be released if he pledged to the *mukhtar* (the village elder—Kanafani making his disdain for older rural power structures clear) to "behave himself." Saad predictably scoffs at this offer and returns with an insult that (literally) belittles the *mukhtar*'s seniority, referring to him as "my son" (*ya ibni*), in a way that marks the passing of communal responsibility to the revolutionaries. The author-narrator, an intellectual and writer standing in for Kanafani himself, pushes back to ask if that was the wisest choice—after all, better to be out of prison than in, no? Um Saad's irate response is first to disparage the difference: "You are out of prison, and what do you do?" ([1969] 2010, 255). Before she continues, her attention is cut off by the radio she'd left on all night and that begins to transmit the latest news broadcast. Her eyes dart between the radio and the narrator. This interruption is not trivial. The dialogue, Kanafani is showing, is broken up by the intrusion of political event. We don't know what the broadcast said, but we know it stiffens Um Saad's resolve. What the scene suggests is that she now understands her son (and by extension herself) as no longer the passive recipient of the actions of others, but as the subject *of* event; she/he makes news. Her track shifts, finding shape in a proliferation of metaphor:

> Do you think we don't live in prison? What else do we do in the camp other than walk around in a strange prison? There are all kinds of prisons, cousin! All kinds! The camp is prison; your house, prison; the newspaper, prison; the radio, prison, the bus and the street and people's eyes... our age, prison; and the last twenty years, prison; the *mukhtar*, prison... you talk about prisons? Your whole life has been spent in a prison... you delude yourself, cousin, into thinking these prison bars are flower vases. Prison, prison, prison. You yourself are prison. (255)

The inside/outside boundaries of prison/camp and refugee subject disappear altogether. The camp-as-prison, which is to say the Palestinian condition, is already in your head. It is already formative or constitutive before you've even begun to contemplate it—"You yourself are prison." Camp, prison, consciousness all collapse into a synchronic chain of equivalence. *To inhabit the camp is to inhabit the prison of one's own consciousness.* There is no interiority, no last bastion of freedom outside of material structures, no neat object/subject divide that might allow for a discrete ego or self beyond historical-spatial conditions. Trembling but certain, she tells him, "Listen up, I know Saad will leave prison. The entire prison! Understand?" (256).

But Kanafani can't leave his narrative in this profuse flux, in this multiplicity of metaphor. He has to mediate back to causes. From where does this prison come? To come to terms with it, with its causes and the means of its overcoming, one has to look elsewhere, beneath the surface, beyond the things (or, rather into the things; into the politics *in* the thing). When Um Saad comes in one day to visit the narrator, he notices her dress is dirty: "I saw the strip of thick mud hanging off the side of her dress as though it were a crown of nails" (271). The intellectual's romanticism transforms, even inverts dirt into a virtue, a Christ-like majesty of sacrifice. But Kanafani is again setting up the writer (that is, himself) only to knock him(self) down. Um Saad, it is true, had spent the best part of the night dealing with flooding rainwater. But there is no sacrificial triumph in this. "I don't want to die here in the mud and dirty kitchens, you understand, cousin?" (271). Instead, the episode reminds her of the night Saad left to join the resistance. That too was a night of heavy rain, the whole neighborhood was out, knee-deep in overflowing water working as hard as they could to stop the small huts being washed away. But Saad just stood there, indulging in what first appears like cynicism: "tonight you're going to be buried in mud." When his father retorts, "What do you expect us to do? Do you think there is a spout in the sky that we can just plug?" everyone laughs. But Um Saad realizes her son is already lost deep in thought, "as though he was going the next day to plug that very spout" (272). The impossibility of camp life, she now understands, is only addressed in the politics that underlie it. The surface/depth metaphor here takes more direct architectural or infrastructural shape. Plugging the master spout is facing the totality that is colonial reality—the hidden political forces that structure the camp's everyday experiences. The run-down houses or the overflowing pathways *appear* as the infrastructural or architectural problems of an impoverished habitat, but they are merely the surface appearances of deeper political inequities. *The concrete is never in the concrete.*

When Kanafani himself in his final interview recalled working and living in the "sad and affective environment of the camp" that left such a mark on him, he quickly adds, "And it was not hard to find the political roots of this environment" (*Shuʾun* 1974, 137). Getting to these "roots" in fiction requires a mediation, the true revealing of the relations between appearance and essence, which is exactly the role Um Saad's emerging insights play in the text, insights that, not coincidentally, she has to keep teaching to the writer himself, of course.[15] The illiterate Um Saad does the work of mediation that the author-narrator, and by extension Kanafani himself as an intellectual, is unable to do. Kanafani marks the political limits of writing within the writing itself. And it's precisely in the form of this text as a skewed dialogical encounter that he manifests his own (Maoist) ethic of learning *from* mass popular struggle.

In all these novels, the struggle against the objective conditions of life has to pass through the camp but also reach beneath it, to the politics that undergird it. Even with Yakhlif's slightly more ambiguous take, the imperative of confronting reality and finding a way out has to take the protagonist beyond the immediate conditions of life. *Tuffah al-Majanin* crescendos in its final pages. The father's close friend and neighbor Tahsil Dar, and the only person among both families with a ration card, has died.[16] Point Four projects are gathering pace with the distinct aim of reducing the numbers of refugees on rations lists.[17] The survey committee begins doing the rounds. The father has been picking up the uncle's rations and now instead of getting his own card (which, of course, never happens), he faces losing the little he gets. "Pressure. Surveys. Rumors. Fear. The Agency. The dead, dying again and again" (2008, 86). The committee eventually "enters the house like a yellow wind" (86). The family decides on a bit of simulation. The militant uncle has to play the role of the older deceased man. Yakhlif takes the symbolism as far as he can. The militant has to dress like the deceased man in the traditional garb of the rural classes, marking himself with precisely the signs of the "regressive" semifeudal structures that the militant generation sought to overthrow. And because Tahsil Dar walked with a pronounced hunch, the symbolic humiliation of the former militant is complete—he has to literally bend his back in a prostrate position "for a fistful of flour" (89).

Three European UN agents and a local translator begin their questioning. But the cover is quickly blown when the foreman's wife (with whom the uncle had been conducting an affair) walks in unexpectedly. "'Why are you wearing those ridiculous clothes?' she laughs out." Rather than take the abuse now being hurled down at him by the translator, the uncle strikes back, throwing him to the floor. This return to bodily action restores the uncle's purpose but is already marked with its own tragic effects—he runs away, "without looking back... leaves us in cuts and fragments" (96). The boys chase him out into the open and watch him fade out of view across the mountains, until he becomes "as small as the head of a pin" (98). It is ambivalent, yes, perhaps even without clear closure, but still insistent on its political task. The uncle only restores a sense of self (and his standing in his nephew's eyes) by leaving and physically moving again across borders to confront the primary political contradiction, reality itself, in militant action. He's walking back to Palestine: "He is returning there, as birds return to a nest" (96).

The almost bewildering range of immediately experienced injustices and lived contradictions—the material lack and humiliating jobs, the fear and police abuses, the punitive paternalism of aid, the crumbling and decrepit houses, and so on—is mediated as but a range of instances of colonial struggle. Without a firm grasp on this reality, these problems are experienced as independent afflictions. To attempt to navigate this world one bit at a time (one ration card here, one evaded police encounter there) is the stuff of illusion, which Yakhlif brings to life in a literal game of make-believe and dress-up. And it is from the depths of this illusion that the shattering realization and its necessary embodiment in corporeal action emerge.

These, then, are novels keenly sincere in their duty to *narrate*. They all employ a tight narrative arc in which the squalid and oppressive conditions of camp life are mediated back into the totality of colonial/imperial order, a realization that sets the protagonist off into the outward movement of insurgent heroism. The novels are solemnly self-tasked with a representational burden, with what Jameson (describing Lukácsian realism) called "the grim duty of a proper reflection of the world" ([1977] 2002, 205). They are didactic and agitational but never simply documentary or evidentiary. They seek not simply to describe the (subjective) conditions of life but to explain its (objective) causes. Things are never described for the sake of description or documentary accuracy alone. Explanation, causality, motivation, totality, the intelligibility and transformability of the present—this is the stuff of the ordering systems of these narratives. That is, these novels are not saying "this is the way things are." They are saying "this is *why* things are the way they are and this is what you need to do about it." The narration is very conscious of its task as instructive mediation.[18] All of these novels were written for local consumption. They're locally idiomatic and accessible, in dialogue pushing formal Arabic prose as far as possible toward colloquial vernacular and common turns of phrase.

These novels are to be used. They were written so as to work on what these authors would have all considered the necessity of forming new *consciousness*, understood as distinct from the reality they encounter and something to be in part shaped in and through literature. The emergence of a subject of militancy is almost always the crescendo of the plot, and it almost always involves the rejection of existing social structures and values: religion, patriarchy, international paternalism, the social hierarchies and obscurantisms of "traditional" rural life but especially refugeehood itself. In Kanafani's literature, says Darwish, we first see how "the revolt over the character of refugeehood emerges as the key to the possibility of return" (1972, 6).[19] If the force of realist narrative "always comes from this painful cancellation of tenaciously held illusions" (Jameson 2015, 5), from the demystifications it effects, then these novels hold true to form. And in most cases, one might say, their aesthetics suffer accordingly: they're often heavy-handed and sentimental, and the character development is transcendent, heroic, masculine, muscular.

Slipping in the Right Place

All of this so far yields a fairly straightforward reading. And yet part of this effect—to mediate causes, to explain why—is somehow complicated by the texts themselves. All these novels employ narrative techniques that run counter to their own narrative drive.[20] They still rely on free indirect discourse and streams of consciousness, what the critic and poet Ahmad Dahbur identifies disapprovingly in Abu Shawir as "the surrender of the author in some instances to a kind of impulsive spontaneity" (1977, 239).[21] In places these novels are written in grammatical moods of uncertainty; they are excessively symbolized and replete with countless scenes of description, often written from the perspective of the omniscient observer, which seems to do little to move the narrative forward, with scenes, tellingly, in which life and domestic things spill over or creep back in over or beneath the politics, in which things exceed their mandate or quarantine. If camps are always about the separation of life and politics, then these novels register a tension, in their very form, precisely along this fault line. In the paragraphs that follow I propose a counter-reading of these novels: one that suggests that the camp and camp life exert a force, symbolically and formally, on these novels that marks the Revolution's tension between a pure, futural politics of insurrection and the present forms of everyday life it came up against.

One way this happens is quite simply when the camp exceeds its symbolic and narrational role (abject, uninhabitable) and appears as *place*—a site of affective relations and belongings, a location or ground from which to think and act, an object of attachment, a site of memory, and so on. For Faisal Darraj, place in Palestinian literature never coincides with the present. Place is either fixed in the past (paradise lost and the object of recovery) or is projected into the future (the redemptive site of return). This absence of place in text, one might argue, is but the expression of the impossibility of place in the world. "In a very literal way," wrote Said, "the Palestinian predicament since 1948 is that to be a Palestinian at all has been to live in a utopia, a nonplace of some sort" ([1979] 1992, 124). The image of the journey back into the future, to the recovery of Palestine and placeness itself, is a movement that always begins in and passes through nondescript space, through the open, through the void of exile.

In a similar vein, Barbara Parmenter writes that landscapes of exile in Palestinian literature tend to lack the attributes of place. These landscapes—desert, city, camp—appear as voids, nonplaces in which the present is suspended (1994, 51). The desert, through which so many Palestinian literary journeys have to pass, is "a kind of anti-place" (56). "This is a landscape shorn of all meaning yet tangibly real, unlike the abstract images of the desert in the poems." The city of exile, likewise, is "unrelenting in its ugliness" (58). This is a stark contrast to the image of the besieged Palestinian city, replete with nobility and its own quiet, if defeated, heroism (Jayyusi 1992). And unlike places in Palestine that always have names, the city of exile often remains anonymous and thus detached and placeless (Parmenter 1994, 60). It lacks definition and substance, and like the desert it "represents the antithesis of a home place" (63).

But as soon as she reaches the camp, Parmenter realizes the difficulty of extending her analytical framework: "The refugee camp, the most squalid of all exile environments, is also the most ambivalent" (1994, 63). There is a "dual quality of camp life" (65). A sense of place is maintained by community living together, and yet the environment is one of squalor, harassment, misery, despair, want, lack. The refugee camp, she concludes, is an "intermediate landscape."[22] It is this intermediateness, this dual quality, that I think is often registered in the novels despite or in excess of its plot structures and generic conventions. And it is registered precisely along the fault lines between life and politics; in fact, this duality is nothing but the impossibility of keeping the camp on either side of the life/politics split.

This occurs on a fairly straightforward symbolic plane, in moments in which this literature registers points of excess in the world of objects themselves. In these works, we apprehend how life *in* and *of* the camps heightened the politics of the object, that is, the object not only as a mimetic representational surface phenomenon that discloses a deeper essence, but as a mediator of political significance in its own right. That is, how, in the camp, the *political* consequentiality of things, especially things that existed around the built, expands and becomes sharper—more fraught, more determining, more literary, even. Things leave "textual residues" (Brown 2003) in ways that constantly exceed their objectness and get entangled with subjects and their political fates. Life slips back into politics.

In *al-'Ushaq*, for example, despite the ideologically unequivocal message and plot structure, it's not only in militant *action* but in the very *work* of building that some characters begin to restore a kind of historical presence. They begin to resist the alienation of the object-world around them though building their own homes. These passages often seem incidental to the plot, but reoccur. In one passage, the main protagonist, Mahmud, observes his comrade's mother, Um Hassan, making mud bricks under the hot sun. The work of turning formless mud into bricks is imbued with an artisanal skill and solemn dignity and, even more importantly, a historical effectuality. The text moves back and forth between Mahmud's internal reflections and his recollection of a poem about the Umayyad Caliph, Hisham, after his palace was destroyed. In the poem the mother of the caliph upbraids him for crying over his destroyed palace—the material world is to be rebuilt, not cried over. The two maternal figures begin to converge: "What is the difference between you and the mother of that caliph? Is she from poetry and you from mud?" (Abu Shawir 1974, 56). The passage moves into a kind of *metamorphic* imagery, common in this literature, in which human bodies begin to cross the object/subject divide and merge with the mud they work with, the buildings they erect, the land on which they dwell, or the trees they plant. There is nothing in terms of narrative happening here for pages on end. Instead, a stream of reflections jumps from past to present, in which the confined, marked body of the refugee reappears with a malleability or plasticity, and the work of building appears like a self-making activity. "She erected [*nasabat*] her body [*jadhʿuha*] in the middle of a mud mountain" (56). The diction is crucial: *nasabat* implies erection of a structure, usually a form of material construction, most commonly a tent, while, *jadhʿuha*, her trunk, is a connotation of arboreal life.

With Kanafani, almost every time Um Saad enters a scene, the narrator views her arms and hands through metamorphic and sensory imagery that opens onto animal or ecological life. So, her folded arms appear "as two animals embrace" ([1969] 2010, 287) or "the embrace of two birds" (305). Elsewhere they are like "the color of the land" (278) or "resemble the skin of land tortured by thirst" (293). In slightly more ambivalent terms, her arms stretch out "as though they were a bridge or a roadblock" (252). In other places, we go back to work, but the image of sight gives way to a sense of smell, when her arms give off a particular odor associated with work, or to sound, when she slaps her palms together "with the sound of wood being cut" (335).

This *slippage* between subject and object marks an ambivalence in camp life. In these sections, the camp appears ambivalent because it is also the product of work that has not been entirely alienated. Yes, it's an object that domesticates, confines, even kills, but one that, through the work of building, has also, in some sense, been returned to common use.

It's self-made and, only as such, inhabited. As metaphor or simile, the self-built world of the camp spills over into a gendered organicity of biological life (*her* trunk-body of mud; *her* hands clapping together like wood being cut). Some of the effects are obvious: these images give the scenes a romantic gloss of an artisanal affinity with materials, the sense of dignity in work, and a focus on the toiling female body, albeit in a way that keeps in place an association between what is constructed as "the feminine" and work. In this sense they mark a certain limit of the Revolution's challenge to gender norms—the sphere of life remained associated with what they considered to be the feminine, and the sphere of politics with the masculine, with figures of insurgent heroism often remaining impoverishedly male. But in another sense, these passages bestow a strong metamorphic capacity to the encamped human body. In this metamorphosis, work itself, and especially work with building matter, is re-visualized or re-conceived—it is not the mastery of engineering turning brute matter into form, but a continuum or flow between life process and material. Work affords the subjects a way beyond the separations of subjecthood itself. In a way this is an even more radical transformative flight than the insurgent heroism, but one that remains incidental to the plot.

To Perhaps Think of Audacity: Uncertainty and Politics

Already we have a sense of how a question of form runs across these texts and their objects. But we can formally read the camp itself in these novels in other ways. All three novels punctuate a narrative drive in a realist style with different modes of grammatical and textual *uncertainty*. In each of them we move from camp-based scenes of description or action—a house, a group of men sitting around a table interrupted by a policeman, Um Saad's entrance into a scene—to either a subjunctive mood or to qualifying phrases that destabilize what we've just seen. With Kanafani it takes the form of a continuous, exaggerated use of simile. There is constant use of a sentence construction that involves qualifying words, like "as though" (*ka∘annaha*) or "it seemed like" (*tabdu/yabdu*); in other places, descriptions start with "I imagined it as . . ." (*khuyyila ilay*), working a subjective, imaginary parallel layer of thought atop the sociological or the descriptive. This is used so frequently and consistently that it creates a pervasive mood of hesitancy, which works itself into the very sentence structure, just as the work of realist narrative seems to be doing the exact opposite.

With Yakhlif, the narrator recounts parts of his childhood and memories of his father and destabilizes clear memories, what he calls "sharp moments," with rhetorical doubt. In one repeated scene, police march his father's friend and neighbor out of the house, and the narrator recalls his father immobilized by fear, unable to act: "My father was exhausted. Even now after all these long years, I remember that sharp moment. My father narrowed down to the capacity of waiting. He stood to walk into the room as though he were walking on a knife blade. *Perchance he was thinking of adventure, perchance he was thinking of boldness*" ([1983] 2008, 27, emphasis added). The sentence construction "Perhaps he was . . ." (*rubama kan*) or "Perchance he was . . ." (*la'lahu kan*) is repeated in the novel, and each time is uttered by the narrator despite the clear sense that his father is either unwilling or unable to act on his thoughts, despite the fact that he had already been, in this scene and in the entire novel, "narrowed down" to nothing but waiting.[23] And yet this sentence construction comes to finish a chain of recollection again and again, as if there is a necessity, grammatical and political, to suspend judgment and even clarity and to entertain doubt.

This scene is repeated with the police again summoning his father's friend Tahsil Dar for another beating at the local station, with the men meekly silent and passive, "fear squirming across their faces like a fish" (45). Again, the narrator's father is left alone, in apparent silence. "Perhaps he was talking to himself, perhaps he was thinking about audacity" (45). To perhaps think about audacity, or boldness, or adventure, is not quite an oxymoronic construction, but it is counterintuitive; it introduces uncertainty, hesitancy, and *thought* into what otherwise might be considered the stuff of conviction, immediacy, and *action*.

How does one explain the textual work of this uncertainty in the frame of a political-revolutionary aesthetic of realism? It makes little sense as a narrational or plot device. Instead, I would argue, that it is the textual registering of camp life's constitutive tension between life and politics. It is not simply that Palestinian refugees navigate a political world defined by its uncertainty, that even at the heights of their insurgent powers they were still hostage to the whims and machinations of others (and always unsympathetic others). It is that everyday camp life is itself defined by punctures and interruptions that—and this is the key—both demand *and* exceed any simple mediation back to political structure. The police beatings, present in every one of these novels, to take one example, are, of course, as the protagonists know well, a symptom of their stateless and encamped condition, a condition that can only ever be overcome in militant politics. And yet at the level of the everyday they become just an ordinary part of camp life that cannot be simply mediated back to the politics of resistance but must be silently endured, survived, avoided, outwitted, and so on. The moods of uncertainty, wittingly or not, mark life in the camps as it is lived beneath meta-politics but above abject survival. They mark, albeit obscurely or even confusedly, a recognition that camp life has to be *lived* imperfectly, unheroically, unresistantly, even apolitically, if only so that heroism and resistance, in short politics, might endure. The "perhaps thinking of audacity" becomes the very necessary prevarication or hesitancy for both life *and* politics in the camp; to "perhaps think of audacity" is as much to consider it as it is to think better of it—in fact, it is to do both at precisely the same time.

It should be clear that I do not have in mind the steadfastness (*sumud*) so often celebrated in representations of popular Palestinian politics. *Sumud* is still a figuration entirely captured by a heroic will to endure and persist (when outright resistance is not possible). Rather, at play here is a simultaneous duality: the ordinary, nonheroic, even evasive, nonnormative daily life that exists alongside, as the necessary scaffolding of, the heroism, and that is the hidden content, I argue, of the moods of hesitancy or uncertainty in the texts. With Yakhlif this is personified in the twin characters of the father and the uncle and the parity they reach at the end (despite the father's defeat, his demonstrable meekness, his submission to waiting). This becomes explicit in the final pages, with the militant uncle restoring pride in violent action, and the father, despite everything, continuing "with self-sufficiency and pride, to overcome misery with the *power of life*" ([1983] 2008, 99, emphasis added). Conversely, given the entire plot, both politics and life briefly establish a kind of correspondence as twin forms of power.

Revolutionary Forms of Entanglement:
Camp, Nation, Novel

What then is left of the image of revolution here, when the camp question spills life right back into politics? The revolutionary novels examined here are narratives of armed struggle, yet, in their treatment of camps and camp life, they cannot but reach past the spectacularity of insurrection and intensity of event to face the everyday experiences, the minor keys of life, the shadows, that were just as much a part of struggle. I have argued that we can approach these constitutive, and perhaps historically unavoidable, tensions in Palestinian revolutionary politics by appreciating how camp life is entangled with these texts in noninstrumental ways, in ways that exceed both the discursive frame of liberation politics and the plot imperatives of the narratives themselves—in other words, by thinking about how built and literary forms intersect.

In hermeneutic terms, this is not a question of context; it is a question of moving away from a strict language-world binary to think about how something like a spatial/material object affects literary texts in ways not confined to symbolism. Form is one word for thinking about precisely that. The very conditions of camp life are indexed in the formal attributes of these novels well beyond plot or genre: episodic and fragmentary structure; multiple narrative voices and constant shifts from first to third person; different modes of address, in which the narrator will suddenly address the reader directly; use of inner voice that is interwoven with character dialogue almost imperceptibly; typographical markings that break the text up, like long parenthetical remarks (in Kanafani, running for almost two pages in places); repetitive use of ellipses and multiple and unclear paragraph breaks; sudden movement between past and present tenses and the constant use of flashbacks; and rapid shifts between metaphors of image, sound, and smell. These do not exist only in the revolutionary novel but are here relatively sharply pronounced *and*, arguably, not just a mediation of the Palestinian condition, but of that condition as captured in camp form; a form that is itself unfinished, transient, fragmented, caught in a perpetual present, and defined by a set of irreducible paradoxes between return/presence and politics/life.

The inability to achieve a bounded *wholeness* in these texts is, I think, but the expression of the inability to achieve a bounded wholeness in the very form the text is performatively inciting: the nation form. In other words, the fragmentation of these novels is in one sense the formal indexing of the fragmentation of the Palestinian body politic, a fragmentation that is both consolidated and contested in camp form. The camp form is defined by its boundedness, but what it binds are only the fragments of a dispersed potential political community. In this very boundedness it reaffirms the impossibility of a bounded Palestinian-national whole. There was no political unity, no bounded territory, no whole nation, or contiguous political community that might function as the conceit and precondition of a whole novel. That fiction existed neither on paper nor beyond it. So, any homology, any easy ideological fit between literary and national space was impossible. At the same time, this boundedness and the fact that camps could become communes of a kind, experimental and, crucially, somewhat insulated zones of revolutionary work and organization, *afforded*, to use Caroline Levine's (2015) useful term, this literature a set of possibilities, horizons, even language. The shared life experiences and idiomatic registers and, just as critically, the material infrastructures and support systems that this literature relied on were preserved only *in* the exceptional, extraterritorial, and excluded character of camp form.

Camp form and novel form are entangled in more ways than one. If as the Invisible Committee, in their book-length homage to the returning imaginary of the commune, write, that *to inhabit* a communal space is always *to write* each other, to tell one's story from a *grounded place* (an association we can still hear in the word geography) (2015, 203), then, here, the camp was both this territorial and communal grounded place from which to tell the story *and* also the very object that stood in the way of that story's culmination. This is not to suggest a direct homology or correspondence between aesthetic and political forms. Rather, I am arguing that the relation between camp form and the Palestinian revolutionary novel form was determinant, even if it was conflictive and tense—these writers tried very hard to etch out a closed ideological whole from the camp experience, but the very restrictions of the camp itself didn't allow for neat narratives, tidy wholes, and sequential conclusions. It did afford authors, however, a common experience, identity, and infrastructure. Form, Levine argues, always indicates an arrangement of elements—an ordering, patterning, or shaping (2015, 3). And if we follow Jacques Rancière, as Levine invites us to, and think of politics as always a matter of distribution and arrangement, of imposing and enforcing boundaries, and of temporal patterned hierarchies, then there is no politics without form.[24]

Palestinian revolutionary politics, I have been arguing, was in some senses an attempt to grapple with a series of interconnected forms: the camp, the nation, and, insofar as it was a medium of politics, the novel. The content of revolutionary politics was often malleable and transferrable; ideologies—left and right, secular and religious—came and went, and most adapted and molded to the formal reality of the camps and the formal imperative of the nation. It remains striking how change in both the camp and the subject is understood through a concept of form or shape—*tahawwul* in Arabic, the movement from one condition to another or the assumption of a different shape, and best translated in English as trans*form*ation.

Yet for all the insistence on the need for transformation, the Palestinian Revolution remained open to the criticism that it failed to achieve a genuine popular mobilization, ultimately failing *as* a revolution. It was too hierarchical, too masculine, too bourgeois, too instrumental, too insurrectionary, too vanguardist, too spectacular. In the camps, the argument went, it saw nothing but the abject ground for the foot soldiers it needed to hide its own inadequacies (Darraj 1996). So, it failed to transform the camps into self-organized popular forms of life that might sustain a revolution beyond an insurrectionary guerrilla war.

True as much of this might be, it misses a reckoning with that category that so much of the revolutionary project was so explicitly about and with which we began: consciousness. In 1981, on the seventeenth anniversary of the launch of the PLO, Arafat responded to a series of question from Elias Sanbar's *Revue d'études palestiniennes*. On the brink of the Israeli invasion of Lebanon and siege of Beirut (where the PLO was headquartered), and arguably what would later be marked as the end of the Revolution itself, the text has a backward revisionist gaze. Where are we seventeen years on? What's the Revolution's gain? Arafat's reply is confident: "We have turned our people from a refugee people *waiting* in queues for charity and alms from UNRWA into a people *fighting* for freedom" (Arafat 1982, 6, emphasis added). This *movement* of people from waiting to fighting, from refugees to militants—a movement, as it was seen, into a new historical time itself—was premised on the transformation of the camps. And *this*—the change in governed subjects and not any seizure of the state apparatus of government—is what appears as the Revolution's achievement. One can argue, then, that the historical production of a collective subjectivity was the enduring revolutionary effect—novel, ruptural, transformative—of what we know and insist on as the Palestinian Revolution. This is revolution not as state capture, but as the formation of revolutionary subjects, as the *becoming revolutionary* of a subject that Gilles Deleuze warned "is not to be confused with the history of revolutions" (2007, 379).

We get at a sense of *both* the potential and limit of this image of revolution as becoming/subject-formation in the entanglement of the novel and camp forms. The tension in the novels between, on the one hand, the realist narrative drive to uncover the essence of totality beyond the camp and face it in a politics of insurrection and, on the other, those moments in which that drive is interrupted by a camp life that appears as not entirely reducible to the imperatives of return and insurrection, is, of course, *the* tension of the Revolution itself. This Revolution was defined by its extra-territoriality and caught between insurrectionist and autonomist poles; between revolution as insurrectionary return to history that might reverse settler negation in a new constitutional moment, and revolution as the autonomist invention of new space-time; between revolution as state-making politics and revolution as a form of autonomy antagonistic to all form of sovereignty; between independence and liberation; between the base and the commune. The camp question was the fault line in this tension—in both the sense that it registered on its surface the Revolution's deep tensions, and also in the sense that how the Revolution answered this question was always going to be deeply consequential.

The abiding virtue of the novels is that they open up the space to ask questions about this tension from within the Revolution itself but outside its teleological order. What does revolution look like from the camps when the work of building homes is as transformative as the heroism of insurgency, or when we make room for uncertainty alongside audacity? How can the camp be both the means of its own overcoming but also a communal place? How do our accounts of revolution change when we look back at the camps not just as the sites of vertically organized insurrection but also as popular, autonomous zones of movement, of living and doing politics otherwise? That is, can we think of camps as sites for a revolutionary politics *of* inhabitation, for ways of producing space differently in which they would not be only the means to another end (elsewhere) but also the *demonstration* of their own idea of life and that life's politics? The camp not just as a "launching pad" to the future of liberation but as an anticipation of that very future in its present.

4 THE CAMP, UNDONE

NEGATION AND RETURN IN THE VANISHING HORIZON OF SETTLER PERMANENCE

"The Core of the Problem"

Consider this sentence by an ostensibly left-wing Israeli politician: "It is clear that the camp inhabitants are the 'hard core' of the refugee problem" (Zakin 1972, 60). Or take this near-identical statement made some twenty years later by an ostensibly left-wing Israeli journalist: "The refugees of the camp are, of course, the core of the problem" (Rubinstein 1991, 35). In certain Israeli political discourse, variations of this statement about the camps are so commonplace, so given and self-evidently obvious, as to be entirely banal. But if we suspend the confident certitude, the "of course" or the "it is clear," of the statements for just a moment, we might ask—What core of what problem exactly? For the journalist Danny Rubinstein, who gives us the latter iteration, the answer is not quite direct but clear enough: "In the refugee camps, the consciousness of exile and the maintenance of customs for sustaining the bonds of the clan and the original village are naturally far more compelling.... In their unrelenting misery, the residents of the camps live on a combination of nostalgia for the past and illusions about the future. Sometimes it seems as though the present is of no import to them" (Rubinstein 1991, 36). These lines are from Rubinstein's book, *The People of Nowhere: The Palestinian Vision of Home*, acclaimed, as its blurbs tell us, for its "remarkable empathy" and its "depth of understanding."[1] I bring up Rubinstein here, a celebrated and award-winning journalist considered an expert in "Palestinian affairs," not to indulge in some facile exercise of unveiling him as nothing more than a colonialist beneath the veneer. His record of criticism is clear enough (which includes his insistence in 2007 on applying the term *apartheid* to the Israeli regime), and his empathy might very well be quite genuine—though neither say anything, *of course*, to the coloniality of his thought and politics. But none of this is the point. I bring this up to signal what I will argue is the consistency of a certain image of the Palestinian refugee camp and its inhabitants in Israeli political discourse as "the core of the problem" that just *has* to be undone, so as to ask: Just what shared political sentiments and assumptions underpin this consistency? What is the point of ideological unity that guarantees this image's reproduction, across the political spectrum and time?

Palestinian refugees, we know, embody what is, for this territorial settler project, the most irreducible and threatening of all political counterclaims: return. Refugee return is *the* political anathema of state Zionism, its master haunting. But, given that the vast majority of the refugees live *outside* the camps, what is it about the camps themselves that multiplies and concentrates this threat? At stake, I want to argue, is something more than the perceived and engendered threat of camps as bases of insurgent refusal, or even the racialized and classed image of their miserable but dangerous urban wretchedness. At stake is something that Rubinstein's sketch indexes without really elaborating, and which will come up again and again in the pages to come—the camps are of a different and recalcitrant political temporality altogether. That is, the camps constitute not just unruly spaces, but the very basis of *a consciousness of an unruly time*. The very *tense* in which encamped refugees live seems, to Rubinstein, a problem: between past nostalgia, future illusion, and no present sits the incorrigible "consciousness of exile" that so palpably irks him across the text. For the politician Dov Zakin who gave us the first iteration we began with here, and who in 1972 was proposing plans for comprehensive camp removal, the language is uncannily similar: "In the camps *the consciousness of being temporary* refugees persists" (1972, 61, emphasis added). Put differently, for Israeli state politics, the trouble with encamped refugees who, in Rubinstein's prose, do nothing less than "live" on this other, presentless time, is that in effect, I argue, they refuse the terms of "settler time" (Rifkin 2017); they refuse inclusion in a historical time inaugurated and defined by the necessity and irreversibility of their own dispossession.

Rubinstein's take finds a past echo in a short fragment in one of Mahmud Darwish's works. In *Journal of Ordinary Grief* (*Yawmiyat al-Huzn al-ʿAdi*), one of his three book-length pieces of prose, published in 1973, Darwish recounts the reaction of an Israeli soldier upon entering a West Bank refugee camp during the 1967 War:

> During the June War many Israeli soldiers were surprised to find that Arabs have a memory and remember a homeland that was lost. What surprised them most was that children born after the loss of the country were still attached to it. An Israeli soldier related that when he went into one of the refugee camps, he discovered that people lived there exactly as they had previously lived in their villages. They were organized as they had been before: the villages were the same and the street was the same. That soldier was shaken. Why?
> —I could not comprehend this. Nineteen years have passed, and they are still saying, "We are from Bir al-Sabiʿ." (2010, 32)

The camp here is both a vehicle of (a)historical continuity—"the villages were the same and the street was the same"—and a site of countertemporality. The soldier's incomprehension comes from encountering this refusal to abide by the givenness of settler time and its sequestering of native life-forms into a finished past—"Nineteen years have passed and they are still saying. . . ." If the camp is a placeholder for the towns and villages of historical Palestine (what Rubinstein construes in Orientalist fashion as an almost primordial remainder, "the bonds of the clan and the original village"), then it is also, in its very material existence, a contestation of not just the settlements constructed atop and among the ruins of those towns and villages but, more fundamentally, the temporal sovereignty that is premised on this very settlement enterprise. What Darwish shows us is that Israeli state politics understood this quite intuitively, understood it to the point that the "soldier was shaken," or, to be more precise, we could say, was *unsettled*. To the soldier's bemused, almost naïve, question—"why?"—the answer of Israeli political policy seems to have been "because of the camps." It was the camps themselves that kept this anomalous political temporality alive; the archival documents abound with statements in which Israeli officials attribute to the camps a kind of effective, even agentic, force, as "evidence," "reminders," "instruments," "symbols." Where Palestinian revolutionary politics sought to both transform and overcome the camp so as to forge and enter a new historical time through liberation and return, Israeli state politics sought to eliminate the camps so as to refute the counterclaim and normalize the state's postcolonial temporal order.

This chapter is concerned with the place of the Palestinian refugee camp in Israeli politics. It follows a set of governmental policies and practices aimed at the refugee camps from the start of the military occupation in 1967 to the popular uprising of 1987, to ask, What makes the camps, in ways not reducible to the "refugee problem," such objects of anxiety and intervention for Israeli political planners? What is it about camps qua camps that means so much energy and destructive power must be expended just to undo them and have their inhabitants dwell in other areas (areas that are sometimes literally only a few hundred meters away)? What do we learn from reading the technologies, calculative logics, and rationales the Israeli State came to deploy in dealing with camps under their control? The chapter argues that how Israeli state policy apprehends the figure and object of the camp provides an insight into the constituent dynamics of settler politics here. The camp tells us about both the negational strategies that structure the settler colony's expansive and dispossessive force and, more critically, the temporal bind—*the vanishing horizon of its permanence*—that continues to define this project. And yet, despite rich histories of the "Arab refugee problem" in Israeli state policy, very little work has been done on the camp in Israeli state politics, or, conceptually speaking, the political stakes of the emergence of the camp as an object of this politics.[2] This is the case despite the fact that the turn to the camp not only extended but also transformed the long-standing Israeli State's goal of permanent refugee resettlement.

Resettlement of the Palestinian refugees has been, and to a certain extent remains, a reoccurring priority (one could say obsession) of Israeli state politics. It occupied Israel's most prominent leaders and its most vaunted academic minds for years. It was a policy that ran for decades and involved huge amounts of money and a raft of organizations: the prime minister's office, the foreign ministry, the military government after 1967, numerous ministerial committees, the Shiloah Institute of Tel Aviv University (later the Moshe Dayan Center of Middle East Studies), and, farther afield, the World Bank, the Rand Corporation, and even expressly constituted and shadowy bodies like the Middle East Arab Refugee Resettlement Organization (MEARRO), based in Zurich. It brought in global personalities: financiers like Baron Edmund Leopold de Rothschild, US politicians like Herbert Hoover (who in 1945 proposed resettling the entire native non-Jewish population of Palestine in Iraq), Jacob K. Javitz, and Edward Kennedy, and celebrated architects like Moshe Safdie. It called on the "expertise" of politicians, urban planners, architects, economists, agronomists, hydrologists, anthropologists, Arabists, and engineers of all kinds. The sheer number of plans, the intensity and frequency of investiture of time, money, and energy, not to mention secrecy and diversion, that went into devising a "solution" is striking. Resettlement was not something a few midtier administrators considered on occasion: it was something deliberated, planned, and organized at the highest ministerial levels of government, year after year—so much so that for decades minister without portfolio effectively became code for minister of refugee resettlement. Between 1948 and the late 1980s more than twenty official (and many more semiofficial) Israeli plans for the resettlement of Palestinian refugees were put forward. The twenty years between the 1967 War and the 1987 Intifada alone gave us more than a dozen Israeli plans for the undoing of the refugee camps in the occupied territories.

Nor was the push for resettlement ever confined to a fixed set of instruments; it was mobile and flexible. Resettlement plans took in everything from elaborate employment schemes (like placing refugees in large projects such as the construction of the Latakia port in Syria or the Aramco oil pipeline from Saudi Arabia to Lebanon), to impromptu opportunism (like the ad hoc and piecemeal distribution of thousands of purchased foreign passports in Gaza in the early 1970s). The plans might target large groups of refugees, as in the large-scale and complicated stealth resettlement projects designed to resettle tens of thousands of refugees everywhere from Libya (where they were to replace returning Italian settlers) to West Germany; or they might target single individuals, as in the Paraguay scheme in which fake work programs lured individual refugees to permanently move to Paraguay through a shell travel agency called Patra and "emigration offices" set up by the military government directly in Gaza's camps.[3] Where the camp became the direct object of intervention, the plans moved across sharply varying scales from the mega ambitions of total camp removal and large resettlement programs designed around things like nuclear desalination plants in Sinai/Gaza (Baron de Rothschild's long-running but abortive pet project), to the more gradual transfer of refugees to modestly designed model "Arab villages." Likewise, the degree of force expended often differed, ranging from eruptively violent demolition and destruction (the razing of entire blocks and thousands of homes, and the forced deportation of their inhabitants) to the seemingly benevolent plans of camp improvement and modernization (that saw camp streets repaved and infrastructure improved, all with the lofty aims of rehabilitation). Yet in all this, there is an unwavering, grinding consistency. In the movement back and forth between improvement and elimination, rehabilitation and demolition, employment and expulsion, there is a unitary and strikingly persistent logic—that of negation.

Settler Negations: "Don't Forget You Were Never Really Here"

To come to terms with the place of the camp in the Israeli State's political imaginary and practice, one has to locate it within the wider drives and dilemmas of settler-state formation. The camp, I argue, is a "privileged" object in the politics of settler *negation*. In his book, Rubinstein, like so many before and after him, figures Palestinian desires for return as a pathological and distinctly irrational dysfunction. In explicitly developmental language that marks its temporal aberration, return is often figured as childlike by Zionists—"a fantasy," a "petulant demand" (Margalit 2018), a "tantrum" or "stomping of the collective foot" (Gitlin 2014). Return, as the insistence on the recoverability of Palestine, is seen by its detractors as the pathological failure to properly mourn the lost object and move on, as part of a broader unhealthy Palestinian resistance to reality itself, one that borders on political psychosis (Massad 2015, 192).

Indeed, for Rubinstein, there is something about the desire for return that runs counter to reason and the evidentiary, counter to the reality principle; it involves, the way a child or a neurotic would, "stubbornly rejecting the evidence" (1991, 66). The camp incubates this infantile but clearly dangerous nostalgia for *places that no longer exist* in the very consciousness of its inhabitants. One of the many similar stories Rubinstein recounts sees a "beggar," who also happens to be a refugee, in Gaza City ordered by an Israeli officer to abide by a curfew and go home. Where is your home, the officer asks, "and in perfect innocence and sincerity the man replies, 'My house is in Majdal.'" Rubinstein adds, as the closing sentence and final judgment, of the entire chapter, if not the book—"Majdal is now the Israeli town of Ashkelon. It hasn't existed for over forty years" (38).

For all its ethnographic Orientalist pastiches that give it the sense of a passing series of observational vignettes, this is the overriding and reinforced message of Rubinstein's book—there is nothing to return to, it does not exist. For all its supposed sympathies and sensitivities, for all the deliberate pathos with which it approaches these stories, in the end, and in essence, the discursive logic of the entire text is *negational*—"There is no (longer) such a thing as Palestine." This logic is openly betrayed in the very title of the book, before a single page has been turned: *The People of Nowhere*.

Settler polities, I argue, demand the work of negation.[4] Settler replacement, we know, is never seamless. "Rather," as Patrick Wolfe had it in one of his more enigmatic but generative sentences, "the process of replacement maintains the refractory imprint of the native counter-claim" (2006, 389). Every act of settler affirmation, every new production is inseparable from the negation that it depends on. As Wolfe goes on, "The positive force that animated the Jewish nation and its individual new-Jewish subjects issued from the *negative process of excluding* Palestine's Indigenous owners" (390, emphasis added). Elimination, then, he tells us, is more than the liquidation of Indigenous people: "In its positive aspect, the logic of elimination marks a return whereby the native repressed continues to structure settler-colonial society" (390). *But* the return of this "native repressed" and the "negative process of excluding" are not quite the same thing; one begets the other in ways that not only structure and animate settler politics but also expose its gaps.

To negate is neither to destroy something nor, as the dictionary definition would have it, to "deny the existence" of something. Negation is related to, but distinct from, both destruction and denial, as well as foreclosure and repudiation. To negate is *to refute the presence of something you also and simultaneously accept exists*. In Freudian terms, it is to lift the repression of an image without ever accepting the repressed content. In the five pages he dedicated to negation, Freud gives us the now-proverbial example of a male patient coming in to talk about a sexual dream, who volunteers the following statement—"You ask who this person in the dream can be. It's not my mother." At which point, Freud tells us, we can be sure it's his mother. "Thus the content of a repressed image or idea can make its way into consciousness, on the condition that it is *negated*" ([1925] 2001, 667). But, writes Alenka Zupančič, we are not dealing simply with an inversion here (no means yes); negation does not deny content, "but transmits it, hands it over" (2017, 482). To negate something is essentially to say "this is something I would prefer to repress, but cannot entirely do so."

The "not-mother" statement, for Freud, is the form of negation. And it is this form, according to Zupančič, more than the content of what is being negated, that is at stake here. The "no" itself "is the hallmark of repression, a certificate of origin" (Zupančič 2017, 483). The negative utterance, "not-mother," is something one has to say but cannot: "It is at the same time imperative and impossible. The result is that the word is uttered as denied, and the repression coexists with the thing being consciously spoken out" (Zupančič 2012).

Negation, then, creates a partial opening in the repressive barrier. But, as Zupančič (2012) (who reads in Freud's short essay "the fascinating knot of practically all the key problems of psychoanalysis") points out, even if one accepts the repressed content, one cannot eliminate the structure of the gap or crack that generates it; even if one succeeds in conquering the negation, the repressive process itself won't be removed.

In his introduction to a book (of mainly clinical essays) about Freud's concept of negation, the clinical psychiatrist and professor of psychiatry Salman Akhtar opts to start with three historical statements by politicians. Between Winston Churchill's wartime imploration to "never give in" and Richard Nixon's self-exposing statement "I'm not a crook" sits Golda Meir's 1969 now-infamous statement to the *Sunday Times*: "There were no such thing as Palestinians. When was there an independent Palestinian people with a Palestinian state? It was either southern Syria before the First World War, and then it was a Palestine including Jordan. It was not as though there was a Palestinian people in Palestine considering itself as a Palestinian people and we came and threw them out and took their country away from them. They did not exist" (*Sunday Times* 1969; cited in O'Neil and Akhtar 2011, 1). Zionist discourse is here, literally, a "textbook example" of negation. For Akthar, Meir's statement is a refutation of the awareness she has that such a people does indeed exist because the recognition is too difficult and distressing to accept. Negation, then, "denotes the appearance in consciousness of something one has desperately attempted to ward off" (3). It only appears, however, in negative form—"not my mother," or "no such people."

If we stretch this beyond the strictly psychoanalytic, we might say the expulsion of thoughts and the expulsion of people—two forms of displacement—share a similar and overlapping structure. Both precede and incite negation—which Freud tellingly described as "the successor to expulsion" ([1925] 2001, 669)—not just when they fail or are unfinished, but when they exceed the mechanics of repression. Indeed, an expulsion of people would seem to necessitate, for most subjects, an expulsion of thoughts.

As with any other colonial enterprise, for territory to be emptied, for Palestine to be rendered "a land without a people," the actual people patently inhabiting it had to be not only disavowed and disappeared, they also, I argue, had to be rendered—in negative—as less than "a people." In conversation with Gilles Deleuze, the Palestinian critic Elias Sanbar draws an intimate connection between emptying land and "evacuating" the settler psyche: "In order to succeed," he writes, "the emptiness of the terrain must be based on the evacuation of the 'other' from the settlers' own head" (Deleuze and Sanbar 1998, 28). In 1948, Sanbar writes, Palestine "was not merely occupied, but was somehow 'disappeared'" (28). For Israeli Jewish settlers coming up against persistent forms of Indigenous life, this necessitated what Sanbar understands as a kind of "blindness." "And this blindness was not physical, *no one was deceived* in the slightest degree, but everyone knows that these people present today were 'on the point of disappearance,' everyone also realized that in order for this disappearance to succeed, it had to function from the start as if it had already taken place, *which is to say by never 'seeing' the existence of the other who was indisputably present all the same*" (28, emphasis added).

The persistence of Palestinian life requires a conscious "blindness" or a "never seeing" that is neither deception nor denial but, I would argue, an effect of the work of settler negation. While disavowal as a concept allows for the contradictory simultaneity of repudiation and awareness, it tells us very little about the apparent necessity of the negational discursive and grammatical form in settler politics. Negation, instead, with its necessary relation to repression, helps us understand how settler politics deals with the *excess* in which Indigenous presence cannot be so summarily unacknowledged, repudiated, or repressed.

Meir's statement is not exactly a disavowal of Palestinian presence as such, but this presence's rendering in negative in a manner completely consistent with a broad part of colonial history—not a people, not citizens, not owners, not a nation, not a sovereignty, not a history, not a civilization, not a culture, and so on. To this day, this is still precisely the discursive logic of so much of Zionism's relationship to Palestinians. The repression of the image of those otherwise "indisputably present" is partially lifted when this image can no longer be warded off, but the repression never really ends and so they are never accepted as just another people (with political rights, audible claims, hearable grievances); the repressed content pierces through, "while at the same time what is essential to the repression persists" (Freud [1925] 2001, 667).

In this respect, it's telling that a large number of the Palestinians left in what became the Israeli State after 1948 were juridically captured and dispossessed by Israel through the category of the "present absentee." Up to a third of the total Palestinian population in Israel became, legally speaking, "present absentees." If negation is "the conscious representation of what is present as being absent" (O'Neil and Akhtar 2011, 7), then the figure of the "present absentees" seems an almost parodic confirmation of the work of negation.[5] These people are undeniably present as living human bodies, but they are absent as a "people" or as a coherent collective with a territorial counterclaim.

Negation here, then, marks both the limit *and* at the same time the reaffirmation of repression. Politically speaking, we might add, that not only does repression persist with negation, but in settler polities it is directed *outward*. If we take them as political concepts beyond strictly psychic mechanisms, settler repression and negation appear performative as much as inwardly directed, causative as much as reflexive. The negational statement "There is nothing to return to" or "They do not exist" is meant as much for other as self. "From the start," Gabriel Piterberg writes, "Israeli officials were well aware of the significance of memory and the need to erase it. Repression of what had been done to create the state was essential among the Jews themselves. It was still more important to eradicate remembrance among Palestinians" (2001, 40). Piterberg draws on one archival file, titled "Operation Refugee," which outlines plans by the Israeli Foreign Ministry to sneak images of the ruins of Palestinian villages and towns into Arabic dailies and newspapers that would reach encamped refugees across the border. The bureaucrat on file notes, "You should be efficiently assisted by propaganda of photos that very tangibly illustrate to them [the refugees] that they have nowhere to return" (cited in Piterberg 2011, 40). Repression-negation here directly cuts to the temporal anxieties of settler politics and its need to overcome its foundational moment.

This remains a formidably constant but somewhat internally inconsistent logic. As Joseph Massad (2015) shows, Zionist discourse on Palestinian senses of loss is marked by an ambivalent double stance. On one hand is the insistence that Palestinians accept the loss of the object as unrecoverable, mourn it properly, and move on (rendering, as all settler states strive for, the foundational act a thing of the past). And, on the other, is the insistence, articulated so explicitly in Meir's negational statement, that the establishment of Israel did not dispossess anyone since no such people existed, and as such the Palestinians have no loss to carry or get over.

To put it differently, to the Palestinians the negational statement ("You do not exist") has always also been an injunction to not only "forget that you were ever here" but also to "remember" that in reality you *never* were, a kind of grammatically aporetic double negative—*"do not forget you were never really here."* What is demanded, then, is a radical self-negation, not of a particular subjectivity but of collective subjectivity *tout court*. It is not good enough to forget a place/homeland, one has to "realize" that one never really knew or possessed it to begin with. This precisely remains the self-negating logic of the demand that Palestinians must accept Israel *as* a Jewish state, that is, to accept the land itself as eternally and exclusively Jewish. There is nothing to return to because there was nothing *really* there to begin with. But we don't need Freud to tell us that nothing comes from nothing. Engendering the nothing, filling the nothing up, making sure the nothing is recognized as nothing is hard and recursive work.

It is not enough to overlay existing memory with official archival history; to target the minds of those in the state's pedagogic wards through schools and curricula; or to frighten those who need frightening with the criminalization of expressions of memory and remembrance (the "Nakba Law").[6] Settler politics also sought out the very geography itself; it sought out the places *of* time and memory, those sites and things that anchor or emplace temporal counterclaims. Israeli state politics changed place-names in a frenetic concern with toponymy; it restlessly reinscribed the landscape with infrastructures that would render it unrecognizable or illegible; it sought to transform ecology itself, devastating indigenous flora and fauna, and—in a self-defeating move that would lead to regular forest fires—replacing them with climatically ill-suited (European) species. And, most strikingly, it erased Palestinian villages, towns, and city centers and then covered the ruins and rubble with trees and parks or housed settlers in them as "re-captured" spoils of war, or else, it transmuted them into fenced-off archaeological sites of abstract mythic history. The Palestinian ruin has received most attention, both as an architectural and landscape object (Kadman 2015; Leshem 2013) and as an aesthetic object of literary (un)representability in Israeli literature, as a trope of "visible invisibility" (Hochberg 2015), or as the written "unsaid" of allegorical topography (Eshel 2011). But this drive and its underlying political anxiety, this sense of an oblique and inchoate but imminent danger, I argue, has also animated official Israel's relation to those built forms—the camps—that kept a material connection to the originary villages and the time of return.

A Permanent Normal

The drive to negate the collective presence and land claims of the Palestinians, to make sure that they remained "no such people" took strongest shape in plans to liquidate "the refugee problem." But after the 1967 War, the refugee camps themselves became direct objects of political intervention. The occupation of the West Bank and Gaza had not only brought the refugees and camps back to the forefront of Israeli politics but also presented a new field of possibilities to an old problem: it allowed for tangible concrete interventions that would go straight to the settler order's anxieties around permanence and normalcy to which negation in essence was a response. Here now were so many of the camps and their refugees confined in a territory the state largely controlled. The temptation for Israeli politicians to bring to bear the full weight of the military, planning, and architectural technologies that had from the start been so integral to their settlement enterprise must have been overwhelming. The question was just where and how to start.

In a reading of the archival record in the first few weeks after the war, the Israeli historian Tom Segev paints a picture of feverish but muddled activity. Although the clamor to do something about the "Arab refugee problem" began immediately after the war, the Israeli prime minister, Levi Eshkol, was raked by vacillation and indecision. "He wanted to get rid of the refugees but did not know how; he was not even considering the hundreds of thousands of 'new refugees,' but only those of the 1948 refugees who were still living in camps, primarily in Gaza" (2008, 524). At Eshkol's urging, the plans began to pour in. Alarmed by the birthrate in Gaza and the youthfulness of its population, and determined to both annex the Strip and do something about this largest concentration of refugees, the early plans all focused on Gaza's encamped refugees. In Cabinet discussions as early as June 15, 1967, a mere five days after the end of the war, figures like Yigal Allon and Menachem Begin (then minister without portfolio in the national unity government) called for clearing all the camps in the occupied territories and resettling their inhabitants in Sinai (Masalha 2003, 105). This was deemed too risky at the offset, though the Sinai Desert would remain fixed in this political imaginary as an ideal open geography, a perfectly remissive space beyond the frontier that might permanently absorb all the refugees (and would return again in the genocidal war launched at the end of 2023 as the site to which all of Gaza's population should be sent). Nonetheless, committees were formed and proposals continued to pour in at a remarkable rate.[7]

Segev's account of the early clamor to do something, anything, about the refugees shows the mixture of strategic urgency and practical disorganization that would mark Israel's attempts to remove the camps and their inhabitants over the next two decades. Eshkol didn't know what he wanted or how to get it, beyond an overriding desire to just be rid of the refugees, especially those of Gaza—"I want them all to go, even if they go to the moon" (cited in Segev 2008, 536). But though the policies may have been muddled and often piecemeal, the drive to remove Palestine's Native inhabitants, of which refugee resettlement was but an unfinished extension, was not just consistent but elementary. All the 1967 War did was open access to a political object of intervention—the camp—that for Israeli politics had come to represent the very "core of the problem," and, as such, it allowed for a *corrective return* to what I argue is the state's foundational impasse.

In the following three sections I follow the attempted undoing of the camps across a set of archival sources. I work mainly from declassified documents in the Israel State Archives (ISA) but also call on personal papers and collections, print journalism, and visual media to track the camps across these sources *not* for some "accurate" picture of this history. The archival documents are, of course, representations only of the forms of knowledge that the Israeli State constructed for the Palestinians it dispossessed and displaced. The point of insight here is in how the archival constructs of camps and refugees *betray* wider organizing—and distinctly temporal—imperatives and anxieties in the colonial state project.

The first section about "removal" traces a series of unrealized visions and plans for the removal and resettlement of encamped refugees, from the earliest large-scale plans of 1969 to some of the last major proposals in 1983. In the following section, regarding "improvement," I turn to look at the relatively more cut-price interventions in the housing and improvement projects actually implemented, mainly in the Gaza Strip in the 1970s. The third section about "demolition" considers the demolition and clearance practices that took shape—and hid—in the shadow of the long counterinsurgency in Gaza's camps. None of this is meant to be comprehensive. There is no doubt much that has been left out, much that hasn't made it into any kind of archival record. And I've chosen to survey a broad number of plans and interventions, instead of a deeper dive into one or two, because what I want to emphasize across these sections is how, despite the diversity and mixture of methods—demolition, improvement, rehousing, jurisdictional incorporation—they are all united in negational logic and intent. All of these practices revolved around the engineered or architectural production, even at their most violent, of *permanence* and *normality*. "The permanent" and "the normal" are here the organizing conceptual principles across the board; the words (or their synonyms and cognates) come up consistently, even incessantly, in the rationales and explanations. Above all, I think, they demonstrate not only how the question of the camps was understood by the state, but also how much this question came to be tied up with the state's reflexive anxieties about its own sense of permanence and normality—after all, the attempt to return to "normal" is precisely what negation and repression are all about.

In this drive for a temporally permanent and normalized state order, it was the camps and not refugeehood per se that was the issue. One of the most striking facts in these plans and interventions is that refugee status was to be left unaffected.[8] When in 1972 Mapam, the ostensibly left political party, jumped on the bandwagon and put forward its own plan for the "voluntary dissolution of the refugee camps by large-scale development enterprises," Zakin (whom we began this chapter with) made clear that their plan had no bearing on refugee status: "Caution must be observed to prevent the impression among the refugees that the evacuation policy will liquidate their status as refugees" (1972, 66). But perhaps the clearest expression of this logic came from then minister of defense Moshe Dayan, insisting in a 1973 statement to the *New York Times* that the aim of camp removal and resettlement was to make all 163,000 inhabitants of the camps in Gaza *"refugees in name only."* The purpose of the project, he went on, "is to improve the standard of living. We have no designs on their political status as refugees. But in the meantime, they will live a better life" (Smith 1973, emphasis added). For so many of the planners and politicians to act on the camps was to act on the refugees at their most essential. It was the camp as *a temporal modality of inhabitation* that was the political object of intervention because at stake was a knot of political claims and temporal subjectivities that were in and of the camps. To act on what Rubinstein and Zakin called "the consciousness of being temporary," to reach this knot, the work of negation has to reach what makes the camp, a camp.

Removal: From the "Father of the Forests" to "Mr. Settlement"

Visions for the removal of the camps were entirely historically consistent with the actual removal of Palestinians from the land—the former have to be understood as an elaboration of the unfinished and stuck status of the latter. It's not, I believe, coincidental that one of the first political figures to take on camp removal was Ra'anan Weitz. We can, in fact, trace a certain history of the filial relation between elimination and replacement in Zionist settler colonialism in the overlapping careers of Ra'anan and his more well-known father, Yosef Weitz. Weitz senior, a figure ostensibly on the Zionist left and a member of Mapai (the Workers' Party of the Land of Israel and the dominant force in early political Zionism, before being merged into today's Labor Party in 1968), was the longtime director of the Jewish National Fund (JNF) land department and a member of the three-man "transfer committee" during the *Nakba*. Gabriel Piterberg describes Weitz as a "great 'redeemer of the land' from the Arabs ... and a formidable ethnic cleanser in the 1948 war and during the 1950s" (2009). As effective head of the JNF, he led the massive afforestation campaigns that saw the ruins and lands of depopulated Palestinian villages covered with trees, earning him the moniker "Father of the Forests." In a sequential elaboration of his father's work, Ra'anan Weitz, a trained agronomist and regional planner, known as "Mr. Settlement" (*Mar bityashvut*), would become a pioneer of "rural settlement," eventually heading the Jewish Agency's land settlement department and later establishing the Settlement Study Center in Rehovot (today bearing his name as the repackaged Weitz Centre for Sustainable Development). Where Weitz senior would depopulate the native countryside and cover the traces in

מידגם ארכיטקטוני להתישבות חקלאית באל-עריש

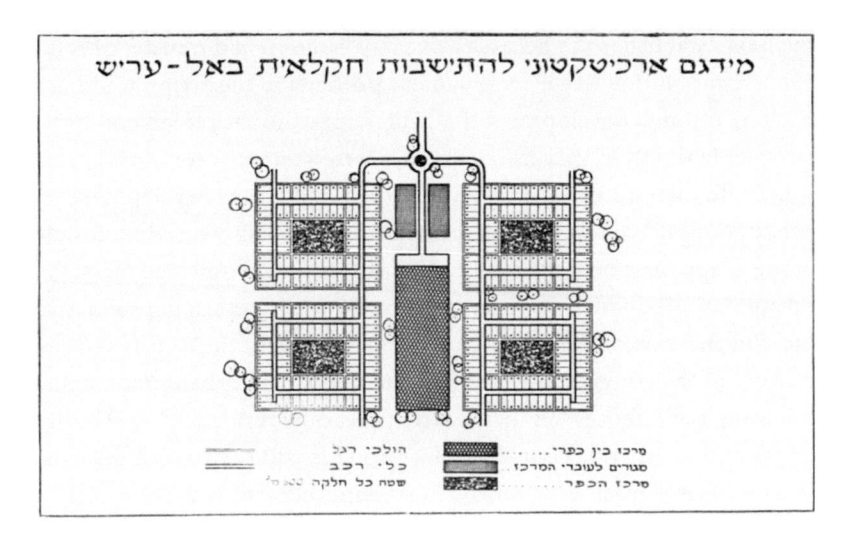

4.1 Weitz plan, architectural sketch of agricultural settlement in al-'Arish. ISA, 1969.

European flora, Weitz junior specialized in its repopulation with settler incomers.[9]

Both father and son were deeply involved in the various "refugee committees" established after the 1948 War, but by 1967 it was the turn of Weitz junior to step up, and in July of that year he was appointed head of a 120-strong team to resettle all of Gaza's encamped refugees. Weitz was to deploy his experience in the comprehensive regional planning of new settlement projects.[10] In June 1969, building on at least three previous plans for resettlement in the occupied Sinai town of al-'Arish, he submitted to the prime minister (at this stage, Golda Meir) what he described as a plan for "comprehensive regional development in the al-'Arish area."[11] This was no overstatement. The document runs for some 230 pages and, in the master planning tradition, elaborates plans for the development of water sources, agriculture, the marketing of agricultural goods, industry, the tertiary sector, and housing. The aim was to start almost immediately and resettle fifty thousand camp-based refugees in new purpose-built quarters around what was to become the "new metropolitan center of al-'Arish," a productively diverse, multisectoral modern city, with peri-urban satellites, that would support full employment for its intended inhabitants (figure 4.1).

Of the plan's four principal premises, the first states that "the main refugee problem, perhaps the only one, concerns the Gaza Strip," and the next establishes the necessity of camp removal and transfer of refugees: "The solution to the employment problem in the Strip should not be done through development that will perpetuate the placement of the refugees in the Strip, and also not within Israeli territory for obvious reasons."[12] To this end, mobilizing an entwined language of development rehabilitation and security, Weitz's plan relies on the same work-based logic of the Clapp Mission—the refugees constitute an unemployed mass, the rehabilitation of which can only be achieved with a return to productive life. *But* the crux of the Weitz plan is the removal of the camps and the transfer of the refugees into planned and permanent urban space. Rehabilitating the refugees "in their current places of residence has security implications that rules out this solution. This will perpetuate the existence of a large number of hostile inhabitants close to Israel's centers."[13] Similarly, the "absorption" of what the report tellingly and chillingly calls "the Strip's demographic surplus" in Israel would have "far reaching negative social (perhaps even security) implications." Transferring them to "Judea and Samaria" (the West Bank) is also "ruled out for security restrictions." Instead the report determines, "The rehabilitation of the refugees in the framework of a comprehensive plan for the development of an area that is distant from the centers of the Jewish population in Israel might meet the security demands of Israel on the one hand, and the possibilities for integral rehabilitation of the refugees in the developed area, on the other."[14] Moving the camp inhabitants to al-'Arish gets them far enough from the racially segregated centers of the heartland and into a sparsely populated (desert) geography supposedly suitable for agricultural cultivation. And though there is talk of how such a project might help redirect water up from the Sinai to serve the needs of Israeli settlements in the south, it is quite clear that the primary advantages lie in removing the refugees and breaking up the camps. To this end, colonizing the Gaza Strip with Jewish settlers is suggested as a kind of reinforcement, blocking, as settlements did elsewhere in historic Palestine, the path of return: "Geopolitically, it is possible to reinforce the advantages of this plan by reinforcing the Jewish settlement in the Ha-Besor area [an agricultural settlement in the south], while extending it west to Rafah [in the Gaza Strip]. This settlement could serve as a kind of barrier between the Arab block in the Gaza Strip and the proposed Arab settlement group in the Rafah-al-'Arish area."[15] What the plan elaborates more than anything else, whether it is in employment generation or the very layout of the city, are mechanisms for *permanent* emplacement. The camps are understood primarily as temporary social structures. And the first "social goal" of the plan is "changing the social structure of the refugees to a social framework that is based on permanent residence and is attached to a permanent employment activity."[16] We get a sense here, and in so many of the other plans, of how the desired permanence of a refugee resettlement outside the camps comes to be felt as critically tied to the still-unachieved permanence of Israel as a polity.

That planning and housing could be forces that would "normalize" the refugees as permanent inhabitants beyond the borders of the settler colony was an idea that became widespread. The period right after the 1967 War also saw proposals pitched to the Israeli government from sources far afield. One such source was Moshe Safdie, the much-feted Israeli-Canadian architect, once mentored by Louis Kahn, who had, a few years earlier in 1965, proposed to the United Nations (UN) plans for a new purpose-built city in Giza, outside Cairo, that could resettle some 250,000 refugees; he simply called this project "City for Palestinian Refugees—the Gyza Plan" (figure 4.2). Spurned at the UN, Safdie returned only three years later, after the 1967 War, to pitch an adjusted proposal to the then Israeli minister of housing, Mordechai Bentov. Bentov was excited by the proposal and put Safdie in touch with Baron de Rothschild (by then himself eagerly trying to get his own resettlement proposals off the ground), in the hope that architect and financier could together cover the conceptual and financial demands of the project.

Safdie shifted the planned location of his city from Giza to the (now more plausible) West Bank and proposed that what he called "the establishment of a Utopian city center" would be both built and inhabited by the refugees.[17] "The model community," Safdie explained, "would incorporate the most advanced concepts in urban design expressing the cultural, social and economic life of its inhabitants." By that, he meant a return to "native" architecture combined with the "factory mass-produced construction" of his famed Habitat model that launched his reputation at the 1967 Montreal Expo. Again, at the heart of the idea is a normalization effected through the built environment: "The basic concept of the proposed program is to design and build a model community (or communities) in which some of the Arab refugees would be settled, obtain housing, employment, and *would be able to return to normal life*" (emphasis added).[18] And like Weitz insisted that his resettlement plan "would be by Arabs and for Arabs" (Feron 1969), Safdie now described his own project as "for and by the Refugees."

In Safdie's case it's striking how much the Gyza plan is entangled with Israel's settler history in ways that only reaffirm the place of the camps at the heart of the foundational impasses of the state project. The Gyza plan came to be recognized as *the* blueprint for Safdie's Habitat model: a low-cost, high-density housing complex of protruding concrete box modules, designed as a futurist but functionalist appeal to mass-produced social housing and the promises of modernist planning (figure 4.3). Safdie himself was at pains to stress that "Habitat is 'Mediterranean,' and inspired by the hills of Haifa." But what is left unrecognized in the words of architectural critic Owen Hatherley is that "the roots of Habitat were based in Israel's bad conscience as much as in its experiments with collective living" (2008). For Hatherley, "This was a return, in a singularly strange form, to the Arab village." With its massing creating peaks, hills, and valleys that, says Hatherley, seem "to be more geological than architectural," Habitat can be read as an homage to the perceived organicity of the "Arab village" seen as continuous with the landscape from which it springs.[19]

Safdie in his own way, then, translates the negational impulse of settler erasure into architectural design. The "Arab village" acts as the remissive repository for what can no longer be repressed in the present, but contains it in fixed temporal and spatial form outside the psychopolitical interiority of national space. The Palestinian villagers/refugees, now camp inhabitants, can only be "seen" and acknowledged insofar as they remain the inhabitants of the "Arab village" *over there* and not native Palestinians with land claims *over here*. There's a striking irony here: Safdie's Gyza plan and Habitat designs emerge from the "bad conscience" (Hatherly 2008) of settler erasure but also function precisely in this case to make that erasure complete (by permanently resettling Palestinian refugees outside Palestine). Safdie's is an architecture of negation in that it responds to the rupture of the repressive barrier precisely in a way that might keep what is essential to that barrier intact.

This sense that the camps are the only thing distinguishing refugees from the surrounding "normal" population framed the most comprehensive plan for camp removal Israel ever put forward, this time from a rightwing Likud government. In 1983, the Ben Porat plan (named after yet another minister without portfolio, Mordechai Ben Porat) outlined a plan for removing every single camp in the West Bank and Gaza and for resettling 30,000 families (some 250,000 people) in new housing projects just outside the old camp boundary, many of them in high-rise apartment buildings of eight to ten floors (*al-Quds* 1983). Speaking to the *New York*

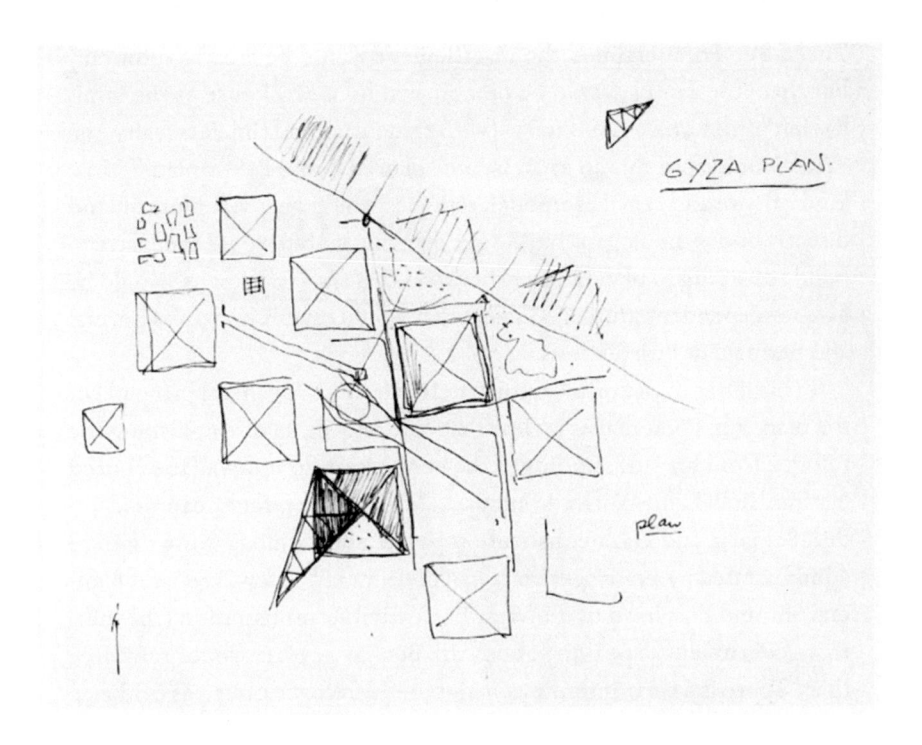

4.2 "City for Palestinian Refugees—the Gyza Plan," concept sketch. Moshe Safdie Archive, 1962.

4.3 Habitat Israel, photomontage. Moshe Safdie, 1969.

Times, Ben Porat claimed the resettlement would be mostly voluntary but that "the camps would be demolished house by house as the families left" (NEW YORK TIMES 1983) (with trademark and timeless fealty, the *Times* would spin this all as an Israeli "plan to house Palestinians"). In a kind of "site and services" model, refugees would be given plots of land directly under the slogan "build your own house" but would then have to build according to plan. The key here was that the "new towns" would be given independent municipal status that would establish them as normal and permanent jurisdictions.

In his letter to the prime minister elaborating the general principle of the plan, Ben Porat makes it clear that "the only thing distinguishing the refugee from his surrounding is the connection to UNRWA [the United Nations Relief and Works Agency].... Most of the refugee camps in Judea, Samaria and Gaza constitute separate autonomous units that are administrated by a manager on behalf of UNRWA."[20] A few days later General Shlomo Ilya, head of the West Bank Civil Administration (the military government), speaking about the Ben Porat plan, would reinforce this: "There is a clear interest to maintain the refugee camps as evidence of the Palestinian problem" (*Globe and Mail* 1983). But, like his predecessors, Ben Porat was at pains to stress that his plan was "humanitarian" and did not affect refugee status: "It does not deal with questions of political autonomy at all" (cited in Hildrew 1983). At stake in all these plans, then, was getting to the material condition that was beneath or prior to refugeehood as a political or legal status. This same supposition, that in acting on the materiality of the camps one could reach the political-temporal claims of the dispossessed, would be carried into the housing and improvement plans actually implemented. And though they paled in comparison to the comprehensive and lofty visions we just went through, they are just as telling of the negational politics that undergirds it all.

Improvement: "There Are No Miniskirts in the Refugee Camps"

None of these plans ever got off the ground in their proposed forms. But, like so many other ambitious colonial designs for native subjects, they were partially implemented in cut-price and decidedly more coercive versions. One such version was cheap housing projects. Over the course of the 1970s, the military government in Gaza expropriated hundreds of acres of land for purpose-built, large-scale housing projects. In 1972, the Canada project was established just across the international border in Sinai on the site of an older military encampment for the Canadian forces of the UN Emergency Force (UNEF).[21] Housing in the Brazil project (named after the camp that housed the Brazilian forces of UNEF) just south of Rafah Camp followed in 1973, and in the same year, the Shuqairi project was initiated outside of Beach Camp. In 1975, these were followed by the more ambitious Sheikh Ridwan project also outside Beach Camp and, later still in 1979, the al-Amal project.

On the whole, these housing projects, carried out by the military government's public works department, mirrored some of the expediency and repeatability of UNRWA's emergency architecture and also reproduced the language of rehabilitation. *But* the emphasis right away was on a sense of permanence and durability, both in aesthetic-built forms and in the instruments of legal ownership. In contrast to the Agency, roofing was provided from the start, usually prefabricated concrete slabs, cast locally on the building sites, and later layered with three-centimeter-thick concrete plaster to waterproof the surface. The foundations were also deeper and stronger, allowing easily for a three-room extension. The finishing also suggested more permanence; in the earlier projects, the Brazil and Canada projects, exterior walls got a rough casting to cover the hollow concrete bricks, and interior walls were plastered or smoothed with cement mortar and washed with paint in a cream color. All the windows, unlike UNRWA's shelters, had glass panes from the start, and courtyards were marked and had doors made of timber, painted in a dark blue.[22] The houses were also infrastructurally better equipped, connected to the electricity grid, with water mains (and individual meters in most of the projects), sewerage (at least in the later projects), and paved roads. Both the housing units and plots of land they sat on (250 square meters) were considerably bigger than UNRWA's allocation (figure 4.4).

Aesthetically the houses were also designed to look more permanent and to conform to what the military government's engineers and architects thought were the correct cultural norms. In the later governmental projects, the aesthetics explicitly appealed to a paternalistic Orientalism and its gendered preoccupations; the military government's chief engineer for these projects pointed out that the houses were designed with arched lintels of precast concrete, "in order to give the building an oriental appearance," and high walls, "at least as high as the height of a person riding an animal ... [keeping] the woman and her activity within the family framework and away from strangers' eyes."[23]

Perhaps most critically, the Israeli military government emphasized forms of legal ownership they hoped would become part of existing private property regimes. These were houses to be purchased and owned by their refugee inhabitants. Units in the housing projects were offered at subsidized prices that could be paid in installments; loans, often interest-free, were also arranged with Gazan banks and guaranteed by the Israeli government. The military government handed out, often in ceremonies attended by top officials, a "certificate for the shelter" signed and stamped by Gaza's military governor. Though as UNRWA officials pointed out, these certificates simply confirmed the allotment of a shelter to a particular refugee; what kind of title, if any, they entailed is unclear: "The validity of these certificates as evidence of title to the land is dubious to say the least."[24] Nonetheless, it was clear in the reception of these projects in the Israeli press at the time that a form of ownership was a central part of the project. Speaking of those that had "elected" to resettle, one journalist wrote, "Only a fool would give up the abundance of benefits that Israel is offering. The refugees who receive the housing complexes are becoming independent the next day, property owners for the first time in their lives, holders of a deed for a quarter-dunam of land and a residential unit."[25] The whole process was meant to "turn the refugees into landlords living in urban neighborhoods rather than in a camp" (Nitzan-Shiftan and Abreek-Zubeidat 2018, 149).

None of this was unconditional. The military government offered houses to refugee families that would accept relocation outside the camp, *but* only on the condition that they first demolish their own house in the camp. As one journalist explained with regard to the Sheikh Ridwan project, "The government assists residents with favorable loans and compensates them on their houses in the camps, which they are obligated to evacuate and demolish by themselves."[26] Typically, an application would be submitted for a new housing unit through the office of the regional administrative governor. A three-person "inspection committee" would visit the refugee applicant in the camp, instruct them to demolish their entire shelter, and agree on an amount of due monetary compensation (paid for the additions the refugees made to the initial structures). After a refugee demolished their home, the military government would prohibit UNRWA from constructing anything else on that plot; the plot of land, the Israeli authorities argued, would in this case revert back to governmen-

4.4 Israeli housing project, Gaza Strip, circa 1973.
Dov Eizenberg Personal Papers.

4.5 "Arabian Refugee House," perspective sketch, MEARRO, 1969.
Israel State Archives.

tal control. UNRWA reported that all the refugees involved in this kind of resettlement felt compelled to demolish their shelters on the orders of the military government.[27] And, rightly sensing in house demolitions an erosion of its own authoritative entitlements over the camps, UNRWA officially protested this "prescribed condition" on more than one occasion, pointing out that what one official dubbed (with more insight than they probably intended) "refugee self-demolition" was "not in connection with any road widening plans of which we are aware, nor even town planning."[28] And though Agency officials even (and unusually) took to the press to lodge their complaints at this "particularly distressing" practice "by which a refugee family must demolish its shelter before moving to a new Israeli project," the "self-demolition" continued across the 1970s.

Undoing the camps, however, need not be restricted to the often tricky stuff of removal. "Improvement" could be just as effective. For the military government, the camps were always a kind of limit to the modernizing pretensions of the early occupation. It is not only that an active insurgency took years to quell in Gaza's camps, or that the camps were hard, if not impossible, to absorb into the narrative of a benevolent occupation that the military governors were so eager to spin. It was also the perception that it was something about the perceived backwardness of the camps that kept them transitory and impermanent and was itself part of the problem. In turn, to modernize or improve the camp, to socialize its inhabitants in settled life, and if possible to turn them into tax-paying residents of local municipalities was to begin to undo the camp as such, just as much as removal.

We get a sense of this logic in the reportage of Walter Schwarz who covered occupied Palestine for much of the 1970s for the *Guardian*. In 1970 in Gaza City, he met with a Colonel Shmuel Liran, then liaison officer in Gaza's military government. Liran, whom Schwarz adoringly gushes over as "a talker, a fine example of the intellectually non-military Israeli soldier...paternal, affectionate, reassuring" (1970) (though this doesn't stop Schwarz from consistently misspelling Liran's name as Liram), is part of the public relations machinery of the occupation and a character that comes up repeatedly in the archives. They meet in his office, previously an office of the Egyptian Administration, and where Liran had kept a picture of the Egyptian president, Gamal Abdel Nasser, hanging above his desk—"because he likes to see the faces of his Arab visitors when they notice it" (McHugh 1972). Liran opens a drawer to show Schwarz some photographs, then mulls on one blown-up image of "a group of laughing college girls walking in the street." He is (almost inevitably) particularly interested in their attire. "Look at the blouses: white blouses—unheard of in the old days. And look again two of the girls have the top buttons undone. And bras underneath. It's a revolution." But, Schwarz goes on, the colonel's punchline was in the hems. And here, at least, Schwarz was not wrong. The photograph apparently showed the hems on the skirts had been rolled up by two or three inches. The colonel explains, "You see? They turn them up but don't cut them. They know, as everyone in Gaza knows, that things have changed but can change back again, as they did when we pulled out in 1957. There's revolution going on all right, but it's inside people's homes and the girls are leading it" (Schwarz 1970).

Schwarz all but fawns at this great modernizing force. "The twentieth century blows in everywhere, but it happens more spectacularly when Israelis with their girl soldiers, their trade unionism and their informality, move into a place like Gaza." "But," Schwarz writes, as though to remind us all of the limits of the onward march of even this irrepressible Israeli century, "there are no miniskirts in the refugee camps." Instead, now letting his contempt come right through, Gaza's camps, "each a seething, muddy mass of corrugated iron, are as grotesquely overcrowded, as smelly with non-sewage, as those around Amman" (1970).

"No miniskirts in the refugee camps" can be read here as the expression of the camp as *limit* to pacification and modernization, to the normative flow of modern historical time itself. Improvement emerges as a corrective normalizing political technology, entirely continuous with removal—and indeed pursued at exactly the same time, often as part of exactly the same plans. If the camps could be upgraded to the topological threshold point at which they were no longer camps, that is no longer *temporary* forms of habitation, then the problem would have been solved by other means.

In 1969, Yisrael Galili, a minister without portfolio, presented a plan called "Rehabilitation of Refugees and Development in the West Bank and Gaza," which emphasized both some new housing projects outside the camp (again, "model villages") and also the renovation of existing camps and their municipal incorporation into neighboring towns. In 1970 yet another minister without portfolio, Shimon Peres, sought to institutionalize camp improvement by establishing a fund precisely to that end: the Trust Fund for the Economic Development and Rehabilitation of Refugees, which would, over the decades to come, finance a series of small "development" projects (sewerage systems, public squares, playgrounds) and elaborate numerous proposals for camp improvement, publishing a confidential yearly report to document the progress.[29] All this was part of a wider push, pursued across the 1970s, in which the military government strongly pursued the jurisdictional incorporation of camps into neighboring municipalities, seeking to act on the legal geography of the camps.

The intent behind improvement incorporation and the housing projects was not really lost on anyone. Even Schwarz (1971a) was able to deduce that the policy "consists of creating economic conditions that will eventually make refugee status wither away." This too was the view of a former UNRWA deputy commissioner, who noted that the improvement policies were "designed to assimilate the refugees to the local resident population and, in time, to erase the special status accorded to them as refugees and the claims which they derive from that status" (Reddaway 1973). Improvement was but one integral part of "Israel's ongoing attempts to liquidate the camps through their normalization by turning them into ordinary rehabilitated neighborhoods" (Nitzan-Shiftan and Abreek-Zubiedat 2018, 153). Like the unimplemented plans, improvement and rehousing projects revolved around the developmental drive to undo the camps and in their place make something permanent and normalized; they sought to produce forms of inhabitation that would close the temporariness of the camps. And yet the clamor to do something about the camps was altogether too strong, too demanding, and too urgent to be restricted to large-scale housing or improvement plans. Alongside all of these projects, as their very scaffolding, was always the more radically eruptive violence of demolition and clearance.

Demolition: "To Teach Them to Wake Up to 1971"

In the summer of 1971, the Israeli army, facing a stubborn insurgency in Gazan camps it found all but ungovernable, embarked on an approach that would see the logics of counterinsurgency and camp removal perfectly align. In July of that year, Ariel Sharon, then the army's Chief of Southern Command, tasked with quelling the insurgents, began mass house demolitions and road widening in the three largest camps in Gaza: Jabalya, Rafah, and Beach. What the army called "thinning out" operations, and what Dayan euphemized as "letting light into the camps"

(Schwarz 1971c), saw Sharon hack away at the camps with something like sheer abandon. The destruction (which peaked in the summer of 1971 and the first months of 1972, but had a third intense phase in 1976) was intense and widespread. Between July and August of 1971 alone, some two thousand homes were ripped down, with about sixteen thousand people displaced. By 1985 ten thousand houses in total would be cleared in the road-widening campaign (displacing a far larger number of refugees than those "voluntarily" rehoused or resettled). Security, as ever, was the pretext, but here I show how much the specter of return and anxieties around the political temporality of the camps were at the heart—often explicitly—of the demolition drive.

The road-widening campaign saw roads "large enough for a half-truck to turn around in" (Farrell 1976), carved through the bigger camps in the strip in a practice that usually involved the clearing of two parallel rows of houses on each side of the road (figures 4.6 and 4.7). Most families were given no more than twenty-four hours' advance notice. In mid-August 1971, to take one example, forced deportation in Rafah Camp in the southern Gaza Strip saw two thousand refugees loaded onto trucks and hauled out to the occupied Egyptian town of al-'Arish in the Sinai Desert. The army had spent one late afternoon marking rows of houses in blocks with large black X's; those who woke up to find their houses marked had less than twenty-four hours to demolish their own houses and board the trucks. Schwarz (1971b), on the ground in al-'Arish, reports "convoy after convoy" arriving in the "hot, sleepy, flyridden desert town." "The refugees looked dazed and exhausted after working around the clock to take their homes to pieces against the deadline." Weitz's al-'Arish plan of 1969 had effectively been stripped to its core essentials: demolition and removal. For all the talk of full employment and integrated planning, the actual operation was little more than blunt forced displacement; the most effort the Israeli State made by way of "rehabilitation" was to renovate some of the barracks-style housing (about 450 units) that had been previously inhabited by the Egyptian workers of the Suez Company.

Road widening is, of course, an old practice in colonial counterinsurgency, as is the resettlement of Native populations in model towns or villages as a means of cutting off insurgents from popular support. Masalha (2003) notes similarities between Israel's Gazan housing projects and Malayan "new villages" or the "strategic hamlets" in Vietnam. And like so many other colonial imaginaries of Native townships, *casbahs*, or reservations, the language here reinforced a certain stock image of the

4.6 Road-widening campaign, Rafah Camp, 1971. Kay Brennan, UNRWA.

4.7 Camp demolition, producing the nothingness, Rafah Camp, 1971. UNRWA.

camp as a febrile and feral space, beyond the limit of law, so often described by both Israeli officials and most Western journalists with some kind of recourse to zoological language: "the hornet's nest," "the snake's pit," a "hive of structures" making law and order impossible (Brilliants 1971), or else a "streetless, tightly packed cluster of houses with rabbit-warren networks of alleys, ideal for terrorists, hopeless for pursuing soldiers" (Farrell 1976).

And yet camp removal was here so clearly an end in its own right. Sharon, whom Gazans dubbed "the Bulldozer" for his role in camp clearance and who himself had long advocated the total elimination of the camps, was altogether less mealy-mouthed than many of his contemporaries about the camp "problem." In his autobiography he dedicated an entire chapter to his time in Gaza and outlined the three interconnected "proposals" that were the basis of his vision for the Strip: counterinsurgency, the establishment of several Jewish settlements (or "Jewish 'fingers,'" as he called them) to divide the Gaza district (which in fact became the basis of the settlements in the Strip), and a plan "to solve the Palestinian refugee problem." "The essence of my plan was to get rid of the Palestinian refugee camps altogether. Despite the UN subsidies the refugees received and despite the powerful economic and educational uplift the camps experienced after 1967, these places still bred the most serious problems for us and always would. It would be to our great advantage to eliminate them once and for all, and in my view such a thing was quite feasible" (2001, 259). For Sharon, "the refugee problem" boils down essentially to the camps. His proposal would have seen all of Gaza's camps razed and their (at the time) 160,000 encamped inhabitants resettled in Gazan and West Bank cities and towns. More critically, Sharon, like many other Israeli politicians, correctly recognized the camps as a *political* reality; no amount of subsidy or economic "uplift" was going to change the fact that they "bred the most serious problems" and "always would." The desire to "eliminate them once and for all," by Sharon's own reasoning, exceeded the demands of counterinsurgency.

That the "problems" the camps posed were about Palestinian return and its land claims is so palpable that it rises up to the surface of historical record with ease. In 1971, one army commander told the (London) *Times* that the security roads being bulldozed through Jabalya Camp "go straight through [the depopulated Palestinian cities inside Israel] Lydda, Jaffa and Haifa" (Marsden and Johnson 1971). Fewer than two years later, Dayan would echo the sentiment, telling the *Jerusalem Post*, "As long as refugees remain in their camps the children will say they come from Jaffa and Haifa; if they move out of the camps, the hope is they will feel an attachment to their new land" (cited in Weizman 2007, 230). Again, the connection between the camps and refugee return was understood in explicitly temporal terms. As the army was razing large parts of Gaza's camps, another Israeli official delivered a striking explanation of the practice, telling a reporter that it had the purpose of "re-education" for the refugees—"*to teach them to wake up to 1971*" (Marsden and Johnson 1971, emphasis added).

These statements are arresting and go to the heart of everything with incredible precision. For one, clearing the camps is explicitly necessary for the *completion* of conquest: without conquering and clearing the camps, you haven't fully conquered the cities of Palestine that fell in 1948. But camp clearance is also a *temporal corrective* that works at the level of subjectivity itself. The demand to return, figured again as an irrational dream or illusion incubated in the camp itself, has to be met with camp clearance as a means of "educating" the dispossessed as to their proper place *in* time. It is a means of waking them up from their dreamy slumber, bringing them into line with the present-as-reality. If for Rubinstein, in the reading we began with, the problem was that "the present is of no import" to camp inhabitants, then the military's response was to raze their camp houses so that this present might be imported straight into their consciousness. The bulldozer here is not simply a device for the clearance of built structures; it is also an instrument of temporal reordering, a device of negation that seeks the clearance of the very "consciousness of exile." That is, the bulldozer seeks to clear not only the houses but the very connections between space and time in the camps that make viable the emergence of a Palestinian people and its territorial counterclaims.

The Return of the Repressed, Doubled

What, then, did the twenty odd years' (1967 to 1987) worth of schemes for camp removal and resettlement achieve? Eventually, between 1971 and 1985, about ten thousand houses in Gaza's camps were demolished, and about thirty-five thousand refugees were resettled (Schiff 1995, 216). All in all, not much of a dent. As Israeli officials themselves bemoaned, this didn't even meet the rate of natural population growth in the camps. Nor did the housing projects seem to be any more successful in producing permanently emplaced, "normalized" subjects. One of the historical ironies is that many of these housing projects would be all but absorbed by the adjacent camps, UNRWA in many cases not making distinctions in the provision of its services. More still, both the Canada and Brazil projects, being on sites of former encampments, are widely referred to today as "camps." Also, all of these new housing projects appear to be just as politically active as the restive camps they were meant to replace. Irony borders absurdity when one considers that the flagship housing project, the Sheikh Ridwan project, which Israeli officials, without a shred of self-awareness, named Kfar Shalom (Village of Peace), and Palestinians called Hay Sharon (Sharon's Neighborhood), became something of a hub for the political organization Hamas.

In 1992, with camp-removal schemes all but shelved, Emmanuel Marx, an Israeli anthropologist based at Tel Aviv University, who built a career as an expert on encamped Palestinian refugees, and was himself involved in resettlement policy, published an assessment of these schemes in the journal *Middle Eastern Studies*. Marx recalls how he and his colleague had published two monographs in the early 1970s (the first with the Rand Corporation and the second with the Shiloah Institute at Tel Aviv University) in which they recommended Israel take full control of the camps and "facilitate their incorporation into the urban fabric" by improving infrastructure and municipal services. This was, by now, a familiar pitch. The government declined to take on their recommendations in full, he writes, but, nonetheless, "I could not help noticing the very considerable changes that have taken place in two decades of Israeli occupation" (1992, 282). He paints a rosy and factually dubious picture: camps are "becoming urban working-class neighborhoods" and are "incorporated" into towns; houses are "fully owned by their occupants and greatly improved"; the camp population is now "mobile."[30] The reality, he writes, is one of growing autonomy, even prosperity. *But*—and you can almost hear the exasperation—"in two areas there was hardly any change: people still consider themselves refugees, and the urban neighborhoods in which they reside are still perceived as refugee camps" (1992, 282–83). The thrust of the article is an attempt to explain why these perceptions and identifications persist (though it's safe to say, he does not reach, and, I would argue, given his colonial preoccupations, *cannot* reach, a compelling explanation).

By any measure, not least its own, camp removal failed. And yet the sense of a strategic need to which it was responding, the sense that the very completion of the settler project demands the undoing of the camps one way or another, remains very much in place. This sense is marked in Marx's retrospective article, both in the rendering of the persistence of the refugee camps as an unsettled "debt" (1992, 293) and "an obstacle to peace" (282) *and* in the insistence, which runs throughout the entire piece, that resettlement and camp removal might have "solved the problem" if they had been done right. It is precisely this sense of *stuckness*—construed here, temporally and spatially, as both debt and obstacle—that "dealing" with the camps was meant to address, and it is what lends, I believe, such a palpable feel of temporal urgency to so much of the primary material one reads on the subject. From academic articles to bureaucratic memos, urgency defines the tenor or the pitch of the writing: urgency in the sense of an imperative, an insistence and a need that demands quick attention, in part because it mediates a source of, not always clear, pressure. This urgency in the image of the camp goes straight to the temporal binds of this settler project.

Colonial order is always unfinished. There is something about colonial settlement, as Ann Stoler has it, that is always unsettled—"Such settlements called 'colonies' are nodes of anxious, uneasy circulations; settlements that are not settled at all" (2016, 121). To follow the colony's range of coordinates, to think through its ambiguous nomenclatures, competing visions, and repeated failures, is, for Stoler, to appreciate it not as a site of settlement but as "an always unstable and precarious project, plagued by the expectant promise (and fear) of its becoming something other than which its visionaries prescribed" (72). The colony is "lived in this anxious future tense" (118). Étienne Balibar gets at precisely this anxiety of permanence and the future in a perceptive observation where he writes that colonial racism, an extreme variant of xenophobia combining fear and scorn, is "perpetuated by the awareness the colonizers have always had, in spite of their claim to have founded a durable order, that *that order rested on a reversible relation of forces*" (Balibar and Wallerstein 1991, 42, emphasis added).

These characterizations seem even more apt for the temporal dilemmas of large-scale settler movements. "Some of the critical aporetic difficulties, those gaps, silences, ambivalences that so indelibly mark the colonial project are resolutely evident in the settler" (Farred 2008, 797). Perhaps nowhere more so than around the question of becoming or self-identity—When does a settler cease to be a settler? When is the lingering question mark overcome? These questions and their "aporetic difficulties" seem even more pressing for political Zionism, which has always been dogged by its own lateness. Wendy Brown's remark that Israel is a project "cursed by a globally rejected past in its present" (2010, 34) might seem a little amiss today when a revisionist colonial common sense is making its own comeback in the West, but the fact remains that Israel's obstacles in its push for normalization and self-supersession are all the more formidable. Despite large-scale and arguably genocidal ethnic cleansing, the native Palestinian population remains numerically inabsorbable, and today it makes up just over half of the population under the effective control of the Israeli State, preventing the more homeostatic turn to liberal-democratic and procedural forms of containment through electoral franchise and citizenship, multicultural policy, assimilation, or modes of recognition. Israel is stuck with a large Native population it considers superfluous and inherently threatening but that it can neither effectively manage nor (for now, at least) totally eliminate.

This is not at all to suggest that other settler colonies are somehow more "complete" or "finished," while this case remains "unfinished." None of this is sequential or stagist or linear in any way—Palestine is not America's or Australia's past. Nor is any of this to skate over the colonial instrumentality, "cunning," or eliminationist logic of things like colonial recognition of Native rights or, indeed, the eruptive violence still integral to the dispossessive machinery of settler states everywhere.[31] All of these different instruments emerge as immanent to settler-Native struggles, often with contradictory effects: the recognition of tribal sovereignty in US federal Indian law, for one, is at once an instrument of settler management and an opening for a disruption of settler control in the articulation of autonomous power against the traps of recognition and inclusion (Blackhawk 2019). My intent here rather is to point to the different, and in some senses blunter, instruments the Israeli settler project depends on, and to stress how these instruments effect this project's (in)ability to present the settler as a finished, historical political category.[32] For one, Israel relies on an order of violence, on all-out colonial war, many scales of magnitude more intense than anything else in the contemporary settler colonial scene. But it also relies on a distribution of this capacity for violence across its fuzzy civilian/military divide; that is, it remains reliant on the work of the settler mob in a distinct way—it cannot close its frontier. In turn, its legal order reflects and reproduces these tensions.

Israel remains dependent not only on legal apartheid and the racial distinction between citizen and subject (in the occupied territories), but even internally among ostensible citizens (of which Palestinians make up nearly one-quarter) on a legally enshrined distinction between Jew/non-Jew and citizenship/nationality.[33] Apartheid here is not at all distinct from settler colonialism; it is in fact the very means of an Israeli settler colonialism forced into physical-jurisdictional cohabitation with a sizable native population.

The reliance on these instruments and the size of the contradiction mean that there is no clear pathway in which the Israeli settler project might normalize its status in the region and world, rule stably over a subject population, close its frontier, end its reliance on discretionary extralegal settler violence and land grabs, and transition out of a permanent war-footing. Israel exists as an open unfinished state of conquest, unable to transition to a constitutional moment that closes conquest into stable and permanent regimes of law and property. There is quite simply no clear given scenario in which "Israel" might itself cease to be an open question, in which it might overcome its own settlerness. The Zionist project is then defined not only by its lateness but more fundamentally, more libidinally we might say, by the obstruction of its drive.

Now, one might argue that the drive to permanence and self-supersession is exactly that, a drive. And, as such, it is not something to be attained, but the very pursuit and enjoyment of loss itself. Settler permanence as drive means it never reaches its object (a racially secure and normalized liberal postcolonial state), just circles around it, and attains enjoyment from the repetitive process of not reaching it. Certainly, there is something of this in Israel's self-perception as a frontier state still in the making—still without declared official borders—and an elastic and expansive force field in which border transgression (the raiding army patrols, or the settler mobs deep in occupied territory) is a kind of masculine spiritual rite. There is here then for the settler state a usable tension at the heart of the project between order/transition and drive/incompletion. Spatially and topologically, this is the tension of a project that is, on the one hand, "deviceful," "overplanned," defined by a will to geometric facts and integrated national planning systems, and, on the other, is defined by an "agenda of precarious formlessness," a "constant cartographic mutability" that seeks to postpone the moment of decisive political contouring or bordering (Efrat 2019, 18). If, as Mladen Dolar explains it, "drive is what prevents an order from stabilizing or closing in on itself, the excess that subverts all attempts to reduce politics to the proper arrangement of subjects and institutions" (2009, 22), then one can see how a settler garrison state, wedded to the notion of an eternal frontier, needs the drive to ever-unfulfilled completion to function as such.

Ultimately, this is a tempting but limited reading. That settler states aspire to and brutally pursue the legal consummation of their settlement, *even* as they need the excess that keeps their politics somewhat unfinished and as such dynamic and expansive, is historically clear enough. In the American settler colony, to take one example, this tension and its attempted resolution can be read in the series of moves made toward the closing of the frontier: that is, in the move away from territorial arrangements based on treaties and toward elimination through assimilation, in the Dawes Act of 1887 (which tried to dissolve tribal affiliation and saw massive rounds of land theft and dispossession), and later, in different terms, in the Snyder Act of 1924 (which granted citizenship). For all their different emphases, these moves attempted to transition the American settler state out of unfinished conquest into the maintenance of consummated order. None of this was easily sequential; it was contradictory, it spurted and reversed, and it didn't end the war on Indigenous life—the assault on Standing Rock in 2016 was an extension of the now differently waged Indian Wars (Estes 2019)—but cumulatively this history marked the start of what Kevin Bruyneel (2007) has called "postcolonial time," not a time after colonialism but a time defined by shifts in both Indigenous resistance and settler colonial instruments of rule in which this struggle no longer takes place along treaty-defined boundaries between nations but in a "third space of sovereignty" that is neither within nor external to the United States.

I don't mean to suggest that American (or any other) settler colonialism is some sort of historical template. What I want to emphasize, again, are structural-temporal tendencies shared across different projects of colonial settlement, notably the tendency toward self-supersession. That the Israeli settler state needs and pursues self-supersession is patently apparent today in the demand it makes to be recognized by its colonized subjects, in the normalization it assiduously pursues within the region, and in the massive campaigns it wages to fight what it calls "delegitimization." Conversely, this drive and its obstruction is also not just apparent in but the very impetus of its consistent recourse to obliterating total violence in the Gaza Strip and West Bank; the genocidal war Israel launched in 2023—aimed so explicitly at annihilation—was above all a search for a way out of its impasse, a corrective return to the open foundational moment of conquest so that it might be closed and overcome. All of this indexes not only a fundamental self-doubt, but also the need to transition beyond the foundational moment of conquest to the moment of stabilization—to overcome the condition of settlerness. The impasse for the Israeli State is that this transition remains distant and unlikely: the frontier cannot be closed and the vanishing horizon of settler permanence defines the Israeli project.

What I have shown in this chapter is how the Palestinian camp for a sustained period in history appeared as not only an object of obstruction in that drive to permanence, but also potentially the key to its solution. Even though the camps historically emerged as devices for the administrative management of the surplus population that a racially defined Jewish state could not perforce accept, they came to occupy a much more troubling place in the political reason of Israeli governmental planners. What was troubling about camps, I argued, was reducible neither to the "refugee problem" per se nor to the threat of insurgency. Camps confined the recalcitrant and came to be seen as constitutive of that very recalcitrance; camps carried, in their very built form, not just the specter but the viability of refugee return. If the camps, more than refugeehood itself, materially "incubated" not just the counterclaims to land but the very temporal consciousness that keeps such claims viable, then they carried the very potential of reversibility itself. In other words, the camp becomes a threatening political object because in its constitution of a temporal politics that affirms a Palestinian presence prior to and *after* conquest, it poses a challenge to replacement as a done deal. The camp enacts a kind of constant return of the repressed. And it's this return—in the double sense—that elicits negation.

Undoing the camps can be seen as acting on the temporal challenges the state faced, as extending the work of negation to those most stubbornly refusing it. This undoing did not always mean physical removal (though it often came down to just that); it meant undoing what keeps camps impermanent, extraordinary, and, in effect, political spaces. And as such, it cut across a diverse set of instruments and calculative logics, from the developmental language of "rehabilitation" to the altogether more prosaic stuff of mass house demolition; it called on the drafts and designs of global architects but could also be achieved with armored bulldozers and explosives; it might keep inhabitants on the same exact sites of the camps or it might move them hundreds of kilometers away across international borders. In this respect, there is little difference between the seemingly benign improvement plans of Shimon Peres's Trust Fund (which, of course, involved their own slower forms of demolition) and the eruptive violence of Ariel Sharon's camp clearance. The conflicts between personalities, departments, and visions are substantively irrelevant; whether the camps were undone through improvement or demolition is beside the point. The abiding and relentlessly consistent drive was the undoing of the camps and the temporal challenge they carried—stopping the return of the repressed.

In all of this, the wider imperative of preventing return and rendering the past as past remains consistent. All of this should be seen, I've argued, within a wider politics of negation that seeks to refute what is not entirely repressible in both settler and Native society. Undoing the camps, by clearing the sites of vanquished villages, changing the names of towns and streets, or banning the commemoration of displacement, seeks to negate the viability of the Palestinian territorial counterclaim; it seeks to undo the political tense that allows for an unsettled and unsettling consciousness of the temporary. Undoing the camps is producing the nothing that was/is/will be Palestine, part of making sure that "no such place exists," and "the people of nowhere" become just that. That this has so monumentally failed, despite over half a century of concerted effort, is above all testament to a power of refusal in Palestinian camps that, from the midst of negation, keeps making its own unruly time so as to remain "the core of the problem."

CODA. THE POLITICS OF INHABITATION

Palestine and "the Encampment of the World"

The Palestinian camps have been neither undone nor overcome. They have, for better or worse, endured. And with time this endurance has begun to appear less like an exceptional divergence from the forward-moving narrative of world history and more like that history's triumphant subtext. The Palestinians have not been "normalized" as yet another nation-state among nation-states, but arguably instead, in their very stateless encampment, have become a prophetic part of the new normal. If the Palestinian question holds such sway in our political imaginations, it is because, as so many have warned us, it no longer points to a historical anomaly but to at least one common imminent future on a burning planet (Collins 2011). Our present, after all, is one in which landlessness and displacement are arguably again the paradigmatic and defining questions of global politics. And, like the Palestinians facing the desert of exile, there really seems to be no place to go.

No place, that is, except for the global string of sites expressly dedicated to those deemed surplus humanity. Ours is a world of camps: refugee camps along borders, reception camps in airport terminals, detention camps under bridges, homeless camps under freeways, reeducation camps in the desert, island internment camps in the middle of the ocean. Today more people and more categories of people inhabit camps than ever before. And though this constantly shifting and always-temporary global ecology makes itself near impossible to definitively empirically assess, most agree that the camps number in the thousands and their inhabitants in the tens of millions. No longer confined to the Global South, camps proliferate beyond any temporal bracket we might think of as "emergency," and with not much respect for the fading distinction between peacetime and wartime. And no longer confined to the rural or the peri-urban, they pop up in and these days are planned for the heart of cities, showing just how elastic and mobile bordering practices have become. The camp is quite simply our go-to solution for "keeping away what disturbs, for containing or rejecting all excess" (Michel Agier, cited in Mbembe 2016, 32). And though these camps range in form from ad hoc self-built formations to centrally planned and imposed state projects, they all come together as networked sites of legal abandonment, temporal suspension, and disciplinary transformation. This is our present of mass encampment, and if displacement and dispossession within a conjoined border/climate crisis are to remain the defining characteristics of our age, it is just as likely our future too. All the world has to offer those deemed surplus is a form of warehousing, a precarious, rightless form of indefinite inhabitation, only shades removed from the carceral.

How did we get here? How did the purported triumph of the liberal idea end in mass encampment and mass incarceration? How did what was only recently celebrated as the flattening of the world in globalization end in such jagged geographies of separation and detention? How did societies governed by the "rule of freedom" come to be so nakedly defined by captivity and capture? Even for those of us that have long insisted that the world of abstract freedom has always been premised on the work of racialized unfreedom, global mass encampment/incarceration seems like a rather obscene late literalization of this bond, one that would seem to signal not so much the triumph of the liberal idea as the exposure of everything it has always sought to hide and defer.

It seems inadequate, even a little risible, to put this down to generic crisis. Crisis, by definition, is temporary and (in theory) ends in decision.

Mass encampment is neither. And yet there is no doubt that the convulsions of the border regime are, at least at one level, but the displaced dynamics of historical crises of capital as they create a vast swathe of surplus humanity that is both ejected from formal economies and subject to enforced immobility: crises that, at once, force movement and capture it in contradictory dynamics that completely undercut *both* the right to remain and the right to move. Perhaps it makes little sense to talk of these dynamics today as "crisis" since they are all but a rule of everyday life under late capitalism. At their most political, which is to say their most violent end, these dynamics coincide with all but permanent warmaking. They form zones, like parts of the Arab world or the Sahel region, that today are integrated into global capitalism precisely *through* continuous war and its adjacent extractive economies and in which millions are displaced. The War on Terror alone, it often needs restating, displaced anywhere between forty million and sixty million people, of whom countless numbers no doubt ended up in camps.

The current phenomenon of surplus population, however, exceeds the effects of imperial war. For Karl Marx (1990) the capitalist mode of production would always make a relative surplus population, as part of the "general law of capitalist accumulation." The conditions of expanded reproduction simply demand the movement in and out of both labor and capital: industries mature, labor-saving technology is integrated, and capital sheds labor to create, among other things, a reserve army of labor that is indispensable to the operations of capital. As commentators have picked up on, for Marx this was a tendency that would invariably move from *cyclical* crises (booms and busts) to a *secular* crisis of reproduction in which capital would undermine the capital-labor relation and its own conditions of accumulation, a limit internal to capital itself (Endnotes and Benanav 2010). Yet as Étienne Balibar (2019) points out, for all its explanatory power, Marx presented this law of population as a structural aspect of an ideal type of capitalism, like the making of a surplus population was the more or less automatic adjustment of accumulation and technological change. Thinking about surplus populations and (im)mobility today demands not just a recognition of the autonomy of migration but a historical appreciation of contemporary capitalism's new mobility regime, starting with what Balibar describes as the brutal pressure that the "nomadism of financialized capital" has exerted on the "sedentariness of labor" (Balibar 2019). If contemporary capitalism increasingly operates as a force of "expulsion" (Sassen 2014), this demands an accounting of those aspects of the post-Fordist historical conjuncture that upend the reabsorption of surplus populations: the "long downturn" of deindustrialization and the stalling of the engine of growth across most of the world, the gutting of public-sector employment in the Global South in structural adjustment programs, increased extractivism and climatic and ecological disaster, the intensification of primitive accumulation and the deracination of the peasantry almost everywhere, and the persistence of dispossession and the plunder of capitalism's "outsides." It's in these historical conditions that *relative* surplus populations become *absolute*. In turn, any equivalence between this new absolute surplus population and the category "reserve army of labor" has collapsed. This surplus humanity can never be absorbed: "It exists now only to be managed: segregated into prisons, marginalized in ghettos and camps, disciplined by the police, and annihilated by war" (Endnotes and Benanav 2010).

It would be a mistake, though, to think of camps in this story simply as effects of causes elsewhere. Camps, we often forget, are not simply devices of management. They are always, as the history in this book attests, sites of transformation. Surplus humanity is not just warehoused in camps; it's also subject to the kinds of force and pressure that ensure that while this life may never be absorbed into formal labor forces it will not be beyond the bounds of the valorization process. We need not subscribe to any kind of economic instrumentalism to recognize how important detention camps are today to the modulation of labor's movement, a "disciplinary decompression valve" that helps form the precarious lives of "irregular"—which is to say, detainable and deportable—labor that is integral to accumulative regimes everywhere (De Genova 2016).

In other words, it's not just that camps are everywhere. It's also that camps exert a shaping force on our world. It's not the border regime that makes camps, but it is camps that make our current border and deportation regimes not just feasible and possible, but increasingly likely. The camp device doesn't just mark: it *forms* ragged but now mobile colonial frontiers in a disjointed line everywhere from the US-Mexico border to Europe's southern boundaries. The new nomos of the earth is also a string of camps. Quite simply, the border zones would not be what they are without the capacities for capture, containment, and disciplinary transformation that camps provide. In turn, the global network of camps is not just the hidden scaffolding of our global regimes of labor (super)exploitation, but in turn also that of our world of circulation; camps are a kind of global infrastructure that, in modulating and disciplining the movement of labor, make possible the logistical world of the circulation of goods and capital (Katz 2017c). They may still often be spatially remote, but in their topological effects camps are at the core of our entire world.

In all this, the camp has not just proliferated; it has been normalized. As an instrument of global government, it has "ceased to scandalize" (Mbembe 2016, 32). The camp has become mundane, unexceptional, entirely routine, even banal—no longer really a question. Like the rest of the immiserating effects of global racial capitalism, today we don't even talk about mass encampment with anguish or pathos, or even surprise (Jameson 2015). It's a given, a seemingly inevitable facet of an equally inevitable border regime.

Palestinian camps—the world's longest-running case of continuous encampment—are in growing company. In hindsight, they are our global harbingers, the great forerunners of all but permanent encampment. "In their very excess and their long history," Palestinian camps, insists Michel Agier, "are exemplary rather than exceptional" (2011, 37). That is nowhere more so than in the region itself. Palestinian camps have exerted a shaping influence on some of the biggest cities in the region—Beirut, Damascus, and Amman are all unimaginable without their entwined histories with the camps—but the camps have also, as long-term holding sites, presaged the very transformation of the Middle East and North Africa into a borderland. Today the Mediterranean Sea, and North Africa as one of its main entry points from the south, is one of the world's most traversed, militarized, and lethal border regions. And the Levant and eastern Turkey have been so engulfed by mass encampment that some now provocatively conceptualize the whole region as a "supercamp" (Knudsen and Berg 2021). Global bordering practices—in their simultaneous unraveling and hardening—rely on mass encampment in the region as a buffer or absorber. In other words, the decades of imperial war, resource extraction, counterrevolutionary violence, and despotic client regimes that have marked the region's place in the global order increasingly rely on the camp form to make it all possible. This was not just anticipated by the region's long historical entanglement with refugeehood and humanitarianism, going back at least to the late nineteenth century, but was also in some ways made possible by the Palestinian camps and the territorial, institutional, and extralegal practices that make encampment on this scale and for this duration feasible.

Yet the Palestinian camps, like camps everywhere, point to changes beyond encampment itself. What then does our present of global mass encampment tell us about our world? Some seventy years after Hannah Arendt declared internment camps to be the new rule of nation-state crisis and statelessness, and some twenty years after Giorgio Agamben, picking up on Arendt, declared the camp and not the city to be the fundamental biopolitical paradigm of Western civilization, what are the stakes of mass encampment today? And how might they be read in the history of Palestine's colonial encampment?

Rather than dwelling on the Agambenian moment in camp studies and its critiques, we should begin, historically and conceptually, by coming to terms with the politics that courses in the camps' very own materiality: not with "the camp" as a paradigm or exemplum, but as a material force of an enduring and de-formed colonial history. The camp-city relation *remains* a political-theoretical problematic. Coming to terms with it, however, requires thinking outside or beyond the juridico-political. Agamben was right: what is at stake in the camp form is the separation between life and politics. But what camps do with and tell us about this separation, and its endurance or collapse, is not an unveiling of the law as a relation of force, the deep affinity between the democratic and the totalitarian, or even the triumph of biopolitics. Agamben's devastating critique of liberalism is entirely compelling; I just don't think the question of liberalism is still what's at stake, or at least primarily at stake, in the question of the camp today. Instead, what is at stake in the ubiquitous and banal camp form, now far removed from the postwar frame of European catastrophe, is what I am calling the politics of inhabitation, that is, the (re)emergence of inhabitation as both an explicit political question and political modality. Camps are devices that manage the fallout of global uninhabitability through an explicit refusal of cohabitation. But they are also where inhabitation in itself, and *not* citizenship or rights, becomes the basis of both political control and contestation and as such the site of politics for those with otherwise no recognized place in the body politic. Thinking through inhabitation as a political question, then, brings *the colonial terms of our border crisis* into full focus; it also keeps us close to the social terrain of migrant and refugee struggle and that struggle's deep implicit affinities with what remains of the worldmaking challenge that was and is decolonization. Inhabitation is the life-making practice of the dispossessed everywhere. And in every migrant struggle, I want to suggest, there is a kernel of anticolonialism, and one—just one—way to see or approach that connection is to read the world *from* Palestine.

The Long Colonial Shadow of Inhabitation

Inhabitation has long been a, maybe *the*, foundational question in colonial history. We know that settler colonial politics is a politics of land dispossession that works through the destruction and replacement of existing forms of inhabitation. But while it may be most pronounced in settler colonial moments, the question of inhabitation has been there in colonialism from the start, perhaps most obviously around the emergence of private property. Inhabitation subtends the property relation. What I mean is that the property relation that emerges from colonial dispossession is about a radical change in modes of inhabitation as much as anything else. I don't mean only that colonial dispossession and property law relied essentially on racializing images of inhabitation: *terra nullius*, the notion of ineffective occupancy, or the figure of nomadism (the itinerant, the unrooted, the unbounded/unbordered) were all primarily images of (wrong or wasteful) inhabitation. I mean also that the entire regime of property depended not only on the enclosure and dispossession of commonly held land but also on the expansion and naturalization of the privately owned, single-family, walled, bounded house on a titled allotment of land as the dominant and normative mode of inhabitation. In a recursive move, this form of inhabiting and using land became the only basis of legal subjectivity; it coproduced the racial subject and the private-property form in a single "racial regime of ownership" (Bhandar 2018). And this directly came at the expense of other ways of inhabiting the world: "Colonialism took root on the grounds of this juridical formation, twinning the production of racial subjects with an economy of private property ownership that continues to prevail over indigenous and alternative modalities of relating to and using land and its resources" (7).

If inhabiting is a faculty that goes to the living "nature" of the human as a dwelling animal, who, as Vilém Flusser (2003, 55) has it, "without a habitual place to live, experiences nothing," then the power of the colonial institution was in welding this ontological need to the relations of exclusion and racial hierarchy we call property. The colonial order takes, then, an arguably ontological need—to inhabit or dwell—and renders it a hierarchical relationship of exclusion. This, the way it brings inhabitation and building, or homing and housing, together in a legal-social exclusionary bond or relation, is arguably colonial history's most signature achievement. That is, it's not simply the institution of property, but property as an entirely different mode of inhabiting the earth that is at stake in colonial history. In other words, property as a relation of exclusion, and the entire legal and financial order eventually grafted atop it, was about the consecration of a certain way of dwelling/residing in the world that became synonymous with the faculty of inhabitation more generally. It demanded not only enclosure and dispossession (and the extinguishment of other modes of inhabitation) but also the gradual reorganization of most metabolic relationships to land and common resources around exclusive relations of use and exhaustion.

This is still patently at the heart of many a political system. If anything, our present seems only to reaffirm that the knot between property, whiteness, and violence remains the foundation of political order in much of the West. If in the 1970s and 1980s this knot was tied together in the credit-fueled visions of the "ownership society," or Margaret Thatcher's "home-owning democracy," then the post-austerity era recasts it in much more paranoid terms around the vigilante defense of property in the wake of "rioting" racialized and colonized subjects.

Yet anterior even to property, in some sense, is the question of separation. This question, as Mbembe reminds us, "lay at the root of the colonial project" (2016, 25) and is inseparable from inhabitation or, more accurately, cohabitation. Our accounts of the colonial have long made this insight clear. Consider how we've understood colonial modes of worlding as defined by an immunological concern with the proper separations of Native and settler living quarters. Recall Frantz Fanon's memorable dissection of colonial geography as "a compartmentalized world," organized around the line between Native and European sectors: "This compartmentalized world, this world divided in two, is inhabited by different species" (2005, 5). Fanon's juxtaposition of the colonial sector, all stone and steel, light and paved roads, with the Native quarter, all hunger and desperation, doesn't just mark the distance between the two—it also marks their intimate and threatening proximities.

For Fanon, colonialism's earliest, and perhaps primary, tension is the lived proximity of colonizer and colonized: "Their first confrontation was colored by violence and their cohabitation" (2005, 2). That colonizer and colonized are "old acquaintances" for Fanon isn't just about the relational constitution of the political subject positions but also arguably about this spatial and habitational intimacy and its inevitable violence. Both the need for a superexploitation of Native labor and the always-incomplete nature of elimination within the unitary jurisdictions of colonial (and often nominally democratic) states produce a spatial, legal, even atmospheric proximity. And it is this cohabitational proximity of and the potential reciprocity between colonial lifeworlds that prompts the anxiogenic and immunological response of separation.

In some readings, the history of racialization itself has to be read as emerging only with and against the prospects of jurisdictional cohabitation in the colonial world. For Patrick Wolfe, the race idea—always but an effect of racialization—only really comes into play in colonial history when the prospect of sharing space and jurisdiction with colonized subjects becomes tangible and near, that is, when physical proximity might become a kind of cohabited mutuality. Race is a foreclosing response precisely to this colonial cohabitation and reciprocity. In the American settler order, to take one example, the full racialization of Native peoples (through blood quantum and biological-hereditary criteria of tribe membership, designed to facilitate their elimination through assimilation policies) didn't really happen until the frontier was effectively closed—until Native peoples couldn't be pushed farther west. Similarly, the codification of anti-Black racist laws in the US South happened only *after* Emancipation and with the prospect of shared political space. Race in this sense is a corollary of democracy; it is a strategic response to the fear and intolerability of sharing political and habitational space with the colonized. Race and place, Wolfe writes, are deeply connected. In terms that recall Fanon's references to vitality and hygiene, Wolfe paraphrases Mary Douglas's well-traveled insight: if dirt is matter out of place, then race is certain peoples being out of place. And—as with any threat to purity—the response to the perceived threat of the "contamination" of cohabitation is to cleanse: "The remedy for a people being out of place, after all, is ethnic cleansing" (Wolfe 2016, 22).

In the context of Palestine, it seems almost trite to belabor a point about politics and inhabitation. We could just pause to consider the sheer brutal ubiquity of the instrument of home demolition, or the use of the single-family suburban housing unit as, today, the primary instrument of colonial expansion. But more than this, the question of inhabitation cuts to the very core of political subjectivity here. Hagar Kotef makes the point that, in the colonization of Palestine, homemaking itself is an act of violent dispossession. It is not only that Jewish Israeli homes were "historically conditioned on the destruction of Palestinians' homes" (2020, xi), but that this becomes integral to Israeli subjectivity itself. What Kotef calls "the colonizing self" is but the effect of an attachment to this site of violence (to the unhoming/homing dyad): "The founding of home as well as homeland, includes a certain longing for and belonging to a past violence that becomes integral to Israelis' self-identity" (xi). When Wolfe made another one of his emblematic statements to write that "settler colonialism destroys to replace," he immediately reached for a line from Theodor Herzl's *Altneuland*: "If I wish to substitute a new building for an old one, I must demolish before I construct" (cited in Wolfe 2006, 388). Wolfe lets this stand as an allegorical image for settler colonialism writ large, but we should also take it quite literally and face the passionate affective attachments that this violence engenders.

Part of what I've shown in this book is how much the colonization of Palestine can be understood through the question of inhabitation and its relationship to time. The stakes of Zionism in one sense rested on the construction of racially separated, settled, propertied, and circulating forms of inhabitation. To do so, the project had to not only expel and eliminate but also target and upend existing Palestinian forms of inhabitation; it had to actively produce the nomadic, the placeless, the unurban, and the ahistorical. Political Zionism's built project was, to borrow Mark Levine's term, premised on its "ability to '*overturn*' the existing modern(izing) geographies in favour of specifically Euro-modern topographies of power and identity" (2005, 1, emphasis added). And it had to do this in a way that historicized or "rooted" settler forms of inhabitation in time (as always there, or as "returning," or as "Indigenous"), in a way that created a new temporal order or beginning *from* these forms that would transition them away from the moment of conquest and foundation.

Yet there is a certain historical irony to this because the urban promise of the settler colony—the promise of a new modern beginning *after* conquest—never arrives. Israel—stuck in the condition of settlerness—still seems spatially defined above all by enclaves and fortifications, by what might be thought of as encampments in their own right. These defensive and paranoid architectures of security stand in stark contrast to the imaginaries of the liberal city of free circulation, light, and air, that vital autoregulative entity that was the foundation of both liberal governmentality and the dialectics of freedom and alienation that have formed such a central plank of critical urban thought. By contrast the architectures and topologies of settlement here materially manifest the fraughtness of the frontier; they mark the anxiousness of settlerness. Settler colonies appear more like the "degenerate utopias" we associate with contemporary gated communities as the antitheses of open urban life, as the monstrous rebirth of Utopian exceptionality (Martin 2010, 20). Here, settler colonialism promises the city but delivers only the camp.

Inhabitation, then, is not a new question or simply a returning old one. If, as I'm arguing, the question of inhabitation is at the heart of migrant and anticolonial struggles today, at the heart of global politics, then this speaks to the way colonial histories and hierarchies are neither simply overcome (in stagist progress) nor eternally present (in seamless continuity) but constantly reworked as endurances and entailments that cling to the present in old and new forms (Stoler 2016). One such old-new form is, of course, the camp.

Learning to Live in the Ruins of the Modern

The question of inhabitation is *the* political question of our time. I don't mean at all to imply that inhabitation, and the entire bundle of questions around the domestic and home, has not been previously political. Feminist thought has long laid that conceit to rest. But one need not subscribe to the fictions at the heart of Western political thought to note a change in the substance of politics. Here I mean simply to point to a more recent set of historical changes around borders and movement that recapitulate but also transform the colonial-racial anxieties of inhabitation that I just mapped out; they do so in part because the border crisis is born out of the dispossessive logics of a racial capitalism that has always been colonial in form.

It is by now trite to say that how we inhabit our cities, our land, and in turn our planet is fatefully consequential on a scale previously unimaginable. And though the so-called mega-cities of the Global South were imagined until quite recently, often in sensationalist terms, as the terrain of "the uninhabitable," we haven't really grappled with inhabitation as a political problem. And yet how we inhabit, with whom, within what boundary, with what metabolic footprint, on what terms, through what relations of production, for how long, and with what, if any, kind of permanence are all urgent questions. The significance of mass encampment to us all today lies simply in the fact that camps manifest the question of inhabitation as something urgent beyond encampment itself, as one of the defining questions of our age, present in everything from sanctuary to eviction and from borders to climate change.

Bruno Latour is in part correct when he says that *the* question of the new climatic regime is the finding of ground on which to inhabit. That is, what defines the sense of vertigo, panic, and anxiety in global politics today is the generalization of the feeling of groundlessness or landlessness in which we all face the "universal lack of shareable space and inhabitable land." Latour's prose here, a mixture of polemic and elegy, warns of an epochal shift in which the mixture of war, inequality, and climate change is producing the displacement of millions of people moving simply "to search for territory they and their children can inhabit" (2018, 10). Today people move, Latour tells us, not strictly to find better work or improved livelihoods but just to find ground to inhabit. We move because our ground is insecure—it's too wet, too hot, or too unsafe. Some of this may sound familiar, but what's new for Latour is the generalization of this experience, the generalization of the specter of uninhabitability. This anxiety, this uneasiness, Latour (more than a bit problematically) claims, "gnaws at everyone equally, the former colonizers and formerly colonized alike" (13).

Now there is much to dislike here. Latour's flat generalization, his unqualified "we," and his gloss on the becoming postcolonial of the world, of course, elide, despite his many moderating caveats, the uneven and racialized distribution of this risk of uninhabitability. There *are* very real points of convergence across the partially collapsing divide between the metropolitan and colonial worlds, or between Global North and Global South (or whatever inadequate pairing you want). But we are *not* all migrants now, even if our climatic regime has scrambled some of the previous complacencies and assurances for the whiter and wealthier among us. And aside from the fact that there is nothing "former" about colonization, the uneasiness does *not* "gnaw at everyone equally." In this suddenly leveled world, Latour woefully misses the enduring colonial terms of the crisis: that is, both the persistence of dispossession and extraction as organizing logics in our regimes of capital accumulation *and* the systemic racism that makes possible the very climate denialism he targets.

But Latour's take *does* have the merit of both returning land to mainstream conversations (even if the idioms of "soil" and "property" with which he engages the land question risk more harm than good) and recognizing inhabitation in itself as a global political question, or, better yet, as a political question that reanimates what "the global" is. He not only takes aim, with a righteous and commendable anger, at a set of "ruling classes" who have systematically abandoned any notion of universal mutuality, but he identifies the effects of this abandonment in the face of the border/climate crisis as a loss of the prospect of shareable ground. In short, he recognizes the present as a global or planetary crisis *of* habitability. This is a crisis, we can add, most clearly at work in precisely those sites with which our border regime deals with the displacements Latour takes as paradigmatic of the age, namely, camps. As one of colonial modernity's most enduring spatial forms, camps are immunological devices for the racializing separation of those we refuse to cohabit with; they are quite simply the single most pervasive way we deal with the escalating impasses of cohabitation in a bordered, unequal, and climatically unstable—which is to say uninhabitable—world, and in turn it's where the question of inhabitation takes on its fullest political expression.

Inhabitation as a concept is one way of coming to terms with the emergent terrain of crisis and struggle. One established narrative of modern politics tells the story of the movement of household management into the political sphere, a story we call (other differences notwithstanding) either biopolitics, the rise of the social, or the technocratic turn. And the completion of this movement, the final indistinction, was, of course, for Agamben what was, at its limit, both marked and made in the camps. But what if camps, today, enact the collapse of the separation between life and politics, or between house and city, *not* as the final triumph of biopolitics or the exception, but by making the very fact of inhabitation in itself an explicit political question and, in turn, the basis of both political control and contestation? Perhaps more than anything else, what camps today demonstrate is how for those not granted the insulations of property, privacy, and settled permanence, the shelter or site of inhabitation becomes the very locus of politics and arguably a different politics, one that, implicitly at least, questions the colonial collapse of inhabitation into relations of property.

The stakes here, then, exceed the cluster of issues we would normally approach through a framework like the politics of housing, dependent as it is on stable forms of possession, patterns of social reproduction, public investment apparatuses, and so on. To talk of a politics of inhabitation is to talk of a change not just in the location but in the substance of politics.[1] By shifting the conceptual focus to inhabitation rather than housing, I want to point to a shifting topology of politics that is not at all contained within questions of ownership, or the housing rights or entitlements that stable forms of citizenship or residency can carry (and indeed the large-scale public apparatuses they assume), or even questions of social reproduction, but often stands in obverse relation to them. In camps the absence of all this is often nonetheless coupled with a domesticating logic that both makes the site of inhabitation a primary means of control/discipline and at the same time seeks to sunder it from any kind of politics (as life or administration). Here the inhabitation, appropriation, or (mis)use of impermanent but enduring structures becomes both the means of a certain regime of domesticating management and the center of a counterpolitics for those with otherwise no place in the body politic.

To inhabit is both to dwell in and to hold. It comes from the Latin verb *habere*, to have, which gave us *habitare*, to dwell.[2] For Agamben (2020) the etymological declension of *habitare* opens having onto being—to have is foremost "to have a certain way of being." It's as such that inhabitation becomes an ontological category, for to inhabit "means to create, to conserve and intensify habits and customs, that is, ways of being." In inhabitation there is a reciprocity and continuous exchange between being and having. The historical challenge, says Agamben, one that confronts architecture in the first order—and here he returns, albeit briefly, nearly thirty years after *Homo Sacer* (1998) to the camp—is that in the modern age the problematic unity of building and inhabitation, of the house-structure (*aedes*) and the house-home (*domus*), is severed. In the face of a historically unprecedented architecture of uninhabitability, from camps to shopping malls, the very concept of inhabitation teeters, for Agamben, on the edge of the obsolete.

Yet there's a way of reading the inhabitation concept as today teetering not on the edge of obsoletion but on that of reformulation and redirection. The narrow historical and geographical purview of accounts like Agamben's (that return again and again to the primal scene of European catastrophe) stops people from seeing how that precisely in its severing from paradigmatic forms of building and ownership—themselves so bound with the property relation—inhabitation might reemerge as a usable political concept. What is missed here is twofold: both how much this "problematic unity" of inhabitation and building in our age is made and mediated by the property relation and colonial dispossession and how the "uninhabitability" of places likes camps is overcome precisely *in* and *as* a politics immanent to the site itself. When millions of people in camps inhabit *temporary* structures that they nonetheless use as a means of making political claims, then it's hard not to see new content for the inhabitation concept.

Even etymologically, the domain supreme of Agamben's political inquiry, inhabitation or the inhabitable carries a productive tension that Agamben misses. It holds, or once held, two opposite senses: both the "not habitable" (in which the Latin prefix *in-* denotes a negation) and that capable of being habited (inhabitable as we understand it now). In a very real sense, to indulge this foray for just a moment, camps today manifest precisely this contradiction—they are that which is habitable and not habitable at the same time, both place and nonplace. This was and remains the defining contradiction of the Palestinian camp: how to live in that which is not to become permanent (and thus *cannot* be inhabited) and at the same time that which is not only to be survived but transformed (and thus *must* be inhabited). Camp life takes shape between the "cannot" and the "must." Dwelling in and holding on to what you have in places that are both habitable and not habitable at once—these are the challenges of contemporary camps and their struggles that we might parse through a notion like the politics of inhabitation.

In camps, in sites designed to be uninhabitable, where people have been reduced to life and disposable labor, to a set of domestic and bodily needs, the site of inhabitation forms the basis of refusal. I don't mean this in the sense of a politics of space, in the sense that people excluded from the body politic will use space to make claims or fashion forms of life. This is undoubtedly true and, here, the building of a solid house, roofing, connections to sewerage, electricity, or water, "encroachments," all become a series of political-temporal thresholds. None of them can be confined to an order of domestic management, and all spill the basic stuff of inhabitation into politics. But here I mean more pointedly how people inhabit a sense of the temporary or the indeterminate as a means of demonstrative refusal.

The contemporary politics of camp life are more than anything defined by the tensions of this double temporal move: to claim something in the camp's here and now (the right to stay, to a site of inhabitation, a claim to ownership, to work, to education, to dignity in the camps) that sits alongside and doesn't undermine the claim to an elsewhere (return, forward movement, even rights and representation). It means opening up a temporality between the *permanence* of the built (camp) and the *temporariness* of the (a)political condition (refugeehood, migrancy): in other words, creating a different political modality of inhabitation. For

Palestinian camp life, this involves negotiating the paradox of built presence in a camp that is meant to be nothing but a means of its own overcoming in the redemptive politics of return: what we might think of as the inhabitation of the *temporary-here* as a claim on a *future-elsewhere*. We see something similar in many camps: an insistence on both holding ground around a site of inhabitation and not being bound by it, regardless of duration or durability. This is only a contradiction if we think of return or forward movement as terminal; if we read returns/movements instead as enactments and desires of circulation and not settledness, then the tension between the camp's meantime and return's future looks very different.

None of this is to suggest that the Palestinian camps are not historically specific. Palestinian camp histories and camp life have their own genealogies and particularities, much of it overlaid with older cases of encampment and displacement in the region. And Palestinian refugees face an order and magnitude of violence that is often starkly different. And yet I *do* want to argue that there is something increasingly resonant about this experience within wider mass encampment, not simply in an analogical sense but in a relational-historical sense. Even the Palestinian insistence on return, often seen as singular, parallels, as I've been arguing, wider migrant practices of circulation and return because all of them are confrontations with and refusals of a connected border regime. In Palestinian camps, the tension is in the insistence on holding ground and a defense of their camps *but only* until return is mirrored in many camps in which refugees and migrants hold ground but only temporarily until the right pathway is opened up (the constant rebuilding of camps in places like Calais or Mt. Gurugu, outside the Spanish colonial enclave of Melilla in Morocco, for example, is a testament to exactly this).

Inhabitation, then, is a concept drawn and reformulated from the struggles that render camps and border zones livable and the means to a kind of life that exceeds both the separations of domestication and the conceits of inclusion. It gives us a way of reading the border crisis from the politics of migrants and refugees and not the politics of states; in other words, centering inhabitation allows us to epistemically and politically start from movement, temporariness, the unsettled. Inhabiting the camp is the making of a life in the *meantime*, without the temporal guarantees of ownership and possession and without a necessary acceptance of the camp as the future. Part of this is simply the insistence of camp inhabitants on remaining in place but *only* for the time being. If, etymologically, to inhabit is both to dwell and to hold, or the simultaneity of holding and dwelling, then we can think of camp life as an inhabitation and holding *of* the temporary. It is to hold and make livable, or to hold so as to make livable in the *meantime*, that is, always with a view to a future or, better yet, a virtuality, not entirely thinkable in the present. All this seems to me not just a change in the locus of politics (going from, say, public square to house) but a change in the topology of politics, not a relocation but an overturning of the content of politics—of what and who counts as politics.

The temporary, AbdouMaliq Simone reminds us, "seems to constantly unsettle what it means to inhabit" (2020, 1128). For Simone, if any urban concept is to work as a way of apprehending contemporary lived practice, it is only by shedding its previous presuppositions and conceits, not least its claims to permanence and settledness. And here, in nodding to settler colonialism's imprint on our modes and imaginaries of urban life, Simone draws a dividing line between settlement and the emergent urban itineraries of the dispossessed: "For, 'to settle' has always been excessively burdened by the imperial practices of the 'settler' and his fascination, obsession in marking a story with a definitive beginning and end" (1129). Instead, he urges us to see contemporary lateral movements through urban territory as the stuff of *provisional* itineraries, an urban life "without subsumption or overarching frame, without settling somewhere" (1128–29). It is a form of what Simone elsewhere called "residing" as a "generalized process of unsettlement," one that entails a more volitional suspension of settlement—an impulsive but determined decision to upend valued ways of living for more provisional circulations (2022, 8). For Simone, the uninhabitable is not so much about the impossibility, for some, of human residency but about those aspects of urbanization that do *not* fundamentally concern the possibilities of inhabitation: the eventful arrangements of times, things, bodies that neither finalize nor foreclose residency but constantly shift what it means to reside—the improvisational jazz of the urban.

Where Simone wants to move beyond inhabitation as a kind of overarching frame, I want to reclaim inhabitation as an antonym of settlement. Inhabitation understood now as the provisional and unsettling life-making practice of the global dispossessed—of which migrants are but a vanguard—can be reclaimed as a concept. In these practices we might see the start of the delinking of the faculty of inhabitation, the ontological need to reside or dwell together, from the property relation and settledness, even from the juridical forms of personal injury and redress premised on the proper legal-civil subject. These practices already exist in various fragments of struggle in life beyond camps: in anti-eviction and antideportation politics; in sanctuary at its most radical ends; in the movements and groundings of migrants and the undocumented in cities; in their presencing that besieges the fort without taking it (Harney and Moten 2013); in their urban lifeworlds that foster a kind of mutual life and exchange subtracted from wider economies and operations of value (migrant Beirut, much of it taking shape in Palestinian camps, for example, or Gulf cities beneath and beyond the *kafala* system). We can see it in the returning figure of the commune, so central today to the revolutionary perspective, and that should be read, above all, as a demonstrative mode of inhabitation, as the enactment of different metabolic relationships to land and common resources beyond the exclusive relations of use and exhaustion we call property; and we can see it too in the persistence of colonized and Indigenous forms of inhabitation in the face of removal, in the obstinacy of rebuilding and re-inhabiting after destruction and against the legalities of colonial law—we see it in Gaza where the active production of the uninhabitable through the obliterating bombardment of homes is met with an insistent inhabitation of the ruin itself. All of these are a politics of inhabitation.

These forms of practice take the very fact of inhabitation as a way not so much of making political claims, as making a (infra)political life. They rely on neither representation nor permanent settledness. They are not, as some have suggested, a post-politics, but they do point to a kind of horizon of politics beyond citizenship and the reparative rationalities of justice, which is not to say a politics beyond rights per se. Mass encampment signals what most agree is a historical, maybe even terminal, crisis of liberal rights, an era of rising open repression across the board. And whether this era is an effect of liberalism *as* crisis, that is, a crisis internal to liberalism and its own repressive tendencies and racial exclusions (the logical rise of "liberal authoritarianism"), or whether it's liberalism *in* crisis, that is, the eclipse or overturning of liberalism (the rise of "illiberal democracy"), is really a moot point. What the politics of inhabitation points to is at once a claim *to* and foundational critique *of* rights. The encamped and dispossessed are not immune from the desires for rights, and they often wage struggles against the eclipse of rights even when these struggles are not and *cannot* be made in the idiom of rights and always function as such as an implicit critique of the limits of liberal-national rights. They are forms of politics that are not quite inclusion or exit.

Inhabitation is the question of our age because it is arguably the question that emerges precisely in the ruins of the liberal modern project, rendering "rights" at once urgent and utterly redundant. Inhabitation emerges in the ruins of the liberal emancipatory promise and the false dawns of citizenship, of the narratives of global development and catch-up, of the self-ingesting collapse of modernization and the pyrrhic triumph of the technocratic, but perhaps most of all in the ruins of the defeated project of decolonization that once promised a humanism genuinely for all. The camp is a kind of name for these ruins. And at one level, what camp life is about is learning to live in the ruins of the modern project.

I should be very clear: there is nothing to romanticize about camp life. The point is not to celebrate some unexpected fragment of urban vitality we find in camps, one that we can read as an implicit critique of the bordered and racialized foundations of our world. I don't think criticism is even the most useful genre or modality of thought here. The point is about the congealment of historical forces in camps; it is about what's at stake in reading the world *from* camps and *with* their inhabitants. To hold ground *and* insist on moving, to assemble political community beyond the territorialities of the colonial border regime and to enact a borderless world in practice, to shape forms that resist the isolation of life, to inhabit without settling and domesticating—these are at once the stakes and the challenges of our world of camps.

NOTES

Introduction

1. It's worth noting how much this reproduces aspects of the legal-discursive rationalities of settler colonial dispossession in other contexts. The term *over-run*, for example, comes up in the majority ruling in Canada's leading case on Aboriginal land title, *St. Catharines Milling and Lumber Co. v R* (1888), which held that Indigenous people "have no idea of a title to the soil itself. It is over-run by them rather than inhabited" (cited in Nichols 2020, 46).
2. Gabriel Piterberg notes that the entire *kibbutz* enterprise relied on the "formative influence" of German agricultural colonies in the pre–First World War colonization project of the German Reich in the Posen province of the east Prussian marches, knowledge that was brought to Palestine by German-Jewish settlement experts like Ruppin and Franz Oppenheimer (2008, 78–88).
3. Peter Lagerqvist (2009) has explored these continuities between British and Zionist colonization in Palestine by tracing the inheritances in built forms and securitized architectures.
4. I am grateful to Samar al-Saleh, whose brilliant master's thesis is the first sustained work I've come across on the British prison labor camps in Palestine. Her thesis helps us come to terms not only with the deep structural synergies between global accumulation practices, British imperialism, and Zionist colonialism in Palestine but also with how critical the almost entirely overlooked issue of prison labor was to this entire history.
5. Often according to settlement plans developed by figures like the agronomist and planner Ra'anan Weitz, then head of the Jewish Agency's Settlement Department, and who later developed similar proposals for the resettlement of Palestinian refugees and the removal of Palestinian camps in Gaza, and whom we will meet in chapter 4.
6. The history of 1948 was written and told by Palestinians as a story of colonial conquest and expulsion from the very start. Numerous Arabic-language memoirs and accounts recounted the expulsions and massacres, notably Muhammad Nimr al-Khatib's *Min Athar al-Nakba* (1951), a combi-

nation of memoir and eyewitness accounts, and 'Arif al-'Arif, who wrote perhaps the most comprehensive early historical account of the expulsion, the six-volume *Al-Nakba: Nakbat Bayt al-Maqdis wal-Firdaws al-Mafqud 1947–1952*, published in 1956. English-language scholarship on the subject quickly followed. As early as 1959, Walid Khalidi (2005) published a historical account of the 1948 expulsions, written from the archives of the Arab Higher Committee and the Arab League. Nafiz Nazzal wrote a doctoral dissertation at Georgetown in 1974 on the expulsion of the Galilee's Palestinian inhabitants, later published as *The Palestinian Exodus from the Galilee* (1978). Later still, we got books by David Gilmour (1980), Elias Sanbar (1984), and Michael Palumbo (1987). Across the 1970s and early 1980s, the Institute for Palestine Studies, *Shu'un Filastiniyya*, and the *Arab Studies Quarterly* published a host of firsthand accounts and oral histories that, in effect, amounted to a historical record. Nonetheless, it took the emergence of revisionist Israeli historians, known as the "new historians," to make a dent in the wider historiographical record of the Western academy.

7   For treatments of Israel as a racial regime, see Ronit Lentin (2018), Yasmeen Abu-Laban and Abigail Bakan (2019), Andy Clarno (2017), and David Theo Goldberg (2008). It needs noting, though, that this is also something of a "return" to categories of race/racism; Palestinian political scholarship had long identified Zionism as a form of colonial racism predicated on multiple racial hierarchies. This scholarship, for one, fed into the drafting of the part of UN General Assembly Resolution 3379 (1975) that declared Zionism a form of state racism, comparable to the racist state structures of Rhodesia and South Africa.

8   In her book, Megan Bradley (2014) demonstrates that over the past three decades, refugee repatriation has been an integral part of *almost every* "post-conflict scenario," with permanent resettlement becoming, after the Cold War, a very rare solution to refugee crises. Indeed, Bradley cites figures from the United Nations High Commissioner on Refugees that show that, between 1998 and 2007, 11.4 million refugees returned to their countries of origin through more than twenty-five large-scale repatriation programs. In this period, for every refugee resettled, fourteen returned to their home countries. This was the result, Bradley shows, of a consensus across global institutions, which held that peace processes and return movements are closely connected: "A strong conviction has emerged that voluntary repatriation movements should be supported because they have the potential to consolidate peace processes" (2014, 5).

9   Letter from Commissioner-General John Rennie to UN Under Secretary General for Special Political Affairs Brian Urquhart, August 14, 1975, file OR 150/1 SC, UNRWA Central Records.

10 This is drawn from a compelling footnote Borges has in a short essay called "Palermo, Buenos Aires" (in Borges 1984), in which he seems to implicitly link the transformative forces of urban capital with the open history of settler conquest. Gabriel Piterberg (2011) uses this footnote as the epigraph to a comparative study of settler literatures.

11 Not only is this conjunction of history and time, for a lack of a better word, historical, and, indeed, as people like David Scott (2014) have argued, decisively coming apart today in a postrevolutionary age defined by time without future, or temporality without historicity. Also, these conceptions and organizations of history and time were only "universalized" in the worldmaking that was colonial capitalism, probably no earlier than the late nineteenth century.

12 In this sense at least, the Palestinian Revolution would appear consistent with aspects of Gary Wilder's (2015) generative reading of the postwar decolonization movement as a struggle over distinct *types* of time and particular political tenses.

13 In a chapter called "Raw Cuts: Palestine, Israel and (Post)colonial Studies," Stoler makes the case that "the dominant definition of what constituted colonial and postcolonial conditions circumvented—and, indeed, seemed defined to exclude—Palestine/Israel and the U.S. presence as sites of inquiry" (2016, 40). In colonial/postcolonial studies, Israel and Palestine's colonial history of the present "remained systematically out of sight, largely absent from what long remained the canon" (40). This exclusion, for Stoler, was symptomatic of a broader set of conceptual and political elisions in the field as a whole.

The pervasive sense of exceptionalism and uniqueness around Zionism and Israel meant that in the Western academy frameworks of colonialism or settler colonialism were until relatively recently avoided. Again, it's worth noting that many Palestinian and Arab accounts were long insistent on the colonial and imperial dimensions of political Zionism. Qustantin Zurayq's book, *Ma'na al-Nakba*, written in the midst of the ethnic cleansing campaign in 1948, and which gave the event its proper name, *Nakba*, located Zionism within the wider historical encounter with European imperialism. Arguably one of the earliest inquiries anywhere into settler colonialism as a distinct political modality came with Fayez Sayegh's English-language book, published in 1965 as *Zionist Colonialism in Palestine*. Abdul-Wahab Kayyali in 1977 wrote a historical analysis of Zionism as a movement emerging at the intersection of the Jewish question, the national question, and the colonial question. Edward Said located Zionism in the longer history of European imperialism and settler colonialism in 1979's *The Question of Palestine*. Joseph Massad later built on this tradition in his 2006 collection of essays, *The Persistence of the Palestinian Question*.

14 Wolfe also made this statement earlier in the opening pages of his 1998 book, *Settler Colonialism and the Transformation of Anthropology*, which is cited much less frequently.

15 Some of the most noticeable effects of the settler colonial turn were not on Palestinian thought, which in some senses had preempted this turn, but rather on the scholarship that actively avoided these frames. On the one hand, in obvious terms, it has upended the work (Rabinowitz 1997; Monterescu 2015) that obscures or ignores the settler colonialism of Zionism through idioms of *ethnicity* or *nationalism*—which have only ever functioned to displace the racial as an analytic. A generally well-received book explicitly brackets "colonialism" as just one more parallel but optional frame of reference to argue that housing is an arena for competing "national claims" (Allweil 2016). It's precisely the kind of elision that allows someone to describe Zionism as a "massive housing regime" that settler colonial studies sought to challenge—no, Zionism was an *un*housing project before and precisely so that it could become a housing project; if anything, it is an ongoing unhousing/housing regime. This kind of crude elision is—and rightly—less tenable than it used to be. On the other hand, the settler colonial turn has also shown the limits of what we can call "the school of occupation studies," a cluster of critical scholarship attentive to the spatial forces of colonialism in Palestine but that tends almost exclusively to restrict itself to studying the 1967 occupation of the West Bank and Gaza, unwittingly reinforcing a separation between the occupation and the wider regime from which, all these scholars agree, it is inseparable (Weizman 2007; Gordon 2008; Ophir et al. 2009; Handel 2014; Berda 2017). Invaluable, in both political and scholarly terms, as this work has been, it contributes to a reoccurring process in which the political border (the 1967 Green Line) becomes an epistemological boundary. This too, in light of the turn not just to the settler "origins" but to the settler *present* of Zionist colonization across historic Palestine, seems just all that less feasible.

16 For example, as Lisa Ford (2010) has shown, once Anglophone colonies in the United States and Australia had been established around mass settlement and the effective exclusion of Indigenous labor, they did not need, in contrast to other moments in colonial governance, to govern through Indigenous hierarchies; these settler polities moved instead to models of jurisdictional-territorial sovereignty that were premised on the intolerability of Indigenous self-government.

17 Lorenzo Veracini (2011b) in an article titled "On Settlerness" develops settlerness as a conceptual category to account, as he has it, for the specificity of the settler colonial situation. He identifies three structuring differentiations of "settlerness" to distinguish it from colonialism: triangular relationships, disavowal, and libidinal economies. Here, I use settlerness

very differently to get at the temporal quality of colonial settlement as it is shaped primarily by the forms of struggle settlers encounter.

18 I refer here to the village of al-ʿAraqib in the Naqab in southern Palestine, which to date has been demolished and rebuilt/reinhabited over 210 times.

19 For a broader engagement with how the open conflict of colonial dispossession is translated into closed juridical terms, including "real estate disputes," see Mor (2024).

20 The very recent appropriation by Zionism of a discourse of Indigeneity (what some have called "brownwashing") is telling; the point is not only how badly this appropriation misunderstands the politics of Indigeneity (which it transmutes into a racial myth of origin), but how much it indexes the temporal drive and anxiety around transition and self-supersession. Zionism, again, is hardly unique in this case (even if it adds an ideological messianism that somewhat sets it apart). Albert Camus's infamous outburst at the 1957 Nobel Prize press conference is usually remembered for his blunt piece of rhetoric: "If I had to choose between justice and my mother, I would choose my mother." But the expression of consummately settler desire that followed is equally instructive: "The Algerian French are likewise [like "the Arabs" of Algeria], and in the strongest meaning of the word, natives" (cited in Prochaska 2004, xvii).

21 Settler colonialism almost always involves a transformation of the natural world, in which the removal and replacement of Indigenous bodies is closely connected to a process of agricultural unplanting and replanting, or unrooting and rerooting. See Mastnak et al. (2014) and, in the context of Palestine, Tesdell (2017).

22 Allweil, for example, writes of the Zionist perception of "housing's role in *re-rooting* Jews as 'natives' in the homeland" (2016, 5, emphasis added). But if we consider this with Farred, much more attuned to the political center of gravity in settler colonies, the image also identifies settler anxieties about time, the past, and origin.

23 Zvi Efrat reproduced the plan in full in his 2018 book, *The Object of Zionism*.

24 Farred briefly brings his reading to bear on Palestine: "That is why, try as it must with all its military might, Israel can never live as anything but a state violently ill at ease with itself; a state dis-eased by the death that is sixty years later, still alive in the memory of al-Nakba, 'the catastrophe' that was the ethnic cleansing of the resident Palestinian population" (2008, 799).

25 Rosemary Sayigh's (1977, 1979) work, combining ethnography, oral history, and a keen attentiveness to the question of political identity, was pioneering in the study of encamped Palestinian refugees and remains relevant. Ilana Feldman (2008, 2012, 2015) has consistently combined ethnography with archival work to study the intersections of humanitarian-

ism and politics in Palestinian refugee lives, with particular attention to the effects of bureaucratic rule and administrative categories. Julie Peteet's (2009) *Landscapes of Hope and Despair: Palestinian Refugee Camps*, which also combines archival and ethnographic work, remains one of the most compelling anthropological accounts of Palestinian refugee camps to take seriously questions around the production of space. Diana Allan's book *Refugees of the Revolution* (2014), which ethnographically engages Shatila Camp's refugees in the aftermath of the collapse of the national liberation movement, urges us to reconsider some of the established terms through which we have apprehended the refugee experience. Similarly, Ruba Salih's (2018) ethnographic work has pushed for a reading of Palestinian refugee politics beyond national frames and the figure of the rights-bearing subject. Sylvain Perdigon's (2015) work on Palestinian refugees in Lebanon, around themes of kinship, poverty, solidarity, and worldliness mixes a fine-brushed ethnographic texture and a theoretical suppleness that sets it apart. The spatial and material turns in social science have also left their mark on studies of Palestinian refugee camps. Adam Ramadan (2009, 2013) has written on concepts of urbicide in a study of Nahr al-Barid Camp in Lebanon, and on the necessity of thinking through the intersections of everyday life and geopolitics in camps, with a compelling case made for assemblage thinking. Nell Gabiam (2012) has studied how UNRWA's shift from "humanitarianism" (to which I would argue it always had an atypical relation) to "development" in the refugee camps forced a shift in Palestinian political narrative. Lucas Oesch (2017) has made the case for thinking through the Palestinian refugee camp as a space of ambiguity and plural subjectivities.

1 The Camp, Inevitable

1. Letter from Michael S. Comay to Pablo Azcarate, UNCCP, March 17, 1949, file: AB-14-4633, Ministry of Foreign Affairs, Hakirya, Israel State Archives (hereafter ISA), emphasis added.
2. Statement to the Special Political Committee of the United Nations General Assembly, Abba Eban, November 18, 1955, Israel Ministry of Foreign Affairs, http://www.mfa.gov.il/MFA/ForeignPolicy/MFADocuments/Yearbook1.aspx.
3. Letter, Comay to Azcarate, ISA.
4. The historian Nur Masalha (2003, 69) notes that by 1950 the slogan coined by senior Israeli Foreign Ministry officials with regard to the refugee question, "If you can't solve it, dissolve it," underlined the logic at play: dissolving politics into economic, or employment-based, instruments.

5 "Authorization of a Contribution by the United States to the United Nations Relief and Works Agency for Palestine Refugees in the Near East," Senate Foreign Relations Committee, Report No. 1275, February 14, 1950, box 2: "UN Economic Survey Mission to the Middle East File, 1949," Gordon R. Clapp Papers, 1933–1963, National Archives and Records Administration, Harry S. Truman Presidential Library, Independence, Missouri (hereafter Clapp Papers).

6 Letter from Gordon R. Clapp to Arthur Z. Gardiner, Department of State, January 10, 1950, box 2: "The Economic Survey Mission to the Middle East," Clapp Papers.

7 In chapter 3 we get a sense of how the survey remained a much-hated part of Palestinian camp life.

8 John G. Rogers, "The Underdeveloped Middle East," *Herald Tribune*, January 21, 1950, box 3: "General Correspondence," Clapp Papers.

9 I. F. Stone, *New York Compass*, January 12, 1950, box 3: "General Correspondence," Clapp Papers.

10 The Clapp quotation is from Gordon R. Clapp, "No Shortcut to Economic Balance," *American Association for the United Nations Newsletter* 22, no. 2 (February 1950), Clapp Papers.

11 "Kushner: Palestinians Not Yet Capable of Governing Themselves," *Middle East Eye*, June 3, 2019, https://www.middleeasteye.net/news/kushner-palestinians-not-yet-capable-governing-themselves.

12 Brandon Tensley, "Jared Kushner's Very Revealing Comment on Black Americans' Desire for Success," CNN, October 26, 2020, https://www.cnn.com/2020/10/26/politics/jared-kushner-black-americans-welfare-queen-racism/index.html.

13 Many of the displaced sheltered in sites of older encampments or barracks, many of which would become official UNRWA camps: French military barracks in Lebanon (Wavel and Gouraud Camps, the latter evacuated in 1963) and Syria (Neirab Camp), a British military prison in Gaza once used for Greek refugees (Nusayrat Camp), older refugee camps in Lebanon that the French had established for Armenian refugees (Rashidiya and al-Buss Camps), and the ruins of old caravansaries on the road to Damascus, two of which would eventually become full UNRWA camps (Khan Dunun and Khan al-Shayh Camps).

14 It's worth noting that it is work and not works that is the important principle here; that is, the key is putting refugees to work and not the broader benefit of public works. This is made clear in the Arabic translation of the word *works* in the UNRWA's name, which becomes the causative verb *tashghil* (to make work) and not *ashghal* (works).

15 Gordon R. Clapp, "An Economic Mission for the Middle East," speech delivered at the conference of the Food and Agriculture Organization (FAO)

in the American University of Beirut, September 15, 1949, box 2: "UN Economic Survey Mission to the Middle East File, 1949," Clapp Papers.

16 "Authorization of a Contribution...," Clapp Papers.

17 Minutes of meeting, "Meeting with the voluntary interests," September 1, 1949, Clapp Papers.

18 In his account of primitive accumulation in England, Karl Marx points to the parish prisons of the Elizabethan Poor Laws of 1601 to show an early example of this historical conjunction of relief, confinement, and forced labor (1990, 882fn9).

19 These continuities would endure beyond the contraband camps. It is no historical coincidence that many of the English vagrancy laws that made possible the transformation of dispossessed peasantry into proletarian labor were taken up, at times verbatim, in the US South after the collapse of Reconstruction and before Jim Crow in what became known as the Black Codes, which were integral to the convict leasing system.

20 UNRWA's first annual report in 1951 points out that, by the end of the year, it became obvious that the program of public works as the first measure in rehabilitation could neither provide the basis for continual employment nor remove anyone from the relief rolls. Indeed, in Gaza, where the language of catastrophe and uninhabitability had already seeped in, the Clapp mission's interim report concedes from the start that these works projects would employ only a "small portion" of refugees.

21 This notion of rehabilitation was seen as so central, and so anterior to everything else, that it would survive the eventual failure of both the small and large works and employment programs—it was immune, that is, to the collapse of the very mechanism designed to bring about its realization. UNRWA's annual report in 1956 would insist on the ongoing importance of rehabilitation, regardless of eventual political scenarios: "It cannot too often be emphasized that a refugee who has lost, or has never acquired, the habit of self-reliance and self-supporting work will be a useless burden on the community, whether he is later to be repatriated or to be resettled." Rehabilitation functioned as a kind of constant discursive reinterpretation of the Agency's practice that allowed for new techniques to be brought to bear on this consistent imperative.

22 Telegram, Sir Desmond Morton to Gordon R. Clapp, November 11, 1949, box 2: "UN Economic Survey Mission to the Middle East File, 1949," Clapp Papers.

23 This separation and disavowal of a discrete sphere called politics obscures, of course, the exceptionally political work that something like technical administration does. In a sense then this story might sound similar to the now-seminal account by James Ferguson (or the anthropology of development that builds on his insights; see Li 2007) that conceptualizes development as an "anti-politics machine," always "whisking political realities out

of sight, all the while performing, almost unnoticed, its own pre-eminently political operation of expanding bureaucratic state power" (1994, xv). More than bureaucratic power, however, what is at stake here, in political terms, is something that cuts much closer to what we can think of in terms of subject formation. That is, technical administration carries not only the force of a negation (the *de*-politicizing), but something more positive and productive; it carries a constitutive power, a power that finds shape in the camp as a device for the production of a settled labor force. It's this power that I argued was at stake for the Clapp mission in work as a form of rehabilitation, a rehabilitation that disavows its own political force even as it seeks to form moral subjects of self-improvement.

24 Letter, Gordon R. Clapp to Morris H. Rubin, editor of *The Progressive*, April 6, 1950, box 3: "General Correspondence," Clapp Papers.
25 Letter, Clapp to Rubin, April 6, 1950.
26 Letter, Clapp to Rubin, April 6, 1950.

2 The Camp, Formalized

1 Elsewhere I've elaborated what I see as the shortcomings of both the Agambenian or juridico-political model *and* its critiques. See Abourahme (2015, 2020).
2 It is worth pointing out that Palestinian inhabitants of the camps have long understood UNRWA in ambivalent terms. Especially in the first two to three decades, the Agency loomed over their lives as an outsized paternalistic but also often punitive disciplinary power: training inhabitants in new bodily habits and comportments, enforcing hygiene standards and regulations, rooting out political activity with local police forces, striking "undeserving" refugees off relief lists, punishing errant behavior by withholding rations, disrupting cultural gatherings that were deemed too political, even, in some accounts, spraying children with DDT at schools (al-Biss 2006). At the same time the Agency provided a modicum of relief, shelter, food support, medical care, employment, and, most especially, education, often regularly helping, as it still does today, refugee students to the top of the test score lists of their host countries. It also, and somewhat paradoxically, inscribed the status of refugees *as* refugees and thus their question as unresolved. Ilana Feldman (2012) has done some of the best work teasing out these ambivalences and their political effects.
3 In Syria, the Palestinian Arab Refugee Institution (PARI) was established in 1949 and renamed the General Administration for Palestinian Arab Refugees (GAPAR) in 1974. In Jordan, there was, first, a Ministry of Refugees (1949–50), which was replaced, naturally enough, given the political anxieties around construction, by the Ministry of Development and

Reconstruction (Wizarat al-Insha' wa al-Ta'mir) (1950–80). This was later effectively renamed the Ministry of Occupied Land Affairs (1980–88) and then replaced with what is still called the Department of Palestinian Affairs (DPA). In Lebanon and Gaza, up to 1969 and 1967, respectively, this task fell to military apparatuses. In Lebanon the military intelligence apparatus effectively administered the camps until 1969, when the Lebanese established the Directorate-General for the Administration of Palestine Refugee Affairs (DAPR). In Gaza the Egyptian Administration (1949–67) established the Department of Refugee Supervision, Government Assistance and Social Affairs, falling under the authority of Gaza's governor general. The Israeli State likewise, when it occupied the West Bank and Gaza Strip, established a Refugee Department in the military government (and what was later called the civil administration) in the occupied territories; that was in addition to the countless ministerial committees that almost every government formed to explore and pursue the dissolution of the "Arab refugee problem." To varying degrees, to construct or modify a shelter needed approval from these authorities as well as UNRWA.

4 Racial figurations of the refugees as naturally and incorrigibly selfish and indolent littered the early reports. Here's a passage from the 1951 annual report: "Owing to his intense individualism, the refugee has little sense of solidarity with his fellows. The concept of giving increased relief to the very needy is incomprehensible to him.... To his natural individualistic tendencies has now been added the characteristics of the typical refugee mentality, and its passive expectation of continued benefits" (UNRWA 1951).

5 Here, the Agency built simple concrete shelters, internal roads, and water distribution networks but handed over administration to state and, where possible, municipal governments. So strong was the drive to emplace and settle people out of the camps that in the peri-urban schemes the award of legal land title was an *obligatory* precondition for the receipt of a basic housing unit. Refugees-turned-landowners, the logic seemed to go, would be "professional refugees" no more. In the 1970s the Israeli State made a similar assumption when it built, sold, and helped finance housing for thousands of resettled Gazan refugees whom it hoped would become settled property owners.

6 The exception to this pattern was the Agency's field office in Syria that generally refrained from building any shelters but provided "roofing grants," roofs being the single most expensive item in the construction of a basic housing unit.

7 "Admittance into UNRWA Camps," memorandum, file RE 420, box RE 107, UNRWA Central Records.

8 "Admittance into UNRWA Camps."

9   "Camp Regulations," undated memorandum, file RE 410 part II, box RE 65, UNRWA Central Records.
10 "Camp Regulations."
11 "Camp Regulations."
12 "Camp Regulations."
13 Letter from UNRWA representative, November 24, 1960, UNRWA Central Records.
14 "Plans of Refugee Camps," letter from UNRWA representative, Gaza, to Director of Operations, HQ, November 24, 1960, file RE 420, box RE 107, UNRWA Central Records.
15 "Plans of Refugee Camps," letter from assistant field operations officer, Jordan, to UNRWA representative, Jordan, February 14, 1961, file RE 420, box RE 107, UNRWA Central Records.
16 "Shelter Planning," letter from director of relief to director of health, December 28, 1961, file RE 410/3, box RE 61, UNRWA Central Records.
17 "Plans of Refugee Camps," February 14, 1961.
18 "Camp Surveys in Jordan," letter from acting director, UNRWA Affairs, Jordan, to special assistant to director of relief, HQ, August 14, 1961, file RE 420, box RE 107, UNRWA Central Records.
19 "Situation in the Refugee Camps in Lebanon," memorandum from UNRWA commissioner-general to the UN Special Political Committee, January 15, 1970, file RE 400, box RE 104, UNRWA Central Records.
20 "Situation in the Refugee Camps in Lebanon."
21 "Situation in the Refugee Camps in Lebanon."
22 "Get Out of the Camps Business," draft report by director of relief services, January 27, 1970, file RE 400, box RE 104, UNRWA Central Records.
23 "The Extent of UNRWA Responsibility in Regard to Refugee Camps," draft paper, April 3, 1970, file RE 400, box RE 104, UNRWA Central Records.
24 "Get Out of the Camps Business."
25 "Administration of Refugee Camps," draft paper, September 12, 1970, file RE 400, box RE 104, UNRWA Central Records. In a later draft of the report, Fisher also added that when the Agency took over the camps, the secretary general himself, in March 1950, wrote to UNRWA's advisory commission and in paragraph 8 stated that part of the UNRWA's operational responsibilities was the "supervision of camps," a section Fisher highlighted and underlined to emphasize. To add to all this, year after year the Agency had been submitting annual reports that showcased its various construction and shelter-based relief efforts, and it received nothing but commend from the General Assembly.
26 "Get Out of the Camps Business."
27 "Get Out of the Camps Business."
28 "Get Out of the Camps Business."
29 "Get Out of the Camps Business."

30 In this sense, the subtitle of the political scientist Edward Buehrig's history of UNRWA, *A Study in Non-territorial Administration* (1972), seems like a contradiction in terms. What Fisher is scratching at, if not in so many words, is that there is no spatially bounded administration (a refugee camp) that is not also territorial, that is, that does not involve the political incorporation of land into power relations (statist or otherwise).

31 "Camps," final report by director of relief, submitted to commissioner-general, April 1, 1970, file RE 400, box RE 104, UNRWA Central Records.

32 "Get Out of the Camp Business."

33 "Agency Camps," letter from director of UNRWA Operations, Jordan, to director of relief, HQ, March 3, 1970, file RE 400, box RE 104, UNRWA Central Records.

34 "Camps."

35 "Camps."

36 "Camps."

37 "Camps."

38 Letter from UNRWA Liaison Office, New York, to director of relief, November 24, 1970, file RE 400, box RE 104, UNRWA Central Records.

39 "Alternatives to the Terms 'Camp' and 'Camp Leader,'" letter from director of relief to acting commissioner-general, December 26, 1970, file RE 400, box RE 104, UNRWA Central Records.

40 "Refugee Camps," letter from chief of Public Information Office to commissioner-general, November 14, 1970, file RE 400, box RE 104, UNRWA Central Records.

41 "Terminology Relating to Refugee Camps," letter from deputy commissioner-general to directors of all fields, February 11, 1971, file RE 400, box RE 104, UNRWA Central Records.

42 "Terminology of Refugee Camps," letter from director of UNRWA Operations, West Bank, to deputy commissioner-general, March 2, 1971, file RE 400, box RE 104, UNRWA Central Records.

43 "Terminology Relating to Refugee Camps," letter from field health officer to director of UNRWA operations WB, February 20, 1971, file RE 400, box RE 104, UNRWA Central Records.

44 "Terminology Relating to Refugee Camps," February 20, 1971.

45 Letter from chairman of the provisional staff committee to director of UNRWA operations WB, February 25, 1971, file RE 400, box RE 104, UNRWA Central Records.

46 "Terminology of Refugee Camps," letter from deputy commissioner-general to director of UNRWA Operations, West Bank, March 5, 1971, file RE 400, box RE 104, UNRWA Central Records.

47 Minutes from General Cabinet meeting, May 25, 1971, file RE 400, box RE 104, UNRWA Central Records.

48 "Report of the Commissioner-General of the United Nations Relief and Works Agency for Palestine Refugees in the Near East," July 1, 1970–June 30, 1971, A/8413, pp. 7–8, para 2.

49 While Arendt could not have read Kojève's reflections, published as they were in French only in 2004, and in English by Verso in 2014, Avital Ronnell (2012) suggests that there is some evidence that Arendt attended Kojève's seminars on the subject while briefly in Paris in the late 1930s.

50 Each of these theorists locates the causal point a little differently: for Kojève, constitutionalism, the rise of the legislature, and the separation of powers eliminate the authority of the father from politics; for Arendt, it is secularization and the splitting of authority from tradition and religion; for Sennett, it is the end of natural hierarchies and the rendering of dependence as unstable. But for all three, the conclusion is the same—the modern age is a protracted crisis of authority.

51 In her excellent anthropology of government in Gaza, Ilana Feldman (2008) tackles something similar when she makes the case that the British Mandate government (1917–48) and the Egyptian Administration (1948–67) in Gaza were effectively groundless; they lacked, she says, implicitly channeling Arendt, "the stable basis for legitimacy" (11). In this context of permanent crisis, the everyday work of government, the very functioning of the bureaucracy (filing, the accumulation of documents, the habits of civil servants, etc.) becomes the stuff of what she calls "reiterative authority" (14–17).

52 I would also distinguish this technocratic iteration, "administrative authority," from a Weberian legal authority of rule-based bureaucracy. The emphasis on competence and authored rules/regulations is shared, but the authority of the camp-regime is a form of authority that has very little to do with "belief" in the *validity* of legal statute, or an identifiable *rationality* of a set of rules, or, indeed, the rational legal subject that might do the work of identification in the first place. In fact, even if we assumed these forms of authority to be similar, Weber ([1946] 1991) was well aware that rule-based authority, as only one type of authority, could never function on its own (without charismatic or historical authority alongside it); on its own, as was the case with the Agency's "administrative authority," it appears startlingly shallow.

53 At one level this sounds similar to a broadly Gramscian notion of hegemony, but it is quite distinct. As it has been conventionally understood, Antonio Gramsci's concept of hegemony is read as a theory of consent. A ruling class secures the consent of other social classes, rather than simply coercing them; that is, it leads or directs (*dirigere*) as opposed to only dominating (*dominare*) other classes. Coercion, or what Gramsci calls "direct domination," might form a part of any hegemonic apparatus (and at times Gramsci defines hegemony as *direzione* + *dominazione*), but "moral

and intellectual leadership" is really made operative in civil society by ideology; it is a form of securing active or passive consent mediated by superstructure. A ruling class must "lead" before and after assuming power if it is ever to become a historical bloc ([1971] 2012, 55–60). In this reading, hegemony "relies more upon subtle mechanisms of ideological integration, cultural influence or even psychological dependency, than upon the threat of censure or violence" (Thomas 2013, 21). And, in fact, as an ethical relationship, this notion of hegemony can be seen as something of a precursor to later theories of subject formation (it's easy to trace a discontinuous line that runs through Gramsci's "hegemony," Althusser's "interpellation," and eventually Foucault's "subjectification," by the time of which, however, we have lost both ideology and consciousness as key terms). In this sense of politics, the inequality in power relations and the hierarchies of class or political formations are either obscured by ideology and formal political equality (citizenship and free contract), or are already constitutive of us as subjects in discourse, such that we obey authority/the law because we "know" it to be just, rational, good, and so on. Hegemony, we might say, moves obedience from injunction ("you must") to ethic ("I should"). This would be something akin to what Slavoj Žižek called, in a slightly different context, an obedience of conviction (as opposed to "real obedience"), obedience already mediated by our subjectivity—"that is, we are not really obeying the authority but simply following our judgment, which tells us that authority deserves to be obeyed in so far as it is good, wise, beneficent" (2008, 35). *However*, while in this version of hegemony and authority, as I'm using it here, both imply an obedience in which subjects retain their freedom (neither are just dominating coercion), they are otherwise quite different concepts. Hegemony here appears as a notion altogether closer to the persuasion that Arendt argues Plato very deliberately distinguished from authority. Authority, by contrast, does not seek to ideologically mediate or obscure hierarchy, but rather to naturalize it precisely *as* hierarchy, as inequality. The power of a father over a child (*the* pre-political authority) does not work by an appeal to persuasion, or with demonstrable proof of its truth, but ultimately by recourse to *the mutually recognized rightness of hierarchy* itself ("because I'm your father . . ."). Recognizing authority as normative and necessary is *not* per se to recognize authority as truth—indeed, authority might remain entirely irrational and incomprehensible. Instead, the legitimacy of an authoritative relation is premised on its very inequality; this is why, for Kojève, authority is defined by the voluntary renunciation of any possibility of resistance and is the very opposite of force. As such, when I talk of the antinomic pairing of force and authority above, I don't mean a mixture of consent-leadership and coercion-domination. I mean the endurance of a self-evident hierarchical inequality as the normative basis of rule (here formed around the technical or administrative expert) *but* ultimately reliant on force in ways that exceed the pure type we find in Arendt and Kojève.

3 The Camp, Overcome

A shorter version of this chapter appeared as "Nothing to Lose but Our Tents: The Camp, the Revolution, the Novel," *Journal of Palestine Studies* 48, no. 1 (Autumn 2018): 33–52.

1. In both Arabic and Hebrew, *adam* or *adama* denotes land or earth, or the surface of the earth. God having made the first man from earth or mud means the name "Adam" and the thing named are one.
2. I have stuck with the term *fugitive* for *farrun* that Humphrey Davies used in his 2006 translation, *Gate of the Sun*, because it captures the tension I'm interested in here: fugitives move and move with consequence, and refugees are beached, encamped, and immobile; fugitives violate the law, and refugees are external to it—two distinct relations to time and politics. The term *fugitive* also hints here at the connections—not simply in gestures of solidarity but in the very political epistemics themselves—between the Palestinian liberation movement and the Black Radical Tradition; for a generative reading of these epistemic and political affinities, see Burris (2019).
3. This, conversely (since she would not have considered any of this to be a politics of any sort), brings to my mind Arendt's comparison between the criminal and the refugee—the latter in contrast to the former exists in a world where "his treatment by others does not depend on what he does or does not do" (1973, 296). Whereas the criminal is still judged by her actions, the refugee has been evicted from the realm of human action itself. "They [refugees] are deprived, not of the right to freedom, but of the right to action; not of the right to think whatever they please, but of the right to opinion" (297).
4. A little earlier in the passage, Khoury also uses the colloquial form *farari*; both terms, *farari* or *farrun*, might involve a sense of shame or cowardice, an escaping or fleeing of the scene, which might be better captured in translation as *runaway*, but it is explicit that refugeehood is here the shameful subject position. In this sense, Khoury, through Yunis, might be revising conventional Arab and Palestinian perceptions of aspects of the *Nakba*: moving, even fleeing to escape danger, are not shameful, but, rather, stopping movement and accepting encampment in exile is the actual source of shame.
5. Of course, the name Khoury chose for his protagonist, Yunis—the Arabic Muslim and Qurʾanic equivalent of the biblical Jonah or Yunan—is telling; Yunis lived inside the belly of the beast (whale) without being digested by it. He entered and exited unscathed.

6 The passage is worth citing in full: "Both for the production on a mass scale of this communist consciousness, and for the success of the cause itself, the alteration of men on a mass scale is necessary, an alteration which can only take place in a practical movement, a *revolution*; the revolution is necessary, therefore, not only because the *ruling* class cannot be overthrown in any other way, but also because the class *overthrowing it* can only in a revolution succeed in ridding itself of all the muck of ages and become fitted to found society anew" (Marx and Engels 1998, 60).

7 If not as old as the career of revolution itself, then certainly around since Marx's writing on the 1848 revolutions. Yet, it should be added, that it seems to have been "resolved" in the anti-imperialist tradition and postcolonial world, in which, as Benedict Anderson ([1983] 1991) pointed out, the national form became so dominant that all socialist revolutions were at once national.

8 *Al-Hadaf* was the official political magazine of the Popular Front for the Liberation of Palestine (PFLP), established in 1969, published weekly in Beirut, and edited by Kanafani from 1969 until his death in 1972.

Tellingly, the word *intilaq* connotes both the start or beginning of something and the physical launching of a body or object into space in a projective or eruptive motion. It also shares the same root verb *t-l-q* (*talaqa*) for the word used (*atlaqa*) for the firing of a bullet, certainly not coincidentally because it points to the old connection between weapons and speed. That the article would also use the term *revolutionary bases* (*qaw'id al-thawra*) synonymously with *launching bases* is also telling, of course; revolution here *is* the very propulsive, kinetic force of insurrection.

9 This arguably resembles an Arendtian distinction, notwithstanding the very different notions of action and politics at play here. Action or *vita activa* is, of course, for Arendt (1998) a deliberative activity, the free exchange of opinion between equals acting in unison that *is* politics. It is very far from, in fact the opposite of, the "militant action" I'm referring to here—violence for Arendt being the stuff of powerlessness and unpredictability, and entirely exterior to politics. This action is closer to a Fanonian immediacy of bodily force in struggle that rises above speech—and in this regard it is significant that in Arabic the word for work and action is one and the same, *'amal*.

10 Though, as we will see, for all the change in gender norms and the instability of the division between life and politics, revolutionary literature itself often slipped back into a gendering of the sphere of life/the domestic as feminine, and the sphere of politics/public as masculine, with figures of insurgent heroism often remaining impoverishedly male.

11 All the novelists considered here were PLO members and belonged to one of the parties. Yahya Yakhlif was the secretary general of the PLO's Union of Writers and Journalists in the 1980s and would eventually become the

Palestinian Authority's minister of culture from 2003 to 2006. Rashad Abu Shawir was the deputy editor of the journal *al-Katib al-Filastini* (*The Palestinian Writer*), published by the Union of Writers and Journalists. Both were members of Fatah (the National Movement for the Liberation of Palestine), the largest party in the PLO. Ghassan Kanafani, a somewhat different kettle of fish, belonged to the Marxist-Leninist Popular Front and was editor of its main journal, *al-Hadaf*, from 1969 until his assassination in 1972. Yakhlif and Abu Shawir were considered bureaucrats and party men through and through and their literature criticized on those grounds. As for Kanafani, admittedly in a league of his own, the consensus is that he was able to write outside the bureaucratic controls and imperatives of party politics—a propagandist without ever doing propaganda, as some had it.

12 This almost existential urge to narrate and write might also explain, as Siddiq suggests, why so many Palestinian writers refused literary specialization and experimented with so many genres, styles, and forms of writing (literary, journalistic, prose, poetry, memoir, etc.) (1995, 99).

13 Notable examples in this respect are the memoirs of As'ad al-As'ad, *Layl al-Banafsaj* ([1988] 2010); Fathi al-Biss, *Inthiyal al-Dhakirah* (2008); and Fawaz Turki's two English-language texts, *The Disinherited* (1972) and *Soul in Exile* (1988). And even where the camp is not foregrounded as setting or context, it exerts a force on many of these texts. In Kanafani's earlier novels, for example, *Men in the Sun* ([1962] 1999) and *All That's Left to You* ([1966] 2004), the camp is not only what is left behind but in part what continues to drive forward the moving, and ultimately doomed, journey of the various protagonists.

14 While the defeat of revolutionary state-led Arab nationalism in the 1967 War had given the mass-based popular movement around the Palestinian Revolution the space to flourish, the 1980s had seen a steady advance of rightwing counterrevolutionary current in the region; the Gulf monarchies and the state regimes in Jordan in particular had never given up the fight. In addition, Sadat's rise to power in Egypt and the Camp David Accords that took Egypt and its army entirely into the imperial US fold (after the partial success of the 1973 War) and Saudi Arabia's massive financial gains during the oil crisis paved the way for a right-wing restoration at the expense of the Palestinian Revolution. It not only consolidated the dictatorships in the region but also opened the door for the strands of conservative Saudi-led political Islam that are very much still with us to this day. The Oslo Accords of 1993 that returned the PLO to the West Bank and Gaza as an interim (and derivative) authority, at the expense of the genuine popular uprising in the 1987 Intifada, were only the latest consolidation of a statist, bureaucratic trend that had its roots in the mid-1970s. For a discussion of how this shift affected the Arabic novel in general, see

Hafez (1994). For the Palestinian novel in particular, see Abu-Manneh (2014). On the transformation of the Palestinian movement from a revolutionary to statist force, see Y. Sayigh (1997) or, for an earlier and prescient glimpse of what was to come, Said ([1979] 1992).

15 The terms *appearance* and *essence* are, of course, borrowed from Lukács's defense of classical realism. For his critique of expressionism and response to Bloch, see Lukács ([1938] 2002). For a more elaborate account of his views on the stakes of realism, including his instructive comparison of horse-race scenes from Zola and Tolstoy, see the essay "Narrate or Describe?" in Lukács (1970).

16 Tahsil Dar, or "the levier," was so-named because, despite his current destitution, he was a former tax collector for Ottoman authorities in Palestine.

17 "Point Four projects" was the shorthand term used to refer to the various projects of technical assistance that the US administration emphasized for "developing countries" after Harry S. Truman's 1949 Point Four speech (a speech taken by some to mark the birth of twentieth-century paradigms of "development"). See Ekbladh (2009). For Palestinian refugees/exiles (and the sense that Yakhlif is pointing to) the Point Four projects were synonymous with resettlement schemes disguised as development.

18 As such, they are very far from today's en vogue forms of mediation in aesthetics that we might associate with naturalism (which eschews all forms of explanation), or even something like Jacques Rancière's (2006) celebration of "indeterminacy" and the resistance to interpretation.

19 It is also worth noting that Kanafani was well versed in the debates around the political and aesthetic stakes of realism and its emphasis on consciousness, and he had written a positive review of Lukács's literary theory in *al-Hadaf*. Faisal Darraj, a Palestinian critic and PLO member, also wrote fairly extensively and critically on Lukács and European literary theory, including in *Shuʿun Filastiniyya*.

20 If we follow Fredric Jameson, this fragmentary textuality and persistent melancholia might be as much of a mark of their "realism" as anything else. For Jameson, realism is not a description exactly, or strictly a genre, but a set of antinomies—"a compromise, an uncertain attempt to do two things at once" (Parker 2015), to both show and tell, describe and narrate, to have both a sense of irrevocable destiny and an eternal present of consciousness. The play of oppositions, Jameson (2015) tells us, is at work *within* realism itself (and not externally with some other kind of discourse, say modernism); what we call realism is nothing but a consequence of the tension between two terms. Realism, then, was dissolving the minute it began emerging. What I'm calling the Palestinian revolutionary novel was a literary form that, with influences from social realism, reproduced some of the tensions and stakes of the realist novel after its time, but in ways that had much more to do with its own political predicaments

than anything internal to the form or genre itself. Whether we can call them a type of social realism (a realism after realism) is a moot point. And though there were marked similarities between the literary debates that raged in the Arab world in the 1950s and 1960s and those that animated parts of the Left in 1930s Europe (Abu-Manneh 2014), the fact remains that any direct mapping of these novels back onto the terms of European literary history, let alone the fierce debates of German Marxist literary theory, makes very little sense.

21 Dahbur also has the merit of being very critical of Abu Shawir's sexism and crude masculinity in certain passages (for example, when describing the hasty retreat of the much-hated Jordanian police from the camp in the 1967 War, Abu Shawir's protagonist notes that they remembered that "government is a feminine word"—in Arabic the noun *hukuma* taking feminine form). Disappointingly, Dahbur (1977, 239) ends up putting this down to "eastern sediments" in Abu Shawir's work.

22 In *Um Saad*, for example, city life outside the camp is always more fraught and crushing. The inside/outside binary of city and camp is almost inverted—it's the camp that appears as community, with the city as a space of alienation. In one scene Um Saad looks out at "the clamorous, crowded, heaping city in the distance...through the dust of a sad evening" (Kanafani [1969] 2010, 219).

23 I translated *la'la* as "perchance" to emphasize (without fully conveying) the semantic sense of wishful sentiment the word has (which *rubama* does not). This semantic difference notwithstanding, both words function to introduce uncertainty and hesitancy into the narrative.

24 In Rancière's somewhat tautological reading of aesthetics and politics, he proposes the now well-trodden notion of a "distribution of sensibility" (*partage du sensible*) to propose an understanding of aesthetics as "a delimitation of spaces and times, of the visible and the invisible, of speech and noise that simultaneously determines the place and the stakes of politics as a form of experience" (2006, 13). Both key terms are doubled—*partage* as sharing *and* partition, and *sensible* as that which is sensory *and* that which is made to make sense. It is worth pointing out that this *distributive* conceptualization of aesthetics/politics was not Rancière's alone. Much earlier, Gilles Deleuze, for one, in his insistence on the importance of Michel Foucault's thought to visuality, gives this conceptualization a distinctly temporal taste to argue that "each stratum or historical formation implies *a distribution of the visible and the articulable* which acts upon itself" (1988, 48, emphasis added).

4 The Camp, Undone

1. This praise is for the 1991 translation, by Ina Friedman, of Rubinstein's 1990 Hebrew-language book, *Hibuk ha-Te'enah* (*Embrace of the Fig Tree*), which had been published by Keter in Jerusalem.
2. Scholars like Nur Masalha (2003) and Elia Zureik have done much to document the history of Israeli resettlement schemes. Masalha, working across Israeli archival sources, has meticulously documented the long litany of plans and proposals aimed at "liquidating the refugee problem," with a focus on the pre-1967 period and especially the various employment schemes. While he does not really delve into the question of the camp in Israeli politics in any substantive sense, he does recognize that the camps became a political object in their own right. Removing the camps, he writes, became urgent not just because they posed "a security threat" but, as he has it, because they were a "visible reminder" of the dispossession, one that he adds had its own "psychological considerations" in Israeli politics. Norma Hazboun (1996), in her doctoral thesis, documented post-1967 plans in Gaza's camps, but she did not have access to the Israel State Archives and stops short of conceptualizing the place of the camp in Israel's settler politics. Alona Nitzan-Shiftan and Fatina Abreek-Zubiedat's (2018) more recent chapter, of which I make use here, also focuses on Israeli plans for Gazan camps. But while they recognize the centrality of return, their focus is on the internal territorial dynamics between cities and camps in the Gaza Strip as they played out in the Israeli State's development projects. There is no engagement with the question of settler colonialism or its temporal politics.
3. The exact numbers of Palestinian refugees lured or pressured into going to Latin America are unclear. The Paraguay scheme ran for three years from 1967 to 1970, and the plan seems to have envisaged tens of thousands, but it's likely that about one thousand were displaced, most of them ending up in the border area between Paraguay and Brazil. Tom Segev writes that at the time, the late summer of 1967, the Israeli Foreign Ministry was functioning in effect as a "global travel agency" that was effectively a displacement machine: "Upon departing the country, the emigrants had to leave behind the identification cards they had received from the military government. They also had to sign a form declaring, in Hebrew and Arabic, that they were leaving willingly and understood that they would not be able to return without a special permit. They signed with thumbprints; if they could, they added their names in writing. Men signed for their wives. The form was occasionally modified, as was the custom in the occupation bureaucracy" (2008, 520).
4. In referring to negation, I am leaving aside, for now, the importance of "negative critique" in the Marxist tradition and post-Marxist continen-

tal theory, as well as the recent calls for a return to the negative/negation and immanent rupture (as distinct from "negative dialects" *and* against the seeming triumph of affirmationist thought in contemporary continental theory) (Noys 2010). As I use it, I mean negation here in a sense closer to Freud than Marx, if ultimately only as a point of departure.

5 "Present absentees" is the juridical category given to those non-Jews who remained in what became the State of Israel but were not in their original villages and towns of residence when the ceasefire was called into effect. In 1948 Israel established a body called the Custodian of Absentee Property that had the capacity to expropriate the property of "present absentees" and transfer it to the state (first carried out under the 1948 "Emergency Regulation Concerning Absentee Property" and then in 1950 as part of the "Absentee Property Law"). In 1950, "present absentees" amounted to almost one-third of the Palestinians in Israel. Today up to 420,000 Palestinian citizens of Israel are considered "present absentees."

6 What came to be known as the "Nakba Law," "Amendment No. 40 to the Budget Foundations Law," passed in the Israeli Knesset in 2011 and allows the finance minister to withdraw state funding from any institution that rejects the legitimacy of Israel as a "Jewish and democratic state" or commemorates "Israel's Independence Day or the day on which the state was established as a day of mourning." The bill's initial form, which failed to pass in full, called for the criminal prosecution of anybody commemorating the *Nakba* or marking Israel's "Independence Day" as a day of mourning.

7 Some pushed for resettling Gaza's refugees in the northern Sinai town of al-'Arish, aware that it had been largely evacuated during the war and now offered vacant houses. Others, including an economist and later director of the Bank of Israel, Michael Bruno, called for removing all of Gaza's camps and resettling their inhabitants in the Jordan Valley camps vanquished during the 1967 War. This had the benefit of preventing the refugees previously encamped in the valley and now displaced for a second time in the 1967 War from returning, and, in the event that the Jordan Valley was returned to Jordan, would mean getting rid of Gaza's refugees for good. But the appetite for settlement in the West Bank was already too strong and Begin, Allon, and Moshe Dayan all opposed this plan on the grounds that the Jordan Valley was (in the summer of 1967) earmarked for Jewish colonization. Bruno and other academics would nonetheless go on to form a committee, dubbed the "Professors Committee," that would spend years researching attitudes and views of Palestinian refugees of the West Bank and Gaza, with a view to their resettlement.

8 It has been reported that in some cases of resettlement the Israeli State demanded that refugees give up their UNRWA registration card (which allows them to draw rations and acts as confirmation of their refugee sta-

tus); I have been told this was the case by refugees, and Nitzan-Shiftan and Abreek-Zubiedat (2018, 147) also reproduce this claim. I have, however, seen no archival evidence of it as a policy; if it was implemented, it was very inconsistent. On the contrary, as seen above, the stated policy was that refugee status as a legal category was to be kept untouched in camp removal or improvement. Moreover, it's not clear what authority the Israeli military government would have had to annul a UN registration card in the first place.

9 It is worth noting that 350 of the 370 new settlements built in the decade between 1948 and 1958 would be built on the lands of the depopulated villages and towns, often directly on the same sites.

10 Weitz wrote numerous articles that drew on his experience of planning the new Jewish settlements of Israel, many of which appeared in international planning and development journals. See, for example, Weitz, Pelley, and Applebaum (1980).

11 "Plan for the Settlement of 50,000 Refugees in the al-'Arish Area," June 30, 1969, Prime Minister's Office, 7440/A6, Israel State Archives.

12 "Plan for the Settlement of 50,000 Refugees."
13 "Plan for the Settlement of 50,000 Refugees."
14 "Plan for the Settlement of 50,000 Refugees."
15 "Plan for the Settlement of 50,000 Refugees."
16 "Plan for the Settlement of 50,000 Refugees."

17 Letter from Moshe Safdie to Mordechai Bentov, January 10, 1968, file RE 300 (14), UNRWA Central Records.

18 Letter, Safdie to Bentov, January 10, 1968.

19 In this sense, we might add, Safdie is firmly part of an early generation of Israeli cultural figures, from architects to novelists, who partook or benefited, one way or another, in the erasure of the Palestinian landscape and then mourned its absence. The "Arab village," an architectural trope in its own right, that prototype of "architecture without architects," and as Owen Hatherley (2008) shows, present in the midcentury swirl between modernism and tradition, became for these Israeli architects a fetishized object of recovery, to the extent that they would quite consciously restage its built syntax in numerous Israeli settlements (even if they always missed the semantics).

20 Letter from Mordechai Ben Porat to Prime Minister Menachem Begin, July 20, 1983, 8197/A-12, Prime Minister's Office, Israel State Archives.

21 Around 4,000 people (516 families) would eventually find themselves resettled in the Canada project on the "wrong" side of the border. They would all eventually be forced to relocate again after the 1979 Camp David Accords, when Egypt made it clear that they refused to add a single Palestinian refugee to their territory. Most of these refugees were rehoused in what become known as Tal al-Sultan, north of Rafah Camp, but it would take until 2000 to move the last families back to the Strip.

22 "Rafah Construction Projects," memorandum, October 19, 1972, file RE 300 (IS-1), UNRWA Central Records.

23 Dov Eizenberg, "The Planning Principles for the Housing Complexes for the Refugees and Bedouins," 1976, personal papers. Eizenberg maintains an online personal record of these projects that is a mixture of memoranda, exchanges, newspaper clippings, and official documents.

24 Memo from commissioner-general to director of UNRWA operations, Gaza, May 16, 1975, file OR 215 (IS-1) II, UNRWA Central Records.

25 Yair Kotler, *Ha'aretz* supplement, December 19, 1975, Eizenberg personal papers.

26 Dani Tzikdoni, "10,000 Refugees Received Apartments in New Neighborhoods," *Davar*, January 12, 1975, Eizenberg personal papers.

27 "Refugee Families Who Demolished Their Shelters," letter from refugee services officer to director of UNRWA operations, Gaza, January 11, 1975, file OR 215 (IS-1) III, UNRWA Central Records.

28 "Demolition and Rehousing in Rafah Camp 1 to 31 December 1974," letter from director of UNRWA operations, Gaza, to commissioner-general, January 4, 1975, file OR 215 (IS-1) III, UNRWA Central Records.

29 "Annual Report—Statistics and Law," Trust Fund for the Economic Development and Rehabilitation of Refugees, December 1971, Prime Minister's Office, file 4124-19/P, Israel State Archives.

30 This kind of inaccuracy runs through the article. What "mobility" amounts to here is very unclear, given that both the Gaza Strip and the West Bank are under siege and closure. As are the claims about ownership, which are much more complicated than what Marx accounts for, and certainly don't extend to any title to land. He later also makes the absurd claim that although only Jordan gave the refugees full citizenship, "the refugees' freedom of movement and employment was never restricted in the other Arab countries" (Marx 1992, 284).

31 For a reading of settler recognition as effectively a technique of further dispossession, see Coulthard (2014) and Povinelli (2002).

32 David Lloyd (2012) gets at this tension in Israeli politics when he points out that Israel at once depends on an image of itself as a besieged representative of "Western civilization," *but* at the same time needs recourse in practice to institutions and measures that "civilized" nations have eschewed (legal distinction between citizenship and nationality, states of siege, severe restrictions of the freedom of movement, military occupation, etc.).

33 It is worth noting that the State of Israel does not recognize an Israeli nationality. Native Palestinians, who make up over one-fifth or 21 percent of the citizenry, are citizens of Israel but not members of the Israeli nation-state, in which only Jews have the *exclusive* right to self-determination. This split between citizen and nation was recently consolidated and con-

stitutionally formalized on July 19, 2018, when the Israeli Knesset voted to approve the "Jewish Nation-State Basic Law," which decreed that "the State of Israel is the nation-state of the Jewish people" and that the "state views the development of Jewish settlement as a national value, and will act to encourage and promote its establishment and consolidation." My point here is that this explicit codification of racial supremacy should be read as an effect of the inability of the settler project to progress toward its own end of self-supersession and cease being a settler colony.

Coda

1. Architects and urbanists have, of course, long insisted that housing is a privileged site of politics. They've shown how housing has been an arena for the regulation of collective life through the reproduction of social norms and the apparatus of the family, how it's been a site through which markets and states have ensured social reproduction, chiefly through real estate development. But what Reinhold Martin, for example, excavates beneath the post-Arendtian clamor about the loss of the public is how the house is itself a site of changing political topology, and as such it is not simply a relocation of the political order but its overturning or reversal. And the fact that, in our own post-Fordist era of immaterial labor and the financialized self, factory and house seem to merge entirely would demand exceeding the terms of Arendtian political thought and seeking "a thought capable of considering the house—and with it, housing—as a site in which agon repeats, daily" (Martin 2016, 107). What gets bundled under the politics of housing is radically changing, in ways, I think, that exceed what this framework can hold.

2. In saying *inhabitation*, I am actively not saying *dwelling*. What I mean is very far from the metaphysics of authenticity and interiority usually associated with the uptake of broadly Heideggerean notions of dwelling.

REFERENCES

Archives

Birzeit University Palestinian Archive, Birzeit University, Ramallah, the West Bank, the Occupied Territories.
Israel State Archives (ISA), Jerusalem, Israel/Palestine.
National Archives and Records Administration, the Harry S. Truman Presidential Library, Independence, Missouri, United States.
Roberta and Stanley Bogen Library and Documentation Center of the Harry S. Truman Research Institute, the Hebrew University, Jerusalem, Israel/Palestine.
United Nations Archives and Records Management Section (UN-ARMS), New York City, New York, United States.
United Nations Relief and Works Agency (UNRWA) Central Records Office, Amman, Jordan.

Published Primary Material and Secondary Material

Abd al-Jawad, Salih. 2007. "Zionist Massacres: The Creation of the Palestinian Refugee Problem in the 1948 War." In *Israel and the Palestinian Refugees*, edited by Emil Benvenisti, Chaim Gans, and Sari Hanafi, 59–127. Heidelberg: Springer.
Abdo, Nahla. 1991. "Racism, Zionism and the Palestinian Working Class, 1920–1947." *Studies in Political Economy* 37 (1): 59–92.
Abourahme, Nasser. 2015. "Assembling and Spilling-Over: Towards an 'Ethnography of Cement' in a Palestinian Refugee Camp." *International Journal of Urban and Regional Research* 39 (2): 200–217.
Abourahme, Nasser. 2016. "The Productive Ambivalences of Post-revolutionary Time." In *Time, Temporality, and Violence in International Relations*, edited by A. Agathangelou and K. Killian, 129–55. London: Routledge.
Abourahme, Nasser. 2020. "The Camp." *Comparative Studies of South Asia, Africa and the Middle East* 40 (1): 35–42.

Abu El-Haj, Nadia. 2002. *Facts on the Ground: Archaeological Practice and Territorial Self-Fashioning in Israeli Society*. Chicago: University of Chicago Press.

Abu-Laban, Yasmeen, and Abigail Bakan. 2019. *Israel, Palestine, and the Politics of Race: Exploring Identity and Power in a Global Context*. London: Bloomsbury.

Abu-Manneh, Bashir. 2014. "Palestinian Trajectories: Novel and Politics since 1948." *Modern Language Quarterly* 75 (4): 511–39. https://doi.org/10.1215/00267929-2796886.

Abu-Manneh, Bashir. 2015. "Tonalities of Defeat and Palestinian Modernism." *Minnesota Review*, no. 85, 56–79. https://doi.org/10.1215/00265667-3144652.

Abu Shawir, Rashad. 1974. *Al-'Ushaq* [The lovers]. Beirut: Daᵉrat al-I'lam wa al-Thaqafa.

Abu Sitta, Salman, and Terry Rempel. 2014. "The ICRC and the Detention of Palestinian Civilians in Israel's 1948 POW/Labor Camps." *Journal of Palestine Studies* 43 (4): 11–38. https://doi.org/10.1525/jps.2014.43.4.11.

Agamben, Giorgio. 1998. *Homo Sacer: Sovereign Power and Bare Life*. Translated by Daniel Heller-Roazen. Stanford, CA: Stanford University Press.

Agamben, Giorgio. 2009. *"What Is an Apparatus?" and Other Essays*. Translated by David Kishik and Stefan Pedatella. Stanford, CA: Stanford University Press.

Agamben, Giorgio. 2020. "Inhabiting and Building." *Ill Will*, June 10. https://illwill.com/inhabiting-and-building.

Agier, Michel. 2011. *Managing the Undesirables: Refugee Camps and Humanitarian Government*. Translated by David Fernbach. Cambridge, UK: Polity.

al-As'ad, As'ad. (1988) 2010. *Layl al-Banafsaj* [Night of the violet]. Amman: Dar al-Shuruq.

al-Biss, Fathi. 2008. *Inthiyal al-Dhakirah* [The overflowing of memory]. Amman: Dar al-Shuruq.

Alderman, Derek H., and Robert N. Brown. 2011. "When a New Deal Is Actually an Old Deal: The Role of TVA in Engineering a Jim Crow Racialized Landscape." In *Engineering Earth*, edited by S. Brunn, 1901–16. Dordrecht: Springer.

al-Khatib, Muhammad Nimr. 1951. *Min Athar al-Nakba*. Damascus: al-Matba'a al-'Umumiyya.

Allan, Diana. 2014. *Refugees of the Revolution: Experiences of Palestinian Exile*. Stanford, CA: Stanford University Press.

Allweil, Yael. 2016. *Homeland: Zionism as Housing Regime, 1860–2011*. New York: Routledge.

Alnajada, Heba. 2023. "'This Camp Is Full of *Hujaj*!': Claims to Land and the Built Environment in a Contested Palestinian Refugee Camp in Amman." *Comparative Studies of South Asia, Africa and the Middle East* 43 (3): 275–92. https://doi.org/10.1215/1089201X-10896858.

al-Quds. 1983. "Khita l'tawtin Laji∍i al-Difa wa Ghaza" [A plan to settle West Bank and Gaza refugees]. November 21.

al-Saleh, Samar. 2022. "Britain's Prison Labor Camps: Imperial-Zionist Class War against Palestinian Men (1917–1948)." Master's thesis, New York University, May 2022.

al-Tha∍r. 1955. "al-Nazihin Yatlubun al-Silah wa Yarfudun at-Tawtin" [The exiles demand arms and refuse settlement projects]. March 10.

Anderson, Benedict. (1983) 1991. *Imagined Communities: Reflections on the Origin and Spread of Nationalism*. Rev. ed. London: Verso.

Appadurai, Arjun. 2002. "Deep Democracy: Urban Governmentality and the Horizon of Politics." *Public Culture* 14 (1): 21–47.

Arafat, Yasser. 1982. "A Discussion with Yasser Arafat." *Journal of Palestine Studies* 11 (2): 3–15. https://doi.org/10.2307/2536267.

Arendt, Hannah. 1973. *The Origins of Totalitarianism*. New York: Harcourt.

Arendt, Hannah. 1998. *The Human Condition*. 2nd ed. Chicago: University of Chicago Press.

Arendt, Hannah. 2000. "What Is Authority?" In *The Portable Hannah Arendt*, edited by Peter Baehr, 462–508. New York: Penguin.

Arneil, Barbara. 2012. "Liberal Colonialism, Domestic Colonies, and Citizenship." *History of Political Thought* 33 (3): 491–523.

'Ashur, Radwa. 1977. *Al-Tariq ila al-Khayma al-Ukhra* [The way to the other tent]. Beirut: Dar al-Adab.

Assi, Seraje. 2018. *The History and Politics of the Bedouin: Reimagining Nomadism in Modern Palestine*. London: Routledge.

Azoulay, Ariella. 2016. "Archive." *Political Concepts*, no. 1. https://www.politicalconcepts.org/archive-ariella-azoulay/.

Azoulay, Ariella, and Adi Ophir. 2009. "The Order of Violence." In *The Power of Inclusive Exclusion: Anatomy of Israeli Rule in the Occupied Palestinian Territories*, edited by A. Ophir, M. Givoni, and S. Hanafi, 99–140. New York: Zone.

Badir, Adnan. 1969. "*al-Hadaf* Tashhad: Tahawul al-Mukhayyamat ila Mu'askarat" [*al-Hadaf* witnesses: The transformation of the camps into bases]. *al-Hadaf* 1 (17): 1.

Balibar, Étienne. 2002. *Politics and the Other Scene*. New York: Verso.

Balibar, Étienne. 2019. "Exiles in the 21st Century: The New 'Population Law' of Absolute Capitalism." Lecture presented at the School of Oriental and African Studies, London, February 19, 2019.

Balibar, Étienne, and Immanuel Wallerstein. 1991. *Race, Nation, Class: Ambiguous Identities*. New York: Verso.

Barakat, Rana. 2017. "Writing/Righting Palestine Studies: Settler Colonialism, Indigenous Sovereignty and Resisting the Ghost(s) of History." *Settler Colonial Studies* 8 (3): 1–15. https://doi.org/10.1080/2201473X.2017.1300048.

Bauman, Zygmunt. 1989. *Modernity and the Holocaust*. Cambridge, UK: Polity.

Baumgarten, Helga. 2006. *Min al-Tahrir ila al-Dawla: Tarikh al-haraka al-wataniya al-filastiniya 1948–1988* [From liberation to the state: The history of the Palestinian national movement 1948–1988]. Translated by Muhamad Abu Zayd. Ramallah: Muwatin.

Ben-Tal, D. 1991. "Welcome to Jabaliya." *Guardian*, August 17.

Ben Zeev, Nimrod. 2020. "'We Built This Country': Palestinian Citizens in Israel's Construction Industry, 1948–73." *Jerusalem Quarterly* 84 (Winter): 10–46.

Ben Zeev, Nimrod. 2021. "Palestine along the Colour Line: Race, Colonialism, and Construction Labour, 1918–1948." *Ethnic and Racial Studies* 44 (12): 2190–212.

Berda, Yael. 2017. *Living Emergency: Israel's Permit Regime in the Occupied West Bank*. Stanford, CA: Stanford University Press.

Berg, Kjersti. 2014. "From Chaos to Order and Back: The Construction of UNRWA Shelters, 1950–1970." In *UNRWA and Palestinian Refugees: From Relief and Works to Human Development*, edited by Sari Hanafi et al., 109–29. London: Routledge.

Bhandar, Brenna. 2018. *Colonial Lives of Property: Land, Law, and Racial Regimes of Ownership*. Durham, NC: Duke University Press.

Blackhawk, Maggie. 2019. "Federal Indian Law as Paradigm within Public Law." *Harvard Law Review* 132 (7): 1787. https://ssrn.com/abstract=3486307.

Borges, Jorge Louis. 1984. *Evaristo Carriego*. Translated by Norman Thomas Di Giovanni. New York: Dutton.

Bradley, Megan. 2014. *Refugee Repatriation: Justice, Responsibility and Redress*. Reprint ed. Cambridge: Cambridge University Press.

Brilliants, Moshe. 1971. "400 Huts Razed in Gaza Camp." *Times*, July 31.

Brown, Bill. 2003. *A Sense of Things: The Object Matter of American Literature*. Chicago: University of Chicago Press.

Brown, Wendy. 2010. *Walled States, Waning Sovereignty*. Princeton, NJ: Princeton University Press.

Bruyneel, Kevin. 2007. *The Third Space of Sovereignty: The Postcolonial Politics of US-Indigenous Relations*. Minneapolis: University of Minnesota Press.

Buehrig, Edward H. 1972. *U.N. and the Palestinian Refugees: A Study in Non-territorial Administration*. Bloomington: Indiana University Press.

Burris, Greg. 2019. *The Palestinian Idea: Film, Media, and the Radical Imagination*. Philadelphia: Temple University Press.

Case, Henry L. 1964. "Gordon R. Clapp: The Role of Faith, Purposes and People in Administration." *Public Administrative Review* 24 (2): 86–91.

Clapp, Gordon R. 1947. "Adventures in Faith and Works." *Ethics* 58 (1): 57–62.

Clapp, Gordon R. 1948a. "Public Administration in an Advancing South." *Public Administration Review* 8 (3): 169–75.

Clapp, Gordon R. 1948b. "TVA: A Democratic Method for the Development of a Region's Resources." *Vanderbilt Law Review* 1 (2): 183–93.

Clarno, Andy. 2017. *Neoliberal Apartheid: Palestine/Israel and South Africa after 1994*. Chicago: University of Chicago Press.

Collins, John. 2011. *Global Palestine*. London: Hurst.

Coulthard, Glen. *Red Skin, White Masks: Rejecting the Colonial Politics of Recognition*. Minneapolis: University of Minnesota Press, 2014.

Dahbur, Ahmad. 1977. "*al-'Ushaq*: Rashad Abu Shawir." *Shu'un Filastiniyya*, no. 72, November.

Darraj, Faisal. 1996. *Bu's al-Thaqafa: Fi al-Mu'sasa al-Filastiniyya* [The poverty of culture: On the Palestinian institution]. Beirut: Dar al-Adab.

Darwish, Mahmud. 1972. "'Urs al-Dam al-Filastini" [The Palestinian blood wedding]. *Shu'un Filastiniyya*, no. 12, August.

Darwish, Mahmud. 1973. *Yawmiyat al-Huzn al-'Adi* [Journal of ordinary grief]. Beirut: Markiz al-Abhath al-Filastini.

Darwish, Mahmud. 2002. "Interview with Raja Shehadeh." BOMB 81, Fall. https://bombmagazine.org/articles/mahmoud-darwish/.

Darwish, Mahmud. 2010. *Journal of an Ordinary Grief*. Translated by Ibrahim Muhawi. Brooklyn, NY: Archipelago.

Davis, John P. 1935. "The Plight of the Negro in the Tennessee Valley." *Crisis*, October.

De Genova, Nicholas. 2016. "The European Question: Migration, Race, and Postcoloniality in Europe." *Social Text* 34 (3): 75–102.

Deleuze, Gilles. 1988. *Foucault*. Translated by Sean Hand. Minneapolis: University of Minnesota Press.

Deleuze, Gilles. 2007. *Two Regimes of Madness: Texts and Interviews, 1975–1995*. Edited by David Lapoujade. Translated by Ames Hodges and Mike Taormina. Cambridge, MA: Semiotext(e).

Deleuze, Gilles, and Elias Sanbar. 1998. "The Indians of Palestine." Translated by Timothy S. Murphy. *Discourse* 20 (3). http://www.jstor.org/stable/41389493.

Dolar, Mladen. 2009. "Freud and the Political." *Theory and Event* 12 (3). https://doi.org/10.1353/tae.0.0085.

Dolar, Mladen. 2021. "The Future of Authority." *Philosopher* 109 (2). https://www.thephilosopher1923.org/post/the-future-of-authority.

Du Bois, W. E. B. (1935) 2013. *Black Reconstruction in America: Toward a History of the Part Which Black Folk Played in the Attempt to Reconstruct Democracy in America, 1860–1880*. London: Routledge.

Efrat, Zvi. 2018. *The Object of Zionism*. Liepzig: Spector Books.

Ekbladh, David. 2009. *The Great American Mission: Modernization and the Construction of an American World Order*. Princeton, NJ: Princeton University Press.

Elmusa, Sharif. 2012. "Portable Absence: My Camp Re-membered." In *Seeking Palestine: New Palestinian Writing on Exile and Home*, edited by Penny Johnson and Raja Shehadeh, 22–43. Delhi: Women Unlimited.

Endnotes and Aaron Benanav. 2010. "Misery and Debt: On the Logic and History of Surplus Populations and Surplus Capital." *Endnotes* 2.

Englert, Sai. 2020. "Settlers, Workers, and the Logic of Accumulation by Dispossession." *Antipode* 52 (6): 1647–66. https://doi.org/10.1111/anti.12659.

Eshel, Amir. 2011. "Writing the Unsaid: Israeli Prose and the Question of Palestinian Flight and Expulsion." Accessed July 20, 2017. http://www.michalgovrin1.com/138470/Writing-the-Unsaid-Amir-Eshel.

Estes, Nick. 2019. *Our History Is the Future*. New York: Verso.

Fanon, Frantz. 2005. *The Wretched of the Earth*. Translated by Richard Philcox. Reprint ed. New York: Grove.

Farred, Grant. 2008. "The Unsettler." *South Atlantic Quarterly* 107 (4): 791–808. https://doi.org/10.1215/00382876-2008-017.

Farrell, William E. 1976. "Israeli Housing for Gaza Refugees Spurs Friction with UN." *New York Times*, November 24.

Fassin, Didier. 2011. *Humanitarian Reason: A Moral History of the Present*. Berkeley: University of California Press.

Feldman, Ilana. 2008. *Governing Gaza: Bureaucracy, Authority, and the Work of Rule, 1917–1967*. Durham, NC: Duke University Press.

Feldman, Ilana. 2012. "The Challenge of Categories: UNRWA and the Definition of a 'Palestine Refugee.'" *Journal of Refugee Studies* 25 (3): 387–406. https://doi.org/10.1093/jrs/fes004.

Feldman, Ilana. 2015. "What Is a Camp? Legitimate Refugee Lives in Spaces of Long-Term Displacement." *Geoforum* 66 (November): 244–52. https://doi.org/10.1016/j.geoforum.2014.11.014.

Ferguson, James. 1994. *The Anti-politics Machine: Development, Depoliticization, and Bureaucratic Power in Lesotho*. New ed. Minneapolis: University of Minnesota Press.

Feron, James. 1969. "Israel Weighs a Refugee Resettlement Plan." *New York Times*, June 9.

Flusser, Vilém. 2003. *The Freedom of the Migrant: Objections to Nationalism*. Translated by Kenneth Kronenberg. Urbana: University of Illinois Press.

Ford, Lisa. 2010. *Settler Sovereignty: Jurisdiction and Indigenous People in America and Australia, 1788–1836*. Cambridge, MA: Harvard University Press.

Forth, Aidan. 2017. *Barbed-Wire Imperialism: Britain's Empire of Camps, 1876–1903*. Berkeley: University of California Press.

Foucault, Michel. 1995. *Discipline and Punish: The Birth of the Prison*. 2nd ed. Translated by Alan Sheridan. New York: Vintage.

Foucault, Michel. 2009. *Security, Territory, Population: Lectures at the Collège de France, 1977–1978*. Edited by Michel Senellart. Translated by Graham Burchell. New York: Picador.

Freud, Sigmund. (1925) 2001. *The Complete Psychological Works of Sigmund Freud: "The Ego and the Id" and Other Works, Vol. 19*. New ed. London: Vintage.

Gabiam, Nell. 2012. "When 'Humanitarianism' Becomes 'Development': The Politics of International Aid in Syria's Palestinian Refugee Camps."

American Anthropologist 114 (1): 95–107. https://doi.org/10.1111/j.1548-1433.2011.01399.x.

Gill, Bikrum Singh. 2023. "A World in Reverse: The Political Ecology of Racial Capitalism." *Politics* 43 (2): 153–68. https://doi.org/10.1177/0263395721994439.

Gilmour, David. 1980. *Dispossessed: The Ordeal of the Palestinians, 1917–1980*. London: Sidgwick and Jackson.

Gitlin, Todd. 2014. "BDS and the Politics of 'Radical' Gestures." *Tablet*, October 27.

Globe and Mail. 1983. "Israel Plans to Rout Palestinians from West Bank Refugee Camps." April 27.

Gniadek, Melissa. 2017. "The Times of Settler Colonialism." *Lateral: Journal of the Cultural Studies Association* 6 (1). https://doi.org/10.25158/L6.1.8.

Goldberg, David Theo. 2008. *The Threat of Race: Reflections on Racial Neoliberalism*. Malden, MA: Wiley-Blackwell.

Goldstone, Brian. 2014. "Life after Sovereignty." *History of the Present* 4 (1): 97–113.

Gordon, Neve. 2008. *Israel's Occupation*. Berkeley: University of California Press.

Gramsci, Antonio. (1971) 2012. *Selections from the Prison Notebooks*. Translated by Quentin Hoare and Geoffrey Nowell Smith. New York: International Publishers.

Grant, Nancy L. 1990. *TVA and Black Americans: Planning for the Status Quo*. Philadelphia: Temple University Press.

Greeman, Richard. 1967. "Literary and Revolutionary Realism in Victor Serge." *Yale French Studies*, no. 39, 146–59. https://doi.org/10.2307/2929489.

Hafez, Sabry. 1994. "The Transformation of Reality and the Arabic Novel's Aesthetic Response." *Bulletin of the School of Oriental and African Studies, University of London* 57 (1): 93–112.

Hage, Ghassan. 2016. "État de Siège: A Dying Domesticating Colonialism?" *American Ethnologist* 43 (1): 38–49. https://doi.org/10.1111/amet.12261.

Handel, Ariel. 2014. "Gated/Gating Community: The Settlement Complex in the West Bank." *Transactions of the Institute of British Geographers* 39 (4): 504–17. https://doi.org/10.1111/tran.12045.

Harney, Stefano, and Fred Moten. 2013. *The Undercommons: Fugitive Planning and Black Study*. Wivenhoe: Minor Compositions.

Hatherley, Owen. 2008. "Apparatus of Capture—Architecture in Israel-Palestine, 60 Years On." *Archinect*. Accessed July 10, 2018. https://archinect.com/features/article/75449/apparatus-of-capture-architecture-in-israel-palestine-60-years-on.

Hazboun, Norma. 1996. "Israeli Resettlement Schemes for Palestinian Refugees in the West Bank and Gaza." *al-Shaml Monograph Series*, no. 4.

Herscher, Andrew. 2017. *Displacements: Architecture and Refugee*. Edited by Nikolaus Hirsch and Markus Miessen. Berlin: Sternberg.

Hever, Shir. 2018. *The Privatization of Israeli Security*. London: Pluto.

Hildrew, Peter. 1983. "Israeli Resettlement Plan Feeds Palestinian Fears." *Guardian*, August 4.

Hochberg, Gil Z. 2015. *Visual Occupations: Violence and Visibility in a Conflict Zone.* Durham, NC: Duke University Press.

Hochberg, Gil Z. 2021. *Becoming Palestine: Toward an Archival Imagination of the Future.* Durham, NC: Duke University Press.

Idris, Yusuf. 2010. "Hayna Tastashhidu Aidan, al-Kalimat . . ." [When words too are martyred . . .]. In Ghassan Kanafani, *al-Athar al-Kamila: al-Mujalad al-Thani—al-Qisas al-Qasira* [The complete works: Volume two: Short stories], 9–31. Beirut: Muʾsasat al-Abhath al-ʿArabiya.

Invisible Committee. 2015. *To Our Friends.* Cambridge, MA: Semiotext(e).

Jabbour, George. 1970. *Settler Colonialism in Southern Africa and the Middle East.* Beirut: Palestine Research Centre.

Jameson, Fredric. (1977) 2002. "Reflections in Conclusion." In *Aesthetics and Politics*, edited by Theodore W. Adorno et al., 196–213. New York: Verso.

Jameson, Fredric. 2015. *The Antinomies of Realism.* Reprint ed. New York: Verso.

Jayyusi, Salma K. 1992. "Introduction: Palestinian Literature in Modern Times." In *Anthology of Modern Palestinian Literature*, edited by Salma K. Jayyusi, 1–80. New York: Columbia University Press.

Joyce, Patrick. 2003. *The Rule of Freedom: Liberalism and the Modern City.* London: Verso.

Kadman, Noga. 2015. *Erased from Space and Consciousness: Israel and the Depopulated Palestinian Villages of 1948.* Translation ed. Bloomington: Indiana University Press.

Kanafani, Ghassan. (1962) 1999. *Men in the Sun and Other Palestinian Stories.* Translated by Hillary Killpatrick. Boulder, CO: Lynne Reiner.

Kanafani, Ghassan. (1966) 2004. *All That's Left to You.* Translated by May Jayyusi and Jeremy Reed. Northampton, MA: Interlink.

Kanafani, Ghassan. 1969. "al-Mukhayyamat: Muʿskarat Iʿtiqal am Qawʿid al-Thawra?" [The camps: Barracks of incarceration or revolutionary bases?]. *al-Hadaf* 16, no. 1 (November 8).

Kanafani, Ghassan. (1969) 2010. *Um Saad.* In Ghassan Kanafani, *al-Athar al-Kamila: al-Mujalad al-Awal: al-Riwayat* [The complete works: Volume one: Novels], 253–337. Beirut: Muʾsasat al-Abhath al-ʿArabiya.

Karaoglan, Aida. 1969. *The Struggle Goes On.* Beirut: Palestine Research Center.

Katz, Irit. 2017a. "Architecture of Control and Struggle: Camps and the Reordering of Populations and Territories in Israel-Palestine." *ABE Journal* 7. https://journals.openedition.org/abe/3966.

Katz, Irit. 2017b. "'The Common Camp': Temporary Settlements as a Spatio-political Instrument in Israel-Palestine." *Journal of Architecture* 22 (1): 54–103. https://doi.org/10.1080/13602365.2016.1276095.

Katz, Irit. 2017c. "The Global Infrastructure of Camps." *Insecurities* (January 10). https://medium.com/insecurities/the-global-infrastructure-of-camps-8153fb61ea30.

Kauanui, J. Kēhlani. 2016. "'A Structure, Not an Event': Settler Colonialism and Enduring Indigeneity." *Lateral: Journal of the Cultural Studies Association* 5 (1). https://csalateral.org/issue/5-1/forum-alt-humanities-settler-colonialism-enduring-indigeneity-kauanui/.

Kayyali, Abdul-Wahab. 1977. "Zionism and Imperialism: The Historical Origins." *Journal of Palestine Studies* 6 (3): 98–112.

Kelley, R. D. G. 2017. "The Rest of Us: Rethinking Settler and Native." *American Quarterly* 69 (2): 267–76.

Khalaf, Salah. 1969. "The Resistance—a Dialogue between al-Fatah and *al-Tali'a*." In *Basic Documents of the Armed Palestinian Resistance*, edited by Lila S. Kadi, 39–100. Beirut: PLO Information Center.

Khalidi, Walid. 2005. "Why Did the Palestinians Leave, Revisited." *Journal of Palestine Studies* 34 (2): 42–54.

Khoury, Elias. 1998. *Bab al-Shams*. Beirut: Dar al-Adab.

Khoury, Elias. 2006. *Gate of the Sun*. Translated by Humphrey Davies. New York: Picador.

Knudsen, Are John, and Kjersti G. Berg. 2021. "Supercamp: The Middle East as a Regional Zone of Containment." *Chr. Michelsen Institute Blog*. https://www.cmi.no/publications/7896-supercamp-the-middle-east-as-a-regional-zone-of-containment.

Kojève, Alexandre. 2014. *The Notion of Authority: A Brief Presentation*. Translated by Hager Weslati. London: Verso.

Kotef, Hagar. 2020. *The Colonizing Self: Or, Home and Homelessness in Israel/Palestine*. Durham, NC: Duke University Press.

Lagerqvist, Peter. 2009. "Tracing Concrete." *Virginia Quarterly Review* 85 (3): 54–71.

Latour, Bruno. 2018. *Down to Earth: Politics in the New Climatic Regime*. Medford, MA: Polity.

Lentin, Ronit. 2018. *Traces of Racial Exception: Racializing Israeli Settler Colonialism*. London: Bloomsbury.

Leshem, Noam. 2013. "Repopulating the Emptiness: A Spatial Critique of Ruination in Israel/Palestine." *Environment and Planning D: Society and Space* 31 (3): 522–37. https://doi.org/10.1068/d15711.

Levine, Caroline. 2015. *Forms: Whole, Rhythm, Hierarchy, Network*. Princeton, NJ: Princeton University Press.

Levine, Mark. 2005. *Overthrowing Geography: Jaffa, Tel Aviv, and the Struggle for Palestine, 1880–1948*. Berkeley: University of California Press.

Li, Tania Murray. 2007. *The Will to Improve: Governmentality, Development, and the Practice of Politics*. Durham, NC: Duke University Press.

Lloyd, David. 2012. "Settler Colonialism and the State of Exception: The Example of Palestine/Israel." *Settler Colonial Studies* 2 (1): 59–80. https://doi.org/10.1080/2201473X.2012.10648826.

Lukács, Georg. (1938) 2002. "Realism in the Balance." In *Aesthetics and Politics*, edited by Theodor W. Adorno et al., 28–59. New York: Verso.

Lukács, Georg. 1970. "Narrate or Describe?" In *Writer and Critic and Other Essays*, 110–48. New York: Merlin.

Margalit, Dan. 2018. "The Arabs Chose to Be Refugees." *Ha'aretz*, May 24.

Marsden, Eric, and Carol Johnson. 1971. "Gaza Strip: Plight of the Palestinians." *Times*, September 3.

Martin, Reinhold. 2010. *Utopia's Ghost: Architecture and Postmodernism, Again*. Minneapolis: University of Minnesota Press.

Martin, Reinhold. 2016. *The Urban Apparatus: Mediapolitics and the City*. Minneapolis: University of Minnesota Press.

Marx, Emanuel. 1992. "Palestinian Refugee Camps in the West Bank and the Gaza Strip." *Middle Eastern Studies* 28 (2): 281–94.

Marx, Karl. 1990. *Capital—Volume One: The Critique of Political Economy*. Translated by Ben Fowkes. London: Penguin Classics.

Marx, Karl, and Friedrich Engels. 1998. *The German Ideology*. New York: Prometheus.

Masalha, Nur. 2003. *The Politics of Denial: Israel and the Palestinian Refugee Problem*. London: Pluto.

Massad, Joseph. 2006. *The Persistence of the Palestinian Question: Essays on Zionism and the Palestinians*. London: Routledge.

Massad, Joseph. 2015. "The Cultural Work of Recovering Palestine." *Boundary 2* 42 (4): 187–219. https://doi.org/10.1215/01903659-3154182.

Mastnak, Tomaz, Julia Elyachar, and Tom Boellstorf. 2014. "Botanical Decolonization: Rethinking Native Plants." *Environment and Planning D: Society and Space* 32 (2): 363–80.

Mbembe, Achille. 2001. *On the Postcolony*. Durham, NC: Duke University Press.

Mbembe, Achille. 2016. "The Society of Enmity." Translated by Giovanni Menegalle. *Radical Philosophy* 200 (1): 23–35.

McHugh, Roy. 1972. "Arab Ghetto a 'Heaven on Earth' since Takeover." *Pittsburgh Press*, November 30.

Mezzadra, Sandro, and Brett Neilson. 2013. *Border as Method, or, The Multiplication of Labor*. Durham, NC: Duke University Press.

Mitchell, Timothy. 2002. *Rule of Experts: Egypt, Techno-politics, Modernity*. Berkeley: University of California Press.

Monterescu, Daniel. 2015. *Jaffa Shared and Shattered: Contrived Coexistence in Israel/Palestine*. Bloomington: Indiana University Press.

Mor, Liron. 2024. *Conflicts: The Poetics and Politics of Palestine-Israel*. New York: Fordham University Press.

Morris, Benny. 1986. "Yosef Weitz and the Transfer Committees, 1948–49." *Middle Eastern Studies* 22 (4): 522–61.

Nazzal, Nafiz. 1978. *The Palestinian Exodus from the Galilee*. Beirut: Institute of Palestine Studies.

New York Times. 1983. "Israel Announces Plan to House Palestinians." November 21.

Nichols, Robert. 2020. *Theft Is Property! Dispossession and Critical Theory*. Durham, NC: Duke University Press.

Nitzan-Shiftan, Alona, and Fatina Abreek-Zubiedat. 2018. "'De-camping' through Development: The Palestinian Refugee Camps in Gaza, 1967–1982." In *Camps Revisited: Multifaceted Spatialities of a Modern Political Technology*, edited by Irit Katz, Diana Martin, and Claudio Minca, 137–57. New York: Rowman and Littlefield.

Noys, Benjamin. 2010. *The Persistence of the Negative: A Critique of Contemporary Continental Theory*. Edinburgh: Edinburgh University Press.

Oesch, Lucas. 2017. "The Refugee Camp as a Space of Multiple Ambiguities and Subjectivities." *Political Geography* 60 (September): 110–20. https://doi.org/10.1016/j.polgeo.2017.05.004.

O'Neil, Mary Kay, and Salman Akhtar, eds. 2011. *On Freud's Negation*. London: Routledge.

Ophir, Adi, Michal Givoni, and Sari Hanafi, eds. 2009. *The Power of Inclusive Exclusion: Anatomy of Israeli Rule in the Occupied Palestinian Territories*. New York: Zone.

Palumbo, Michael. 1987. *The Palestinian Catastrophe*. London: Quartet.

Pappe, Ilan. 2007. *The Ethnic Cleansing of Palestine*. 2nd ed. London: Oneworld.

Parker, Ben. 2015. "The Moments of Realism." *Los Angeles Review of Books*, July 28. https://lareviewofbooks.org/article/the-antinomies-of-realism/#!.

Parmenter, Barbara McKean. 1994. *Giving Voice to Stones: Place and Identity in Palestinian Literature*. Austin: University of Texas Press.

Perdigon, Sylvain. 2015. "'For Us It Is Otherwise': Three Sketches on Making Poverty Sensible in the Palestinian Refugee Camps of Lebanon." *Current Anthropology* 56 (s11): s88–96. https://doi.org/10.1086/682354.

Peteet, Julie. 2009. *Landscape of Hope and Despair: Palestinian Refugee Camps*. Pittsburgh: University of Pennsylvania Press.

Peteet, Julie. 2016. "Camps and Enclaves: Palestine in the Time of Closure." *Journal of Refugee Studies* 29 (2): 208–28. https://doi.org/10.1093/jrs/fev014.

Piterberg, Gabriel. 2001. "Erasures." *New Left Review* 10 (July–August).

Piterberg, Gabriel. 2008. *The Returns of Zionism: Myths, Politics and Scholarship in Israel*. New York: Verso.

Piterberg, Gabriel. 2009. "Cleanser to Cleansed." *London Review of Books*, February 26.

Piterberg, Gabriel. 2011. "Literature of Settler Societies: Albert Camus, S. Yizhar and Amos Oz." *Settler Colonial Studies* 1 (2): 1–52. https://doi.org/10.1080/2201473X.2011.10648811.

Povinelli, Elizabeth. *The Cunning of Recognition: Indigenous Alterities and the Making of Australian Multiculturalism*. Durham, NC: Duke University Press, 2002.

Prochaska, David. 2004. *Making Algeria French: Colonialism in Bône, 1870–1920*. Cambridge: Cambridge University Press.

Puar, Jasbir K. 2017. *The Right to Maim: Debility, Capacity, Disability*. Durham, NC: Duke University Press.

Qaddumi, Faruq. 1969. "A Conversation with Abu al-Lutuf." In *Basic Documents of the Armed Palestinian Resistance*, edited by Lila S. Kadi, 101–10. Beirut: PLO Information Center.

Rabie, Kareem. 2021. *Palestine Is Throwing a Party and the Whole World Is Invited: Capital and State Building in the West Bank*. Durham, NC: Duke University Press.

Rabinow, Paul. 1995. *French Modern: Norms and Forms of the Social Environment*. Reprint ed. Chicago: University of Chicago Press.

Rabinowitz, Dan. 1997. *Overlooking Nazareth: The Ethnography of Exclusion in Galilee*. New York: Cambridge University Press.

Ramadan, Adam. 2009. "Destroying Nahr El-Bared: Sovereignty and Urbicide in the Space of Exception." *Political Geography* 28 (3): 153–63. https://doi.org/10.1016/j.polgeo.2009.02.004.

Ramadan, Adam. 2013. "Spatialising the Refugee Camp." *Transactions of the Institute of British Geographers* 38 (1): 65–77. https://doi.org/10.1111/j.1475-5661.2012.00509.x.

Rancière, Jacques. 2006. *The Politics of Aesthetics*. Translated by Gabriel Rockhill. London: Bloomsbury Academic.

Raz, Adam. 2020. "When Israel Placed Arabs in Ghettos Fenced by Barbed Wire." *Ha'aretz*, May 28.

Raz-Krakotzkin, Amnon. 2013. "Exile, History, and the Nationalization of Jewish Memory: Some Reflections on the Zionist Notion of History and Return." *Journal of Levantine Studies* 3 (2): 37–70.

Reddaway, John. 1973. "No Man's Land." *Guardian*, May 4.

Rifkin, Mark. 2017. *Beyond Settler Time: Temporal Sovereignty and Indigenous Self-Determination*. Durham, NC: Duke University Press.

Ronnell, Avital. 2012. "Authority." *Political Concepts: A Critical Lexicon*, no. 3. https://www.politicalconcepts.org/category/issue-3/.

Rook, Robert. 2004. "Race, Water, and Foreign Policy: The Tennessee Valley Authority's Global Agenda Meets 'Jim Crow.'" *Diplomatic History* 28, no. 1 (January): 55–81.

Ross, Andrew. 2019. *Stone Men: The Palestinians Who Built Israel*. New York: Verso.

Rothbard, Sharon. 2003. "Wall and Tower." In *A Civilian Occupation: The Politics of Israeli Architecture*, edited by Rafi Segal and Eyal Weizman, 23–27. New York: Verso.

Rubinstein, Danny. 1991. *The People of Nowhere: The Palestinian Vision of Home*. Translated by Ina Friedman. New York: Crown.

Said, Edward W. (1979) 1992. *The Question of Palestine*. Reissue ed. New York: Vintage.

Said, Edward W. 1998. *After the Last Sky: Palestinian Lives*. Photographs by Jean Mohr. New York: Columbia University Press.
Salih, Ruba. 2018. "Refugees and Cathartic Politics: From Human Rights to the Right to Be Human." *South Atlantic Quarterly* 117 (1): 135–55. https://doi.org/https://doi.org/10.1215/00382876-428207.
Sanbar, Elias. 1984. *Palestine 1948: L'expulsion*. Paris: Institute of Palestine Studies.
Sarhan, Basim. 1975. "al-Mukhayyam al-Filastini fi Thil al-Thawra" [The Palestinian camp under the revolution]. *Shuʿun Filastiniyya*, no. 41–42 (January): 423–40.
Sassen, Saskia. 2008. *Territory, Authority, Rights: From Medieval to Global Assemblages*. Updated ed. Princeton, NJ: Princeton University Press.
Sassen, Saskia. 2014. *Expulsions: Brutality and Complexity in the Global Economy*. Cambridge, MA: Belknap.
Sayegh, Fayez. 1965. *Zionist Colonialism in Palestine*. Beirut: Palestine Research Center.
Sayigh, Rosemary. 1977. "The Palestinian Identity among Camp Residents." *Journal of Palestine Studies* 6 (3): 3–22. https://doi.org/10.2307/2535577.
Sayigh, Rosemary. 1979. *The Palestinians: From Peasants to Revolutionaries*. London: Zed.
Sayigh, Yezid. 1997. *Armed Struggle and the Search for State: The Palestinian National Movement, 1949–1993*. Oxford: Oxford University Press.
Schiff, Benjamin. 1995. *Refugees unto the Third Generation: UN Aid to Palestinians*. Syracuse, NY: Syracuse University Press.
Schwarz, Walter. 1970. "A Quiet Revolution." *Guardian*, November 10.
Schwarz, Walter. 1971a. "Dayan Fishing for Photos." *Guardian*, May 24.
Schwarz, Walter. 1971b. "Gaza Refugees Go West." *Guardian*, August 19.
Schwarz, Walter. 1971c. "'New Homes for Old' Plan Upsets Refugee Families." *Guardian*, July 28.
Scott, David. 2014. *Omens of Adversity: Tragedy, Time, Memory, Justice*. Durham, NC: Duke University Press.
Segev, Tom. 2008. *1967: Israel, the War, and the Year That Transformed the Middle East*. First American ed. New York: Picador.
Sennett, Richard. (1980) 1993. *Authority*. New York: Norton.
Shafir, Gershon. 1996. *Land, Labor and the Origins of the Israeli-Palestinian Conflict, 1882–1914*. Updated ed. Berkeley: University of California Press.
Sharon, Ariel. 2001. *Warrior: An Autobiography*. New York: Simon and Schuster.
Shuʿun Filastiniyya. 1974. "Hadith Yunshar l'Awali Maratan maʿ al-Shahid Ghassan Kanafani" [A dialogue published for the first time with the martyr Ghassan Kanafani]. *Shuʿun Filastiniyya*, no. 35, 136–42.
Siddiq, Muhammad. 1984. *Man Is a Cause: Political Consciousness and the Fiction of Ghassan Kanafani*. Seattle: University of Washington Press.
Siddiq, Muhammad. 1995. "On Ropes of Memory: Narrating the Palestinian Refu-

gees." In *Mistrusting Refugees,* edited by E. Valentine Daniel and Lal Jayawardena, 87–101. Berkeley: University of California Press.

Simone, AbdouMaliq. 2020. "To Extend: Temporariness in a World of Itineraries." *Urban Studies* 67 (6): 1127–42.

Simone, AbdouMaliq. 2022. *The Surrounds.* Durham, NC: Duke University Press.

Simpson, Audra. 2016. "Whither Settler Colonialism?" *Settler Colonial Studies* 6 (4): 438–45. https://doi.org/10.1080/2201473X.2015.1124427.

Simpson, Audra. 2017. "The Ruse of Consent and the Anatomy of 'Refusal': Cases from Indigenous North America and Australia." *Postcolonial Studies* 20 (1): 18–33. https://doi.org/10.1080/13688790.2017.1334283.

Smith, Terrence. 1973. "Israel's Refugee-Resettling Project Is Transforming Gaza Strip." *New York Times,* April 2.

Stoler, Ann Laura. 2011. "Colony." *Political Concepts: A Critical Lexicon,* no. 1. https://www.politicalconcepts.org/colony-stoler/.

Stoler, Ann Laura. 2016. *Duress: Imperial Durabilities in Our Times.* Durham, NC: Duke University Press.

Sunday Times. 1969. "Interview with Golda Meir." June 15.

Tadiar, Neferti. 2022. *Remaindered Life.* Durham, NC: Duke University Press.

Tawil-Souri, Helga. 2017. "Checkpoint Time." *Qui Parle* 26 (2): 383–422. https://doi.org/10.1215/10418385-4208442.

Tesdell, Omar. 2017. "Wild Wheat to Productive Drylands: Global Scientific Practice and the Agroecological Remaking of Palestine." *Geoforum* 78: 43–51.

Thomas, Peter. 2013. "Hegemony, Passive Revolution and the Modern Prince." *Thesis Eleven* 117 (1): 20–39. https://doi.org/10.1177/0725513613493991.

Turki, Fawaz. 1972. *The Disinherited: Journal of a Palestinian Exile.* New York: Monthly Review Press.

Turki, Fawaz. 1988. *Soul in Exile.* New York: Monthly Review Press.

United Nations Conciliation Commission on Palestine (UNCCP). 1949a. *The Final Report of the United Nations Economic Survey Mission to the Middle East: An Approach to Economic Development in the Middle East,* A/AC.25/6, December 28.

United Nations Conciliation Commission on Palestine (UNCCP). 1949b. *First Interim Report of the United Nations Economic Survey Mission for the Middle East,* A/1106, November 16.

United Nations Conciliation Commission on Palestine (UNCCP). 1949c. "Memorandum Dated 28 July 1949, Submitted to the Technical Committee by Mr. G. Meron of the Government of Israel: On Principles Guiding the Resettlement of Arab Refugees," A/AC.25/Com.Tech/8, August 8.

United Nations Conciliation Commission on Palestine (UNCCP). 1949d. "Report of the Technical Committee on Refugees to the Conciliation Commission," A/AC.25/Com.Tech/9, August 20.

United Nations Conciliation Commission on Palestine (UNCCP). 1949e. "The Second Progress Report of the Conciliation Commission," A/838, April 19.

United Nations Conciliation Commission on Palestine (UNCCP). 1949f. "Summary Record of a Meeting between the Conciliation Commission and His Excellency Mr. David Ben Gurion, Prime Minister of Israel," A/AC.25/SR/G/16, April 7.

United Nations General Assembly. 1948. Resolution 194. "Palestine—Progress Report of the United Nations Mediator," A/RES/194 (III).

United Nations General Assembly. 1951. Resolution 429. "Convention Relating to the Status of Refugees," A/CONF.2/108.

United Nations Relief and Works Agency (UNRWA). 1950. "Interim Report of the Director of the United Nations Relief and Works Agency for Palestine Refugees in the Near East," A/1451/Rev.1, October 6.

United Nations Relief and Works Agency (UNRWA). 1951. "Annual Report of the Director of the United Nations Relief and Works Agency for Palestine Refugees in the Near East," A/1905, September 28.

United Nations Relief and Works Agency (UNRWA). 1952. "Annual Report of the Director of the United Nations Relief and Works Agency for Palestine Refugees in the Near East," A/2171, June 30.

United Nations Relief and Works Agency (UNRWA). 1956. "Annual Report of the Director of the United Nations Relief and Works Agency for Palestine Refugees in the Near East," A/3212, June 30.

Veracini, Lorenzo. 2011a. "Introducing: Settler Colonial Studies." *Settler Colonial Studies* 1 (1): 1–12. https://doi.org/10.1080/2201473X.2011.10648799.

Veracini, Lorenzo. 2011b. "On Settlerness." *Borderlands* 10 (1): 1–17.

Viorst, Milton. 1984. *UNRWA and Peace in the Middle East*. Washington, DC: Middle East Institute.

Walker, Robert B. J. 1996. "Space/Time/Sovereignty." In *Perspectives on Third World Sovereignty*, edited by Mark Denham and Mark Owen Lombardi, 13–27. New York: St. Martin's.

Weber, Max. (1946) 1991. "Politics as Vocation." In *From Max Weber*, edited by H. H. Gerth and C. Wright Mills, 77–128. London: Routledge.

Weber, Samuel. 2012. "Bare Life and Life in General." *Grey Room* 46 (January): 7–24. https://doi.org/10.1162/GREY_a_00058.

Weitz, Ra'anan, David Pelley, and Levia Applebaum. 1980. "A Model for the Planning of New Settlement Projects." *World Development* 8 (9): 705–23. https://doi.org/10.1016/0305-750X(80)90058-3.

Weizman, Eyal. 2007. *Hollow Land: Israel's Architecture of Occupation*. New York: Verso.

Wilder, Gary. 2015. *Freedom Time: Negritude, Decolonization, and the Future of the World*. Durham, NC: Duke University Press.

Wolfe, Patrick. 1998. *Settler Colonialism and the Transformation of Anthropology: The Politics and Poetics of an Ethnographic Event*. New York: Continuum.

Wolfe, Patrick. 2006. "Settler Colonialism and the Elimination of the Native." *Journal of Genocide Research* 8 (4): 387–409. https://doi.org/10.1080/14623520601056240.

Wolfe, Patrick. 2016. *Traces of History: Elementary Structures of Race*. New York: Verso.

Yakhlif, Yayha. (1983) 2008. *Tuffah al-Majanin* [Apples of the crazed]. Beirut: Dar al-Adab.

Zakin, Dov. 1972. "Rehabilitation of the Refugees." *New Outlook* 15 (7): 59–67.

Zangwill, Israel. 1921. *The Voice of Jerusalem*. London: Macmillan.

Žižek, Slavoj. 2008. *The Sublime Object of Ideology*. London: Verso.

Zupančič, Alenka. 2012. "Not-Mother: On Freud's *Verneinung*." *E-flux*, no. 33. https://www.e-flux.com/journal/33/68292/not-mother-on-freud-s-verneinung/.

Zupančič, Alenka. 2017. "Hegel and Freud: Between *Aufhebung* and *Verneinung*." *Crisis and Critique* 4 (1): 481–96.

INDEX

Note: Page numbers followed by f refer to figures.

Abu Shawir, Rashad, 31, 102, 110, 116, 118, 199n11, 201n21; *al-'Ushaq*, 102, 104, 109–10, 117–18
administration, 57–60, 67, 79–80, 92, 98, 177; of camps, 10, 53, 68, 81, 91, 192n5, 194n30; nonpolitical, 68, 77; public, 34; spatial, 68, 81, 85–86, 90; technical, 35, 57–59, 190–91n23
aesthetics, 103, 115, 147, 200n18, 201n24; of Palestinian liberation movement, 99, 102–3
Agamben, Giorgio, 57, 169, 176–78
Agency, the. *See* United Nations Relief and Works Agency (UNRWA)
Al-Hadaf, 96, 198n8, 199n11, 200n19
Allon, Yigal, 138, 203n7
anticolonial struggle, 24, 29, 174
anxiety, 15, 48, 79, 129, 158, 187n20; border, 47; political, 32, 137, 175
apartheid, 27, 127, 160
Arab Nationalist Movement (ANM), 99–100
Arab refugee problem. *See* refugee problem
Arabs, 4–5, 38, 47, 61, 128, 140, 143, 187n20
Arafat, Yasser, 78, 95–96, 124. *See also* Palestine Liberation Organization (PLO)
architects, 89, 130, 147, 162, 204n19
architecture, 6, 8, 26, 89, 177, 204n9; emergency, 147; native, 143; of negation, 144; securitized, 183n3; of security, 173; of settlement, 174
Arendt, Hannah, 37, 57, 87–89, 169, 195nn49–51, 196–97n53, 197n3, 198n9

authority, 11–12, 30, 57, 65, 79, 87–92, 109, 195–96nn50–53, 199n14; administrative, 31, 59, 67, 80–81, 87, 89–90, 92, 195n52; archival, 29; of Gaza's governor general, 192n3; of Israeli military government, 204n8; of knowledge, 58; of military intelligence apparatus, 78; reiterative, 195n51; UNRWA's, 31, 58–59, 66–68, 71–72, 77, 80–82, 85–87, 89–91, 111, 195n52
autonomy, 102, 125, 146, 157; of migration, 166

Balibar, Étienne, 73, 158, 166
Begin, Menachem, 138, 203n7
Beirut, 40, 50, 103, 168, 198n8; Bourj al-Barajneh Camp, 64; Israeli invasion and siege of, 101, 106, 124; migrant, 181
Ben-Gurion, David, 7, 37
Ben Porat, Mordechai, 144, 146
besiegement, 16, 22
biopolitics, 169, 176
Borges, Jorge Luis, 16, 185n10
built environment, 13, 55, 64–67, 84, 143; UNRWA regulation of, 31, 72, 77, 79, 81, 86, 90–91

Cairo Agreement, 31, 68, 78, 82, 96
Camp David Accords, 106, 199n14, 204n21
camp form, 6–7, 15, 29, 35, 52–55, 168–69; colonial and racial histories of, 63; displacement and, 105; novel form and, 31, 99, 122–24; separation and, 61

camp life, 13–14, 69–70, 77, 104–5, 108–10, 115–18, 120–22, 125, 178, 180, 182; early, 64; impossibility of, 113; stillness of, 94; survey and, 189n7

camp regime, 30, 34–36, 47, 51–52, 56, 61, 64, 66, 98; authority of, 195n52; UNRWA, 54

capital, 27, 166, 168; accumulation, 175; critiques of, 19; private, 91; real estate, 7, 46; settler, 20; urban, 185n10

capitalism, 19–21, 52, 166–67; colonial, 185n11; racial, 168, 174

citizenship, 27, 32, 159–61, 169, 177, 181–82, 196n53, 205n30, 205n32; nationality and, 27, 160, 205n32

Clapp, Gordon R., 30–31, 33–35, 39–47, 49–55, 57–62, 64, 67. *See also* Tennessee Valley Authority (TVA); United Nations Relief and Works Agency (UNRWA)

Clapp mission, 34, 39–43, 45–46, 60, 69, 142, 190n20; closure of politics and, 36, 45, 92; humanitarianism and, 55; Lausanne Conference and, 36, 41; work and, 47, 51–53, 68, 191n23

colonialism, 26, 60, 106, 161, 170–71, 173, 185n13, 186n15, 186n17; American, 47; anticolonialism, 169; liberal, 43, 53; metropole, 21; residual, 66; Zionist, 6, 183n4. *See also* settler colonialism

colonial order, 35, 158, 170; Israeli, 12

colonial struggle, 2, 9, 24, 114; settler, 5

colonization, 21, 175, 183n2; of the Americas, 47; of Palestine, 6, 8, 45, 172–73, 183n3, 186n15, 203n7; settler, 17

Comay, Michael, 36–37

confinement, 5, 31, 35, 53, 94, 105, 190n18

conquest, 3–4, 16–17, 21, 24, 44, 156, 160–62, 173; colonial, 183n6; of land, 6; settler, 15, 185n10; Spanish, 60; Zionism and, 28

consciousness of the temporary, 12, 32, 163

construction, 27, 64–68, 70, 72, 74f, 76f, 77, 90, 118, 130; the Agency and, 86, 89, 193n25; factory mass-produced, 143; political anxieties around, 191n3; roofing and, 192n6; sector, 20; of settlement towns, 9; Zionism and, 173

counterinsurgency, 139, 152–53, 155

Dahbur, Ahmad, 116, 201n21
Darraj, Faisal, 116, 201n19
Darwish, Mahmud, 33, 103, 115, 128
Dayan, Moshe, 139, 152, 155, 203n7
decolonization, 17, 30, 35, 60, 169, 182, 185n12
Deheishe Camp, 74f, 76f
Deleuze, Gilles, 124, 134, 201n24
demolition, 12, 90–91, 131, 139, 153, 163; camp, 13, 154f; house/home, 86, 150, 152, 162, 172
demoralization, 49, 54
depoliticization, 30, 35
development, 34, 40, 56–58, 142, 200n17; anthropology of, 190n23; of camps, 73; economic, 44; enterprises, 139; global, 182; human, 67; humanitarianism and, 188n25; journals, 204n10; programs, 39; projects, 42, 69, 100, 152, 202n2; real estate, 206n1; regional, 141; towns, 7; TVA-led, 46
dislocation, 2; economic, 39, 69; psychological, 109
dispossession, 2, 22–28, 35–36, 52, 54–55, 61, 167, 170–73; camp removal and, 202n2; colonial, 2, 54, 170, 175, 177, 183n1, 187n19; encampment and, 8, 54–56, 165; land, 26, 40–42, 161, 170; nomadic life and, 5; original, 12; settler recognition as, 205n31; time of, 2–3, 23, 27, 128
Dolar, Mladen, 90, 160
domestication, 25, 179; of the camp, 98

Economic Survey Mission. *See* Clapp mission
Ekbladh, David, 44, 50
elimination, 19–22, 69, 131–32, 140, 161, 171–72; of camps, 155; of the native, 25
Elmusa, Sharif, 14–15
employment, 41, 131, 188n4, 191n2, 205n30; of Black workers, 46; continual, 190n20;

full, 141, 143, 153; in Gaza Strip, 142; programs, 190n21; public sector, 167; schemes, 130, 202n2; TVA practices of, 45

encampment, 5, 6, 8, 10, 12, 35, 53, 63–65, 82, 106, 108–9, 173, 189n13; dispossession and, 8, 54–56, 165; in exile, 197n4; housing projects and, 157; inhabitation and, 175; mass, 32, 60, 92, 165–66, 168–69, 174, 179, 181; military, 147; permanent, 52, 168; practices of, 91; as regime, 67; settlement, 23; stateless, 164; temporary, 48; urban, 7; voluntary, 2

engineers, 55, 90, 130, 147

Eshkol, Levi, 137–38

ethnic cleansing, 6, 36, 159, 172, 185n13, 187n24

exile, 18, 48, 107, 116–17, 126, 164; consciousness of, 14, 127, 156; encampment in, 197n4; permanent, 2

expertise, 8, 36, 58, 60, 130

exploitation, 19–22; super-exploitation, 54, 167, 171

expropriation, 25; land, 45, 52

expulsion, 9–10, 28, 47–48, 131, 134, 166, 183–84n6; settler, 96

extraction, 7, 22, 60, 168, 175

Fanon, Frantz, 16, 171–72

Farred, Grant, 25, 27, 187n22, 187n24

Fatah, 101, 199n11

Feldman, Ilana, 187n25, 191n2, 195n51

Fisher, R. L., 79–83, 85, 193n25, 194n30

Flusser, Vilém, 48, 170

force, 3–4, 31, 57, 169; authority and, 58, 67, 87–88, 90–91, 196–97n53; bodily, 198n9; disciplinary, 35; environmental, 108; of negation, 191n23; normative, 44, 51; political, 85, 94, 191n23; regulatory, 111; surplus humanity and, 167

form, 7, 67, 95, 107, 119, 123; of authority, 77, 79, 81, 86; built, 91, 105, 162; camp as architectural, 35; camp as placeless, 5; narrative, 21, 31, 99, 102, 105; national, 102, 105, 122, 198n7; of negation, 133–34; novel, 31, 99, 106, 116, 123–24, 200–201n20; private-property, 170; property, 41; spatial, 92, 107, 144; temporal, 144. *See also* camp form

Forth, Aidan, 52, 54

Foucault, Michel, 51, 59, 196n53, 201n24

Freud, Sigmund, 88, 132–36, 203n4

Gaza Strip, 1, 73, 107, 130–31, 141–42, 155, 161; camps in, 10, 130, 137, 139, 144, 146, 150–52, 155–56, 183n5, 189n13, 202n2, 203n7; government in, 195n51; governor general of, 192n3; inhabitation and, 181; Israeli housing projects in, 149*f*; military government in, 147, 150; military governor of, 148; occupation of, 32, 86, 137, 186n15, 192n3; PLO in, 199n14; public works projects in, 190n20; refugees in, 138, 141, 153, 192n3, 203n7; shelters in, 70; siege of, 205n30

Global South, 44, 165, 167, 174–75

Gramsci, Antonio, 195–96n53

Great Depression, 45, 50

Haifa, 7, 144, 155–56

Hatherley, Owen, 144, 204n19

heroism, 94, 106, 117, 121; insurgent, 115, 119, 125, 198n10

Herscher, Andrew, 52–53

hierarchy, 35, 60, 88–90, 196n53; of elders, 13; racial, 44, 46–47, 170; of technical competence, 57

historical time, 2, 11, 33, 108, 110–11, 128–29; modern, 151; mythico-historical time, 18; new, 31, 124; revolutionary, 98

historicity, 16, 185n11

homing, 28, 170, 172

housing, 69–71, 77, 86, 141, 143, 170, 172, 186n15, 192nn5–6, 206n1; complexes, 17, 144, 148; policies, 45; politics of, 176; projects, 26, 64–65, 100, 139, 144, 146–49, 151–53, 157; rights, 177

idleness, 44, 47, 49, 51–54, 57; of workers, 46

imperialism: British, 6, 52, 183n4; European, 21, 185n13; liberal, 60
improvement, 13, 44, 46, 70, 139, 146, 150–52, 163; camp, 131, 151–52, 204n8; of refugee living conditions, 69; self-improvement, 35, 50, 191n23
independence, 125; postcolonial, 60; settler declarations of, 16
Indigeneity, 21–22, 25, 187n20
Indigenous life, 134, 161
inhabitation, 4, 9, 17, 30, 32, 65, 152, 167, 169–82, 206n2; camp as temporal modality of, 140; encampment and, 67; indefinite, 165; politics of, 32, 55, 77, 125, 169, 176, 178, 181; restless, 22. *See also* uninhabitability
insurrection, 31, 98, 121, 125, 198n8; camps as sites of, 101, 125; politics of, 116, 124
Israel, 1, 11, 27–28, 37–38, 48, 135–36, 142–43, 148, 155, 159–61, 185n13, 187n24, 205n32; border with Lebanon, 94; camps and, 137–38, 144, 152, 157; establishment of, 10; Gazan housing projects of, 153; Independence Day, 203n6; Jewish settlements of, 203n10; as Jewish State, 10, 15, 136, 162, 203n6; leaders of, 129; Ministry of Foreign Affairs, 36, 38; murder of Kanafani and, 103; nationality and, 205–6n33; National Plan of 1950, 26; non-Jews in, 40, 203n5; occupation of Palestine, 18, 61, 86; planning in, 26; as racial regime, 184n7; settlement towns of, 9; as settler colonial project, 2, 23; as settler colony, 2, 8, 19–20, 25, 129, 143, 173, 206n33; settlerness and, 173; settler politics of, 202n2
Israeli military government, 86–87, 129–30, 146–48, 150, 152, 192n3, 204n8
Israeli State, 13, 24, 131, 135, 138, 159, 162, 192n5; development projects of, 202n2; Refugee Department of, 192n3; rehabilitation and, 153; resettlement and, 129, 203n8; War on Infiltration, 48
Israel State Archives, 29, 31, 138, 202n2

Jabalya Camp, 152, 155
Jaffa, 7, 155–56
Jameson, Fredric, 106, 115, 200n20
Jewish Agency, 140, 183n5
Jewish National Fund (JNF), 48, 140
Jim Crow, 45, 190n19
Jordan, 133, 191n3, 199n14, 203n7, 205n30; Amman, 69, 107, 151, 168; camps in, 10, 73, 101
jurisdictional incorporation, 13, 139, 152
justice, 37–39, 61, 108, 181, 187n20

Kanafani, Ghassan, 31, 96, 102–5, 109, 115, 122, 199n13, 200n19; *al-Hadaf* and, 198n8, 199n11; *Um Saad*, 102, 104, 111–13, 118–19, 201n22
Khoury, Elias, 48, 93–95, 197nn4–5
Kojève, Alexandre, 87, 89, 195nn49–50, 196–97n53
Kotef, Hagar, 172–73

labor, 6, 19–20, 41–42, 53–54, 106, 140, 166–67, 190n19; disposable, 178; forced, 190n18; immaterial, 206n1; Indigenous, 19, 186n16; Native, 171
labor camps, 7, 183n4
labor force, 46, 51, 54, 167, 191n23
labor markets, 55, 77
land, 2, 4–6, 10, 16–17, 20, 24–28, 35, 40–42, 65, 70, 72, 118, 134, 136, 140, 146, 148, 156, 170–71, 174, 181, 194n30, 197n1; claims to, 12, 137, 144, 155, 162; dispossession, 26, 40–42, 161, 170; expropriation of, 45, 52, 147; Indigenous, 44; inhabitable, 175; liberation of, 101; occupied, 86; settler colonies and, 19; titles, 69, 183n1, 192n5, 205n30
land grabs, 160
landlessness, 35, 164, 175
Latour, Bruno, 175–76
Lausanne Conference, 36–38, 40–41, 58
law, 24, 59, 67, 85, 90, 95, 160, 196n53; civil, 22; colonial, 181; Indian, 159; limit of, 155; and order, 14, 71–72, 81, 91, 155; prop-

erty, 170; refugees and, 197n4; as relation of force, 169
Lebanon, 48, 101; Aramco oil pipeline and, 130; border with Israel, 94; camps in, 10, 31, 65, 68, 78, 96, 99, 189n13, 192n3; Israeli invasion of, 124; Palestinian refugees in, 188n25. *See also* Beirut
liberalism, 169, 181
liberation, 122, 125, 129
literature, 99, 102–3, 110, 115, 117–18, 123, 199n11; Israeli, 137; Palestinian, 105–8, 116; political, 101; revolutionary, 103, 198n10; settler, 185n10
loss, 65, 136, 160

Mandate, 6–7, 40, 51, 60, 195n51
Marx, Emmanuel, 157–58, 205n30
Marx, Karl, 53, 89, 95–96, 166, 190n18, 198n7, 203n4. *See also* primitive accumulation
Massad, Joseph, 136, 185n13
Meir, Golda, 133–34, 136, 141
Michelmore, Laurence, 78–79
militancy, 31, 98–99, 102, 104, 109, 115; clandestine, 93; Palestinian, 96
Mitchell, Timothy, 41, 58
model villages, 69, 131, 151, 153
modernism, 58, 106, 200n20, 204n19
modernity, 54; colonial, 176; of colonialism, 26
modernization, 43–44, 46, 50, 60, 131, 151, 182

Nakba, 9, 11, 94, 140, 185n13, 187n24, 197n4, 203n6
Nakba Law, 136, 203n6
Nasser, Gamal Abdel, 78, 150
nationalism, 186n15; anticolonial, 35, 43, 60, 101; Arab, 199n14
nationality, 27, 56, 160, 205nn32–33
national liberation, 98f; movement, 2, 188
Native peoples, 5, 17, 172
negation, 5, 30, 32, 96, 131–35, 137, 139–40, 162, 178, 191n23, 202–3n4; architecture of, 144; bulldozer as device of, 156; of exile, 18; politics of, 131, 146, 163; self-negation, 95, 136; settler, 125, 131, 134
New Deal, 42, 45, 50
1987 Intifada, 130, 199n14
1967 War, 104, 128, 130, 137–38, 143, 201n21, 203n7; Arab nationalism and, 101, 199n14
nomadism, 4–6, 170; of financialized capital, 166

occupation, 18, 150, 157; bureaucracy, 202n3; military, 1, 27, 86, 129, 205n32; regime, 2; studies, 186n15; of the West Bank and Gaza, 32, 86, 137, 186n15
ownership, 72, 148, 170, 177–79, 205n30; landownership, 71; legal, 147–48; society, 171; state, 28

Palestine Liberation Organization (PLO), 31, 65, 68, 78, 96, 101, 124, 199n14
Palestinian Authority (PA), 91, 199n11
Palestinian liberation movement, 2, 95, 98–99, 101, 188n25, 197n2
Palestinian Revolution, 13, 17, 31, 66, 96–98, 101–3, 116, 124–25, 199n14; collapse of, 94; decolonization and, 185n12; gender norms and, 119
Palestinian revolutionaries, 12–13, 65, 87, 101, 104, 109, 111
Parmenter, Barbara, 116–17
paternalism, 108, 114–15
peace processes, 2, 184n8
Peres, Shimon, 151, 163
periodization, 15, 107; in Palestinian novel, 106
permanence, 13, 24, 27, 64, 71, 147, 174, 180; anxiety and, 137, 139, 158; of the built, 178; of refugee resettlement, 143; settled, 176; settler, 160, 162; of settler colony, 129; of status quo, 84
Piterberg, Gabriel, 135, 140, 183n2, 185n10
planners, 140; Israeli, 13, 129, 162; UNRWA, 89; urban, 15, 130

INDEX 227

Plato, 57, 88–89, 196n53
Point Four projects, 61, 113, 200n17
politicians, 133, 140; Israeli, 14, 137, 155; US, 130
politics, 13, 29, 30, 37, 42–43, 46, 58–63, 65–68, 88–92, 105–6, 112, 119, 161, 176–77, 179–80, 182, 188n4, 190n23, 196n53, 197n3, 198n9; administration and, 57, 60; aesthetics and, 103, 201n24; authority of the father and, 195n50; camp life and, 113, 178; closure of, 36, 45, 92; colonial, 19, 22, 29, 170; coloniality of, 127; global, 35, 91, 164, 174–75; of housing, 17, 176, 206n1; humanitarianism and, 187–88n25; of Indigeneity, 187n20; of inhabitation, 32, 55, 77, 125, 169, 172, 176, 178, 181; of insurrection, 116, 124; Israeli, 31, 128–29, 136–38, 202n2, 205n32; law and, 197n2; liberationist, 11; life and, 31, 56, 66–67, 98–99, 102, 113, 116–17, 120–22, 169, 176, 198n10; of naming, 84; of negation, 131, 146, 163; party, 199n11; of recognition, 27; of return, 12, 101, 179; revolutionary, 95, 122–23, 125, 129; securitized, 16; settler, 24, 32, 129, 132, 134–36, 202n2; settler colonial, 22, 170; state-making, 125; the technical and, 81; temporal, 162, 202n2; of temporality, 15, 18, 25; of temporariness, 66; of time, 15, 18; TVA and, 45
Popular Front for the Liberation of Palestine (PFLP), 99, 101, 198n8. See also *Al-Hadaf*
pragmatism, 37; administrative, 61
present absentees, 135, 203n5
primitive accumulation, 19–20, 52–53, 167, 190n18
professional refugee, 13, 69, 192n5
property, 24–25, 37, 39, 41, 170–71, 176; expropriation of, 203n5; owners, 192n5; private, 19, 27, 148, 170; regimes, 22, 24, 28, 148, 160; relations, 27, 170, 176–77, 181

racialization, 54, 61, 172; of Palestinians, 5, 20

racial world formation, 30, 35
Rafah Camp, 142, 147, 152–53, 154f, 204n21
Rancière, Jacques, 123, 200n18, 201n24
Rand Corporation, 130, 157
realism, 99, 102, 106–7, 115, 120, 200n15, 200–201nn19–20
Reconstruction, 45–46, 190n19
refugee camps, 1, 7–10, 12, 14, 57, 28–29, 31, 34, 54, 117, 127, 151, 155, 165, 189n13; built history of, 68; defense of, 23; exile and, 126; Israeli politics and, 129–30; as neighborhoods, 157; 1967 War and, 137; Palestinian Revolution and, 96, 101–2; persistence of, 158; production of space and, 188n25; regime, 35; settler colony and, 28; settlerness and, 25; UNRWA, 79, 83, 146, 194n30; voluntary dissolution of, 139; West Bank, 128
refugeehood, 13, 41, 94, 109, 139, 162, 168, 178; consciousness of the temporary and, 32; legal status of, 56, 146; shame and, 197n4; subject of militancy and, 115
refugee problem, 10–12, 38, 141, 192n3; camps and, 126, 129, 155, 162; liquidation of, 11, 137, 202n2
refugees, 1, 11, 13–15, 36–43, 46–50, 53–56, 61, 64–65, 68–72, 80–81, 83–86, 94–96, 110, 124, 126, 130, 137–40, 142–44, 152–53, 155–56, 189n13, 191n2, 197nn2–3, 203–4n8; citizenship and, 205n30; encamped, 2, 90, 101, 127–28, 135, 138, 141, 157, 187n25; Gaza's, 192n5, 203n7, 204n21; housing and, 146, 148; idle, 30, 34; Palestinian, 10, 14, 29, 46, 64, 67, 84, 120, 127, 129–30, 157, 179, 183n5, 187–88n25, 200n17, 202n3, 203n7; Point Four projects and, 113; professional, 192n5; racial figurations of, 192n4; refugees-turned-landowners, 192n5; resettlement and, 150, 156; return and, 184n8; stateless, 109; transfer of, 131, 142; works projects and, 190n20
refusal, 14, 22–24, 61, 94–95, 127–28, 163, 178–79; anticolonial, 15–16, 22, 24; of co-

habitation, 169; of colonial wardship, 62; of humanitarian capture, 98f; of resettlement housing projects, 65; return as, 3

rehabilitation, 54, 57, 131, 142, 153, 190nn20–21, 191n23; language of, 142, 147, 162; of subjects, 50; work as, 53; work-based, 11–12

rehousing, 139, 152

removal, 9, 138, 150–51, 153, 181, 187n21; camp, 127, 130, 139–40, 142, 144, 152, 155–58, 183n5, 204n8; physical, 162; spatial, 53

repatriation, 11, 36, 38–40, 42, 184n8

replacement, 22, 25, 28, 140, 162, 170, 187n21; settler, 21, 27, 132

representation, 68, 79, 81, 135, 178, 181

repression, 15, 132–35, 139, 181; collective, 9; double, 4

resettlement, 39–40, 42, 64, 67, 100, 139, 141, 146, 150, 156, 158, 183n5; camps, 8; forced, 53; housing projects, 65; Israeli schemes of, 202n2; mass, 54; of Native populations, 153; permanent, 10–11, 52, 184n8; Point Four projects and, 200n17; policy, 157; programs, 99, 130; projects, 108, 130; refugee, 129–30, 138, 143, 203nn7–8; reintegration as, 69

return, 10–11, 28, 38, 56, 61, 64–65, 98f, 115–16, 122, 125, 127, 129, 142, 144, 155–56, 162–63, 178, 202nn2–3; desire for, 131; fever, 48; movements, 184n8; negation and, 32, 132, 135–36; Palestinian insistence on, 3; politics of, 12, 101, 179; practices of, 23; specter of, 153; time of, 137

revolution, 17, 30, 95–96, 101–3, 106, 121, 124–25, 151, 198nn6–8

rights, 32, 38–39, 43, 59, 77, 91, 169, 178, 181–82; of the displaced, 36; housing, 177; Native, 159; nonpolitical, 71; political, 135; of refugees, 55, 84, 188n25; territorial-political, 42; voting, 45

Ronnell, Avital, 88, 195n49

Rothschild, Edmund Leopold de, 130–31, 143

Rubinstein, Danny, 126–28, 131–32, 140, 156, 202n1

Ruppin, Arthur, 6, 183n2

Sadat, Anwar, 106, 199n14

Safdie, Moshe, 130, 143–44, 145f, 204n19

Said, Edward, 2, 18, 107, 116, 185n13, 200n14

Sanbar, Elias, 124, 134, 184n6

Sayegh, Fayez, 21, 185n13

Schwarz, Walter, 150–53

Segev, Tom, 137–38, 202n3

self-determination, 34–35, 60, 205n33

self-government, 46, 51, 60; Indigenous, 186n16; Jewish, 3

Sennett, Richard, 88–89, 195n50

separation, 35, 58–59, 61, 171–72; domestication and, 179; geographies of, 165; between life and politics, 58, 62, 66, 116, 169, 176, 190n23; racial, 38, 176; of subjecthood, 119

settlement, 3–6, 9–10, 17, 21–29, 82, 84, 128, 137, 174; agricultural, 26, 141–42; colonial, 16, 19, 25, 28, 158, 161, 187n17; forced, 35; inhabitation and, 180; Jewish, 206n33; Jewish National Fund and, 48; mass, 186n16; permanent, 64; plans, 183n5; rural, 140; in the West Bank, 203n7

settler colonialism, 2, 15–16, 21–24, 66, 161, 173–74, 180, 185n13, 187n21, 202n2; apartheid and, 160; colonialism and, 173; elimination and, 19–20; inhabitation and, 4; Zionist, 21, 140, 186n15

settler colonial studies, 18–21, 25, 186n15

settler colonies, 8, 16, 19, 22, 27, 159, 174, 187n22

settlerness, 22–28, 36, 66, 160, 162, 173–74, 186n17

settler order, 12, 52, 137; American, 172

settlers, 8, 19, 23, 136, 187n17; Italian, 130; Jewish, 134, 142

settler states, 15–16, 27, 136, 159, 161

settler time, 3, 12, 17, 23, 96, 128

shame, 14, 194n4

Sharon, Arieh, 26–27

INDEX 229

Sharon, Ariel, 152–53, 155, 163
Siddiq, Muhammad, 104, 109, 199n12
siege, 18, 205n30; of Beirut, 106, 124; states of, 27, 205n32
Simone, AbdouMaliq, 180
Sinai Desert, 131, 138, 142, 147, 153
social evolutionism, 42, 46
social reproduction, 41, 176–77, 206n1
South Africa, 20, 184n7
sovereign power, 59, 110
sovereign time, 16, 92
sovereignty, 26, 31, 59–60, 68, 82, 87–88, 91–92, 125, 134; jurisdictional-territorial, 186n16; settler, 17; temporal, 128; third space of, 161; tribal, 159
spatial administration, 81, 90
spatial regulation, 66, 77, 79
statelessness, 11, 63, 109–11, 169
steadfastness, 23, 121
Stoler, Ann, 8, 21, 158, 185n13
stuckness, 22, 158
subjectivity, 156, 173, 196n53; collective, 124, 136; Israeli political, 15, 172; legal, 170
surveying, 72; Clapp mission and, 40–42
Syria, 133, 191n3; Damascus, 168, 189n13; refugee camps in, 10, 99, 101, 189n13; resettlement plans and, 130; UNRWA field office in, 192n6

technical, the, 35, 39, 46, 57–58, 60–61, 81; as imperial alibi, 30, 60
technical assistance, 43, 60–62, 200n17. *See also* Point Four projects
technomorality, 30, 57; racialized, 35, 57, 61
temporality, 15, 27, 92, 162, 178; of the camps, 32, 153; countertemporality, 128; of encampment, 65; without historicity, 185n11; political, 65, 127, 129, 153; politics of, 18, 25; of settler sovereignty, 17
temporariness, 5, 65, 178–79; of camps, 84, 152; permanent, 2, 18; politics of, 66
temporary, the, 18, 178, 180
Tennessee Valley Authority (TVA), 30, 33–34, 39, 43–47, 51–53, 56, 61, 69; abroad, 44, 50, 60
tragedy, 36–38, 55
Truman, Harry S., 43, 200n17. *See also* Point Four projects
Turki, Fawaz, 64–65, 108, 199n13

uncertainty, 116, 119–21, 125, 201n23
unhoming, 28, 172
uninhabitability, 169, 175, 177, 190n20
United Nations (UN), 10, 85, 143; administrators, 11, 14; forces in Egypt, 104; General Assembly Resolution 194, 36, 38; General Assembly Resolution 3379, 184n7; High Commissioner on Refugees, 184n8; Palestinian camp regime of, 30; Refugee Convention, 56; subsidies, 155
United Nations Conciliation Commission on Palestine (UNCCP), 36–37, 39, 61
United Nations Relief and Works Agency (UNRWA), 10–11, 29–31, 34, 38, 43, 55–56, 64–73, 77–87, 100, 104, 110–11, 114, 124, 146–47, 157, 189n14, 191n2, 192nn5–6; administrators, 12–13; annual reports, 190nn20–21; authority of, 31, 58–59, 66, 68, 72, 80–81, 86–87, 89–91, 195n52 (*see also* authority: administrative); built environment of camps and, 67, 90; camp regime of, 54; camps, 111, 189n13, 191n2, 193n25; emergency architecture of, 147; housing in camps and, 55, 70–71; Mandate system and, 51–52; officials, 148, 150, 152; refugee self-demolition and, 150; registration card, 203n8; rehabilitation and, 190n21; schools, 109
United States, 42, 46, 92, 161, 186n16; Senate Foreign Relations Committee, 38, 50. *See also* US South
unruly time, 127, 163
unsettlement, 28, 180
US South, 30, 35, 190n19; segregation in, 34, 51, 172; TVA and, 44–47, 51–54

Veracini, Lorenzo, 25, 186n17
violence, 9, 23, 55–57, 61, 66, 84, 92, 152, 159,

161, 171, 173, 179, 198n9; authority and, 89; of camp clearance, 163; counterrevolutionary, 168; of displacement, 15; foundational, 2, 15, 22, 27–28; hegemony and, 196n53; racist, 45; reason and, 90; settler, 27, 160
Vreeland, Frederick Dalziel, 78–79

waiting, 18, 95, 110–11, 120–21, 124
wardship, 51, 60; colonial, 62
Weber, Max, 88, 108, 195n52
Weitz, Ra'anan, 140–43, 183n5, 204n10
Weitz, Yosef, 48, 140, 153
West, the, 10, 16, 159, 171
West Bank, 142–43, 151, 155, 205n30; camps in, 10, 23, 128, 144; Civil Administration, 146; model villages in, 69; occupation of, 1, 32, 84, 86, 137, 186n15, 192n3; PLO and, 199n14; settlement in, 203n7; violence in, 161
Wolfe, Patrick, 4, 19–21, 25, 132, 172–73, 186n14
work, 18, 30, 34–35, 43–44, 47, 49–56, 64, 98, 118–19, 142, 175, 178, 198n9; of building, 117–18, 125; of government, 195n51; political, 190n23; programs, 130; projects, 31; refugees and, 42, 50, 68, 189n14, 190n21; rehabilitation and, 11–12, 191n23; revolutionary, 123; social reproduction and, 41; will to, 57, 60
work-relief, 39, 43, 61
World Bank, 91, 130

Yakhlif, Yayha, 31, 105–6, 198–99n11, 200n17; *Tuffah al-Majanin*, 102, 104, 109–10, 113–14, 120–21
yishuv, 5–6

Zakin, Dov, 127, 139–40
Zangwill, Israel, 3–6, 8
Zionism, 3–4, 6, 8–9, 18–19, 26, 135, 185n13; Indigeneity and, 187n20; political, 140, 159, 173, 185n133; as racism, 184n7; refusal and, 23; settler colonialism of, 186n15; as settler colonial project, 21; state, 127; Stone and, 42; territorial, 28
Zionists, 131; Labor, 4
Zupančič, Alenka, 133

Printed and bound by CPI Group (UK) Ltd, Croydon, CR0 4YY
02/04/2025
14651937-0001